Make a
WINDSOR
CHAIR
with Mike Dunbar

POPULAR WOODWORKING BOOKS
CINCINNATI, OHIO
www.popularwoodworking.com

Table of Contents

Introduction

Scientists tell us that before the universe began there was a singularity, an infinitesimally small point. That singularity exploded as the Big Bang, and all that exists radiated out — and still is radiating out — from that event. That's how the phenomenon I call the Windsor Revival began. The Revival is the rediscovery of Windsor chairmaking's long-forgotten secrets and re-establishing it as a thriving craft. The Windsor Revival's singularity was a small, black chair sitting on a porch in Sutton, Massachusetts in the spring of 1971. The Windsor Big Bang occurred when I stumbled across that chair and bought it. Before that event there was nothing. Everything related to Windsor chairmaking — the craftsmen making Windsor chairs (even if they are unaware of it), sources for chairmaking tools, customers buying handmade Windsors - all came into being as a result of that one event, and all continue to radiate out from it. I told that little black chair's story in the original introduction.

I wrote *Make a Windsor Chair with Michael Dunbar* in 1983. (It was published in 1984.) After a remarkably long run for a woodworking book, *Make a Windsor* went out of print about a decade ago. However, demand for it never disappeared. Woodworkers began to bid up used copies on Ebay and Amazon.com, until at one point the price was bumping around $300. I regularly receive inquiries as to whether or not I have any copies for sale. Obviously, the book was missed, and I have decided to bring it back to serve another generation of chairmakers. I made a minor change to the title, as I have always called myself Mike. Michael sounds too pretentious.

I began teaching chairmaking in 1980 as an itinerant. For a little over a decade I travelled around the country conducting classes in a variety of venues: colleges, woodworking stores, woodworking clubs, etc. I was 45 when my son – my only child – was born. I was present at his birth, but he and my wife Susanna, were no sooner home than I went off to Detroit to teach for a week. I returned to New Hampshire and jumped on a plane to Halifax, NS. While there, I called my wife and told her I couldn't keep traveling. My heart ached too much. She said she had a solution. We would start our own school so I could stay home.

In 1994 we began regularly scheduled classes in a rented building in Portsmouth, NH. We grew so quickly that first year we knew we had to relocate to a bigger facility. We purchased 60 acres in nearby Hampton. While we were teaching our second year of classes, we were also building our new school with our home nearby. Our Hampton location was good for us. We continued to grow so fast it was hard to keep up. Along with more classes and more work benches, we added two additional buildings, and expanded both our faculty and parking. I estimate some 6,500 people have now made a Windsor chair with Mike Dunbar.

Conducting all those classes on a regular basis made my school a chairmaking laboratory where all sorts of new ideas, techniques, tools, and designs have been developed. I am never content with the status quo. For me, teaching is a perpetual quest for better ways to explain chairmaking and easier ways for students to work. Because we continually seek to improve all things related to Windsor chairmaking, we named the school The Windsor Institute. That is what the place remains: an institute dedicated to the advancement of Windsor chairmaking.

I did not stop learning in 1983. My chairmaking knowledge continued to grow. Releasing this new edition of *Make a Windsor Chair* has provided some desirable opportunities; foremost is to disseminate that new knowledge. In this new edition I also changed and/or eliminated some things, including the biggest blooper of all. I have removed the whole wet wood/dry tenon process, what I disparagingly call the "Lily Tomlin Joint". In 1981 that actress starred in an embarrassingly bad movie titled *The Incredible Shrinking Woman*. The wet and dry wood technique is the embarrassingly wrong "incredible shrinking joint". I strongly recommend against the joint (and the movie) as being a waste of effort. I deeply regret I ever included the technique in the original book. It was a boneheaded blunder that resulted in untold numbers of chairmakers drying tenons in hot sand. This is the guiding principal in making a Windsor. Every piece in the chair should be thoroughly dry. You can work the wood wet, but it must be dried before assembling the chair. The joinery described in the new chapter on Windsor joints is what one needs. Employ those techniques and you will create chairs that, like the antique originals, remain tight for generations, even centuries.

In spite of my mistakes I am fond of the original book and am happy to bring it back. It was quite good and a lot of people made Windsor chairs using it. However, how to present all the new knowledge? This is my decision and how I made it. I was 36 years old when I wrote *Make a Windsor Chair*. I had been making chairs for 11 years and teaching for three. Today, at age 66, I have been making chairs for 41 years and teaching for 33. When I wrote the original book I knew a lot and I was pretty good at my craft. Today, I'm a lot better and I know a whole lot more. As I reread the book I felt close to that chairmaker who in 1983 was entering his middle age. *Make a Windsor Chair* was his book, and it felt wrong to take it away from him. It's a bit bizarre, but I began to see my younger self as a colleague and this new edition as a collaboration with him.

That is what you are holding, a joint endeavor, but one that is primarily his. I invite you to read the book imagining two Mike Dunbars looking over your shoulder as you work. The younger man is teaching you to make his chairs. The older man defers to the younger and only speaks to add his wisdom and extended knowledge. It will not be hard to hear our two voices, as I write differently than I did in 1983. However, to make the older man's contribution more obvious, **I have put it in semibold face type**.

The original book included lots of measured drawings and sketches of the sack back and continuous arm that I made in the early '80s. Today, I make different designs of sack back and continuous arm, although they are mature versions of my earlier chairs (as I am a mature version of that younger man.) However, the chairs I made in the 1970s and 1980s using the patterns in this book are still being sat in by the people who purchased them from me. They are comfortable and strong. While my eye has improved so that I better see and better understand Windsor forms, the Windsors I made in the original edition were perfectly good. The younger Mike Dunbar has no reason to apologize for his chairs.

In the event you wish to make my current designs I point out the changes. A lot of these changes are no more than procedure. I do things differently because the new ways are easier for students to understand or accomplish. Other changes are to dimensions – thickness, length, a different spacing, a different sized bit. The most significant changes between 1983 and today are the seat templates. Both are new. I have added them to the pertinent chapters.

I use some different tools, although not as many as you might guess. For example, today I drill holes with a cordless drill and brad point bits. While spoon bits are great, they are a high-skill tool, and a class of new chairmakers is overwhelmed by them. As I said, they are wonderful tools, and if you want to practice with them and learn their intricacies, they are worthwhile. You will not be disappointed. In all the woodworking literature there is no other complete account of using these tools. I decided the information about spoon bits in the 1984 edition is so important it had to be retained; having said that, a cordless and brad points are equally good. The decision is yours.

In 1984, I rived the wood for the chairs I made each week. However, like spoon bits, riving is high-skill and is only learned with a lot of practice. Until you get it down, your early attempts result in lots of waste. When I began teaching on my own and watched the waste occurring, I realized there were not enough forests in New England. So, at The Institute the staff prepares in advance the bending and spindle stock for most of a year. We still split the logs into eighths, but now cut the billets on a monster Hitachi resaw. Doing so, we are able to follow the grain and obtain stock that is just as good as if it were completely riven. Preparing all this bending and spindle stock is a time consuming and labor-intensive process. Few people making chairs would want to undertake it on their own. The first edition included a chapter describing riving, and like the information about spoon bits, this is the most complete source on the subject. So, I retained it, as this is the way you will most likely work.

When writing the original edition, I sharpened my tools using a grinding wheel and oil stones. Since that way of sharpening remains valid, I decided to retain the sharpening chapter. However, I developed my sandpaper sharpening system specifically for teaching on the road. Because it is so effective and easy I continue to use this method. Sharpening and tuning tools are never-ending activities at The Institute. We maintain scores of tools for students use, and it is much easier with the sandpaper system.

Because today, I teach chairmaking rather than making chairs for sale, I changed my set-ups. I provide identical work stations for every student, so I no longer use the holding forms shown in the original edition for shaping seats and drilling holes in them. However, if I were still in the chairmaking business and working by myself, I would. These devices are handy. My old bench is disassembled and stored in the loft of an outbuilding. My tin knocker's vise is stored with it. Today, I and my students all use Record #53 vises, as these are the universal woodworking standard. I do not use a shaving horse. They are so inefficient compared to a vise; working on one is like taking a self-imposed pay cut. I strongly urge you not to get sucked into a shave horse.

I retained the finishing chapter as I still finish with milk paint for the same reasons described in it.

Over the years, I developed a steam box that is far superior to the one I used in 1983. In fact, the new one is so efficient we dubbed it the Ultimate Steam Box. In this edition I substituted a photo of my new model, replacing the more primitive one shown in the 1984 edition. In a class we bend so many parts at one time The Institute has two boxes of eight-inch, schedule-80 PVC. They can handle almost all the parts for a class in one filling. You do not need a box this large and can use four-inch pipe. You will find Schedule-80 PVC is expensive. I also generate steam in a metal utility can. These are no longer available. I have a supply that will last me for the foreseeable future, but I have no suggestions as to a substitute. You will have to innovate.

Chairmakers use their own jargon and vocabulary. However, other groups also have their own vocabularies for talking about chairs. The first group is antique collectors. These people have been talking and writing about chairs since the 1876 Centennial, and their vocabulary is deeply ingrained. Their terms tend to be quaint and familiar. An example is *love seat or courting bench* instead of *settee*. Their vocabulary is also inexact. For example, collectors are inclined to call both high back and fan back chairs comb backs, although they are two distinct forms. American Furniture scholarship began in earnest during the 1970s and scholars and museum people developed their own Windsor terminology. It tends to be stilted and artificial. For example, they refer to the ends of most parts as a terminal. They are not inclined to distinguish between a stump and a stile, calling both either posts or uprights.

I am a chairmaker and in this book I use our vocabulary. It is a hybrid, but has been around for four decades. Many of our terms were taken from the old guys, the original chairmakers. Much of it is anthropomorphic, resulting from the fact chairs have many of the same parts as a human body. For chairmakers, Windsors have legs, arms, backs, hands, knuckles and ears. Some of our jargon overlaps with mainstream woodworking (we are after all woodworkers.) I suggest you use and become familiar with this chairmakers' vocabulary as it allows us to communicate with each other. By the way, we shortened continuous arm to c-arm.

The 1984 edition contained a section called the Windsor Gallery – several pages of pictures of some chairs I had made, as well as some antique Windsors. Today, my repertoire is far more expansive, as every year we add a new chair to our curriculum at The Institute. So, to give you a better feel for the variety of forms known as Windsor chairs, I have expanded the Gallery.

Thanks for buying a copy of *Make a Windsor Chair with Mike Dunbar*. I hope you discover that you enjoy chairmaking as much as I do.

— Mike Dunbar, Hampton, NH, 2013

If you have purchased this book, you can download the author's bonus section of Windsor chairmaking advice by visiting the site below.

http://www.popularwoodworking.com/form/make-a-windsor-chair-download

Chapter One

Making the Seat

A Windsor chair begins with the seat. It is the one element common to all Windsor chairs, benches, and stools. Windsor chair backs vary in shape — some have bows, some have crests. The spindles of the backs also vary — some are turned to look like bamboo, others are whittled with more or less of a swelling. Some are even arrow-shaped. Legs can be baluster, double-bobbin, or bamboo shaped. Some stools have only three legs, and some settees have a dozen. The stretchers usually form an H pattern or box pattern, but some form an X or even a crescent with spurs. The solid wood seat, into which the legs and back are joined is the one constant, and is what distinguishes Windsor chairs from all other types.

There are other reasons why a Windsor begins with the seat. Most of the other parts of a Windsor chair radiate from this point. The angles at which the leg sockets are bored into the seat determine the splay of the legs and the lengths of the stretchers. The angles of the spindle sockets dictate how much the back will recline. The cant of the arm stumps results from the angles of the stump sockets. This cant determines the length of the stumps as well as the length of the arm.

The seat is the key to the legendary durability of Windsors. The two major systems of the chair — the back and undercarriage — are secured into this solid block of wood. The chair is engineered so that the parts of these systems are always pushing and pulling against each other. The seat is a reliable anchor that allows the chairmaker to strengthen the chair by stressing its parts in such a way that use tightens rather than loosens the joints.

The seat is also the visual center of the chair. By separating the back and the undercarriage, the seat prevents them from competing with each other, and forces them to contribute instead to the artistic success of the chair. No matter where the viewer's eye is drawn by the sweeping curves of the back and its radiating spindles, or by the bold rake of the legs, it is pulled back by the robust and dynamic form of the seat.

Wood Selection

The seat should be made of wood that is lightweight, soft, and stable, with little figure. I usually use eastern white pine. If you cannot get this species you will probably want to work with one native to your area. When teaching in the western United States, I have made seats of sugar pine and ponderosa pine. Teaching in Ohio I have used tulip (also called yellow poplar). I have also used basswood, and even once made a set of chairs with Honduras mahogany seats. A friend in Georgia makes his seats of cypress. If you are using a local wood, avoid those that are hard and difficult to sculpt, such as maple, birch, cherry, walnut, oak, and hickory.

I purchase 2"-thick rough sawn planks of white pine directly from the mill and air-dry them myself for at least one year. I do this because it is less costly, but kiln-dried wood will work fine, too. The planks will eventually be cut into short sections, so their length is not important. I try to buy wide planks that do not have too much sapwood, because pine heartwood is much easier to work. Clear planks would be ideal, but I usually end up sawing the seats out from between clusters of knots.

Today, I buy pine in much larger quantities. I order it from a wholesaler who delivers to The Institute.

Wood constantly reacts to changes in humidity - shrinking when the weather is dry and swelling when it is wet. If you live in the Southwest where the air is continually dry, or the Northwest where it is always moist, the humidity probably does not change enough to affect your wood. If you live in the Frost Belt, like I do, you must be concerned with wood movement because the humidity fluctuates widely. In the summer, when the humidity is high we open our windows and allow the warm moist air to move freely about. In the winter, we seal our houses and pump them full of hot, dry air. Wooden furniture is constantly swelling and shrinking in these conditions. This movement creates stresses that sometimes crack or check a chair's seat. The largest and longest checks will occur in seats made of single boards. A seat glued up of two or more pieces is more resistant to splitting because the stresses are broken by each joint.

My customers usually have a strong traditional bent and often request a single-piece seat. Therefore, I usually work with a single piece of wood, even though I know it is not necessarily the best possible seat. The seat for the sack back chair is 15¾"-wide, the seat for the continuous arm Windsor is 18"-wide. If I am out of 18"-wide planks, I have no qualms about gluing a strip to one of the narrower planks.

Experience with cracked seats in antique chairs and in my own early production has prejudiced me against single board seats. Today, I glue my seat blanks exclusively. I buy my pine in 8" and 10" widths as these yield most of the shapes and sizes of seats we make. I have the wholesaler plane the wood to 1¾". We make seat blanks 24" long, as this accommodates the seats for most of our chair designs.

If you glue up seat blanks make sure that the grain is running in the same direction on all the pieces. If the grain on one piece is rising and on the other dipping, any cut along the joint will tear no matter which direction the tool is worked. When gluing, look at the mating edges of the boards and make sure that the slope of the grain on each is running in the same direction. Avoid any black knots, which may loosen in time. I occasionally work bright, also called live knots. These will not loosen, but they do increase the amount of work needed to shape the seat.

The two most common Windsor-seat shapes are the oval, used here for the sack back chair, and the shield, used for the continuous arm chair. The grain of the oval seat runs from side to side; that of the shield seat runs from front to back. The sack back is a shallow yet commodious chair; the continuous arm is deep and supportive of the sitter's torso. All the techniques required to make the oval seat are used when making the shield, so I will describe how to make the shield seat first. Then I will outline the making of an oval seat, drawing your attention to any different processes needed.

Chapter Two

Making the Shield Seat

The shield seat requires a blank that is 18" square. If the chair is to have a back brace (two spindles connecting to the seat) the seat blank should be 18" and 21" long to allow for the tail.

About a decade after writing the 1984 edition I added an inch of width to my c-arm seat. When we glue up seats for c-arm classes we join two pieces of 10" pine, yielding a blank 20" by 24".

The brace is a desirable feature on the continuous arm chair. Its bent back is anchored to only the stumps and short spindles, and all the stress created when the chair is in use is transmitted to the spindles of the back. The brace regulates just how much the spindles can flex, and it transfers some of the stress down to the robust tailpiece.

Examining antique continuous arms has revealed the forward bend (under the sitter's elbows) to be their weak spot. While the wood is new and flexible, this bend acts like a spring, absorbing the sitter's weight. As it ages, the wood in the arm becomes more brittle and loses its flexibility. Then, it is likely to break at these points. A brace limits the amount these bends can flex and over the long term protects the chair. I recommend this feature.

The faces of a rough-sawn blank must be planed so that you can see the grain to judge which face will be the top of the seat. A thickness planer will do the job, but I do not have one, so I hand-plane the seat blanks. I use a wooden plane about 16" long, known as a jack plane or foreplane. The plane blade has a convex cutting edge that removes heavy, coarse shavings and quickly disposes of the rough surface.

After planing, inspect the surfaces and decide which will be the top. Do not be concerned with the direction in which the wood will cup if it should warp. The seat is so short in relation to its width, and its surface is so undulate that no one will notice. A lot of wood will be removed from the top surface of the seat, so place any spike knots, pitch pockets or other blemishes that do not run completely through the blank on the seat bottom, to avoid hav-

CLEAN UP THE ROUGH FACES *of the seat blank so you can decide which is the best face for the top surface.*

ing to work them. Try to place through knots at the rear of the seat - you can probably arrange the spindles on either side of knot.

Once you have chosen the top surface plane, it flat. I use a wooden smoothing plane with a straight, sharp cutting edge. Though most of this surface will be removed when the seat is excavated (or saddled), if it were not finish-planed, the tracks of the foreplane would remain where the spindles meet the seat.

Next, make a pattern for the seat. Because I use my patterns over and over, I make them of ¼" luan plywood. The shape of the seat is shown in the measured drawings. Mark the position of the sockets for the legs, stumps and spindles on the pattern. When you cut out the pattern, make sure that all the curves are smooth. Trace the outline of the seat onto the blank. Pay attention to knots and the blemishes when placing the pattern, and when possible, keep them out of the area that will be excavated. Draw in

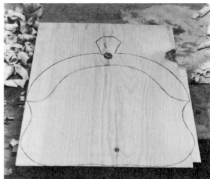

MAKE A PATTERN FOR THE *seat out of ¼"*
luan plywood. If possible, position the pat-
tern so that knots and other blemishes are
located out of the area to be excavated.

the groove that circumscribes the saddle and separates it from the spindles and stumps. Draw this free hand, judging the distance from the back edge of the seat by eye. You could use a compass or a pattern if you do not trust your eye. I do not bother at this point to mark any of the sockets.

I cut out the seat with a 25" bow saw. It takes so little time to do this that I have never been tempted to buy a band saw.

The bow saw is a fast and efficient tool. It was fine when I was young and I made only two seats a week. Today, I have two 14" band saws for cutting out students seats.

I clamp the blank to the corner of a bench with wooden hand screw clamps, and I saw right to the line – this saves clean up later. I prefer hand screws, because the wooden screws flex and can accept more torque. The flexibility also gives the clamps a spring-like quality. If the blank shifts and loosens the clamp slightly, the springy back screw will adjust for the slack, whereas a hand screw clamp with metal screws will fall to the floor. There is only one drawback to an all-wood hand screw clamp: The threads are vulnerable to damages from bumps and bangs. Screws that have been damaged, however, can be discarded and new ones made with a screw box. With a threaded die and its corresponding tap (I use a ¾"), you can make all the clamps that you could possibly want or need.

Though I have seen it suggested that the some excavating be done prior to cutting out the seat, I prefer to do all operations that require the same tools at one time. When I am finished with the oper-

ation, I put the tools the away and thus avoid a cluttered work bench (benches have a natural tendency to become cluttered).

Shaping the Edge

The first step in shaping the seat is to contour the edges. This contour is complex, changing several times as it moves around the outline of the seat as shown in the photos and drawings. Along the back and up to the stumps, the shape is very nearly quarter round. Adjacent to the stumps, where the shield shape is indented, the edge changes abruptly. Here, a long, low incline beneath the indentation rises to meet the slightly sloping top surface of the seat. This incline on the seat bottom develops into a large radius curve under the front corners of the seat. Between the corners, the bottom profile becomes an incline once again. A distinct arris runs around the edge from stump to stump, delineating the top and bottom surfaces and sharply defining the shape of the seat. I establish the line of the arris by eye while sculpting the seat. It might help you to sketch it on the edge with a pencil.

There are two steps in shaping the edge of a seat. First remove the bulk of the waste with a drawknife. Second finish the edge with spokeshaves and planes. I shape the edge in sections, moving back and forth between the drawknife, two spokeshaves, a smoothing plane, and a compass plane. This alternation is merely my habit and I urge you to find a way of working that is comfortable for you. Before describing the edge-shaping process, I will discuss the shaping tools.

A 25″ BOW SAW MAKES *short work of cutting out the seat. Clamp the blank securely to a corner of the bench. Saw with the full length of the blade and use your whole body, not just your arms, for the strokes.*

DRAWKNIFE The general progression in most woodworking is to move from coarse tools that remove large amounts of wood through a series of increasingly refined tools that are easier to control. The coarse tool for this job is a drawknife. The one I use is a traditional Anglo-American pattern, 12″ long overall, with a 7½″ long blade. A drawknife that is longer than this is awkward to control and one that is shorter is too light and too short to take a complete cut. The handles are about 5″ long and lie in nearly the same plane as the blade. I find this tool easier to control than drawknives with handles that are offset from the blade. They have a tendency to dive into the grain. I have never been comfortable with Continental-style drawknives which have egg shaped handles.

When I use a drawknife I grip it very securely. My wrists are stiff to prevent the tool from diving into the wood. Because I am right handed, I hold the right handle closest to me. In this position, the blade slices through the wood at a skewed angle. As you work around the seat's outline you move from edge grain into end grain and back into edge grain again. A skewed slicing cut, using as much of the length of the blade as possible is less likely to chatter or dig into end grain. Do not try to hew away the wood as if you were using a two-handled hatchet. When used properly, the drawknife will remove a lot of wood very quickly, and with a surprising amount of control.

I like to work the drawknife at about the height of my sternum. My elbows and shoulders act as a natural stop, so I do not worry about cutting myself. Each drawknife cut has three distinct motions. Begin the cut by gradually entering the blade into the wood. Slice through the shaving with a second long motion. Then separate the shaving and end the cut. Most people have trouble with this third action. Think of it as you would the follow-through of a swing with a golf club or a baseball bat. You must follow through with edge tools to prevent digging and tearing the grain. This greatly reduces cleanup with abrasives and scrapers.

THE EDGE OF A WINDSOR *seat is roughly shaped with a drawknife. Use as much of the drawknife blade as possible.*

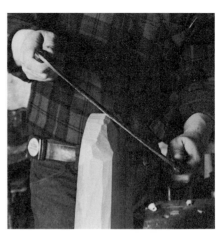

Spokeshaves

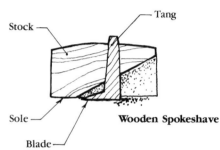

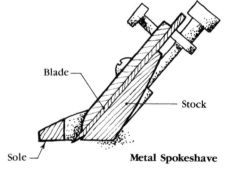

FINISH SHAPING THE EDGE WITH *spokeshaves and planes. The large and small spokeshaves can work concave as well as convex surfaces. The smoothing plane (right) works convex surfaces and the compass plane is useful for the incline along the front of the seat.*

SPOKESHAVES AND PLANES I finish shaping the edge with two wooden spokeshaves and two wooden planes. I like my tools to wear to fit the work they do. The sole of the wooden smoothing plane has a distinct hollow worn in front of the mouth, which helps the plane to track on a rounded surface. The small spokeshave has a wear spot on the sole where I whittle spindles. This wear spot also allows the tool to get down into a tight radius such as in the concave area of the seat edge. The compass plane is shaped very much like the smoothing plane but its sole is curved from front to back. I use it on the inclined front edge of the seat.

I prefer wooden spokeshaves to metal ones. A metal spokeshave is really a plane with two handles. The blade is set at 45 degrees in the stock, bezel down. **(thefreedictionary.com Be-zel 1. A slanting surface or bevel on the edge of a cutting tool, such as a chisel.)** The sole has a mouth just like the sole of a plane, as shown in the drawing. The blade is held in place by a set screw, which must be loosened and tightened during adjustment. A wooden spokeshave is a true shave. The blade is very nearly parallel to the sole which means that it makes a paring cut, very much like the cut made by a knife or chisel. This paring cut is ideal for working end grain.

The blade has a tang at each end, bent at right angles to the length of the cutting edge. The tangs are press fitted into holes in the stock. The depth of cut is increased by tapping the ends of the tangs and decreased by striking the flat of the blade beneath each tang. This tapping can be done on any handy surface, like the corner of a bench or the vise, so adjustments can be made quickly, with one hand. For finishing the seat edge I set the spokeshave blade by cocking the two tangs so that the blade protrudes beneath the sole farther at one end than at the other. By working back and forth along the length of the cutting edge, you can find just the right spot to cut a shaving of the thickness that you desire. With practice selecting this spot becomes second nature.

My comparison of the little black chair to the Big Bang also applies to chairmaking tools. When I started teaching few of the tools I needed for classes were still available, and those that were being sold were horrible. The drawknife sold in catalogs (still is) was all wrong. It was ground like a chisel, not a knife. As a result, it could not be controlled. In order to get through a class, I had to let students use my antique tools and they were wearing them out.

I needed to develop sources for correctly made tools. I set about finding toolmakers willing to bring traditional chairmaking tools back into production. I promised them the support of The Windsor Institute. It would generate the large number of customers they needed to make their efforts worthwhile. I worked with these toolmakers, explaining what features are required by each tool, not only so it would work, but so it would work well. I lent them my tools to copy. Today, because of the demand created by The Windsor Institute, chairmaking tools have made a comeback.

The new demand for chairmaking tools attracted others that have started making tools on their own, without my guidance. Many of those tools are less than satisfactory and I discourage our students from buying them. That means that you too have to be knowledgeable. It is not sufficient that a catalog says a tool is for chairmaking. You have to know what to look for.

I no longer use antique tools. I have come to consider myself a custodian with a responsibility to preserve these items for the future.

SHAPING I prefer to hold the seat in a vise while shaping most of the edge, keeping the area being worked more or less horizontal. Begin draw knifing with the quarter round profile on the back edge. This shape can be roughed out with drawknife cuts at three angles as shown in the drawing. Make the first slice at about 15 degrees from the perpendicular. This should be a heavy cut. In pine I take off as much as ¼" Now make two shallower cuts above and below the first cut and at a smaller angle. Be careful to leave some of the sawn edge near the top of the contour so that you do not lose the shape. The tailpiece creates two corners that are difficult to work. Slice up to it as closely as you can with the drawknife. The tailpiece and area adjacent to it will be finished later using a chisel. Work the quarter round shape up to the position of the stump on one side.

On an oval seat or a shield seat with no tailpiece I need only the smoothing plane to finish the quarter round. The surface is rough from the drawknife and the plane brings it to the desired contour

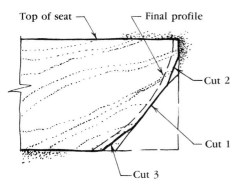

To ROUGH OUT THE QUARTER *round back edge of the shield seat, make three cuts with the drawknife. The three are shown in the drawing and show how little wood needs to be removed with spokeshaves.*

COMPLETE THE QUARTER ROUND WITH *spokeshaves.*
Skew the small spokeshave to clean up the chatter
marks on the end grain.

CLEAN UP THE EDGES OF *the tailpiece and carve the bevels with*
a wide chisel. You can take a heavy cut when beveling. Trim the
quarter round back edge up to the bevel. Grasp the tailpiece and
chisel with one hand to help control the cut.

USE THE LARGE AND SMALL *spoke shaves to continue roughing out the edge profile for the shield indentation and the front corner. Next, rough out the incline along the front edge.*

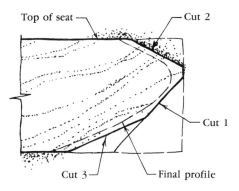

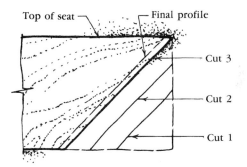

TO SHAPE THE FRONT CORNER *of the shield seat and the front, follow the sequence of cuts*

more quickly than even the large spokeshave. But the plane will bump into a tailpiece, so I use the large spokeshave when necessary to avoid this. Even this tool will not get down completely into the corner formed by the back of the seat and the tail. This area has to be cleaned up with a wide chisel. I do this when shaping the tailpiece.

The plane and large spokeshave are heavy tools set to take a heavy cut. Therefore they might dig in slightly on the end grain. These marks can be quickly cleaned up with the smaller spokeshave which is easy to set for a fine cut. This tool is so

light however, that it will chatter as it hits the alternating hard late growth and soft early growth of the annual rings. To prevent this chattering I skew the spokeshave at right angles to the rings so that the cutting edge runs across several rings at a time and is not able to burrow into the softer areas.

When the rear edge is cleaned up, shape the tailpiece with a wide chisel. The lower edge of the tailpiece is beveled. I like this bevel to account for about three fifths of the thickness of the seat. This makes the tailpiece appear more three dimensional and thinner than it really is. While working on the

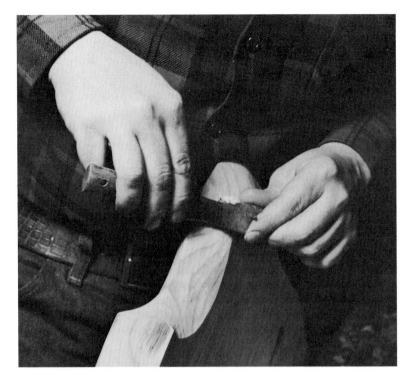

TO ROUGH OUT THE EDGE *in front of the stumps, first remove the arris at the front corner. Then shape the concavities at the indentation of the shield on both top and bottom surfaces. Finally, make a low-angled cut on the top surface at the corner.*

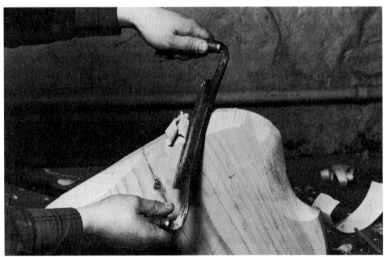

tailpiece clean up the corners where the tailpiece meets the seat.

Next, shape the edge in front of the stump. This area is complicated. It may help you to refer frequently to the photos and drawings at the end when reading the description and when making the seat. Where the shield shape is indented the top surface of the seat slopes slightly down, meeting a long low, slightly convex incline rising from the bottom. This bottom incline develops into a large radius curve under the front corners of the seat. The top surface of the corner is also a slight convex slope.

First make a heavy 45 degree cut with the drawknife to remove the bottom arris of the front corner of the seat. The shield indentation is perhaps the most difficult area of the seat to clean up because end grain is exposed on both sides of the concave curves. Cut down the sides toward the bottom of the curve with the drawknife. If you cut upward, the cutting edge will get buried in the end grain.

Rough out the rest of the front corner. You have made the first cut eliminating the bottom arris. A second cut below the first should be at a shallower angle as shown in the drawing. A third cut removes the upper corner.

Continue work on the edge with the large and small spokeshaves.

A lot of wood needs to be removed from both

A SIMPLE WOODEN FRAME WILL *hold the seat on the bench while shaping. Two threaded wooden screws fit through the back of the frame into the bench top. Bore and tap a series of holes in the bench top so that the frame can be positioned for several different jobs.*

the top and the bottom surfaces of the indentations in the side of the shield, as well as from the front corner. I remove as much as possible now, but leave the final shaping until later when the seat is flat on the bench top.

Next, begin the incline in front. Shape the incline with a series of slicing cuts at 45 degrees as shown in the drawing. Usually I can work only as far as the pommel without changing the position of the seat in the vise.

About half of the seat edge is roughly to shape now. The seat is symmetrical, so follow the same process on the other half. When I switch the seat around in the vise to work on the concave area of the opposite side I am able to finish cutting away the rest of the front edge profile at the same time.

FINISH SHAPING Take the seat from the vise and place it upside down on the bench. I have made a frame to hold the seat on the bench for shaping. The remainder of the edge shaping, most of the saddling on the top surface, and all the socket boring is done with the seat held in the frame. The frame is designed to hold the seat by gripping the tailpiece and either the top or bottom surface of the seat can be placed up. The frame is secured to the bench with two threaded wooden screws for which you will need a screw box and tap. These come in sets of various sizes – a ¾" set will do for the frame as well as for making wooden hand screw clamps. Several rows of threaded holes in the bench top permit positioning the frame appropriately for different tasks. When shaping the edge, the front half of the seat should extend beyond the bench top so that the edge can be easily worked. Two hand screw clamps, carefully placed so that the jaws grip the seat along the back edge, will also work. If you are clamping, place the seat on the corner of the bench top so that the two shield indentations overhang and give

plenty of free space in which to work.

Finish shaping the bottom inclines at the indentations on each side of the shield with the small spokeshave. As mentioned earlier the grain changes direction in this area, so it is necessary to cut from back to center and front to center to avoid digging into the grain.

Proper completion of this shape is important. The continuous arm Windsor is a delicate and complex chair, a symphony of curves. The seat is a block of wood in the center of a sensuous, undulate form. If it reads as a static lump, the visual success of the chair is impaired. When the chair is viewed from the side, the long slope of the incline on the bottom of the seat makes it appear thinner than it really is. This illusion of thinness is important. However, you must make sure that it is only an illusion. If the seat is too thin where the leg and stump sockets are, the chair will be weak. An ample amount of wood must remain at the joints, but the shaping of the seat between these points must flow naturally.

With the seat upside down I complete the incline along the front edge with a compass plane. This tool with its curved sole creates a gentle concavity across the lower front edge. (If you do not have a compass plane a large spokeshave can be used to give the same effect.) Because the plane blade is set at 45 degrees it will often tear out the soft early growth, so this surface should be cleaned up with the small spokeshave using the same skew technique described earlier. While I have the spokeshave in hand I make all the transitions flow together - from the incline of the front into the radius of the corners, and from the corners into the incline under the indented edges.

The bottom of the seat is now finished. The planes, spokeshaves, and chisel each leave their own individual track. You may wish to sand these

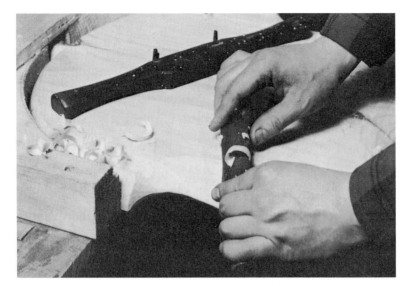

SHAPE THE CURVE UNDER EACH *shield indentation carefully. Work the spokeshave with the grain so that it won't dig in. The small spokeshave fits curves of a shorter radius than the large one in the background. A simple wooden frame will hold the seat on the bench while shaping. Two threaded wooden screws fit through the back of the frame into the bench top. Bore and tap a series of holes in the bench top so that the frame can be positioned for several*

COMPLETE THE INCLINE ALONG THE *front edge of the seat with a compass plane.*

out and can do so quite easily because the evidence of good handwork is subtle. However, I am neither ashamed of, nor offended by these tracks and they remain on any chair I make.

Saddling the Shield Seat

Saddling After shaping the edge, the top surface of the seat needs to be excavated. The area where this is to be done begins at the line for the carved channel and continues to the front edge of the chair. The completed shape looks like a saddle, so the process is often called saddling. The tool used to cut away the majority of the waste is the gutter adze. I use an antique gutter adze, but these are uncommon. Similar adzes are made today but I find their curves less satisfactory than mine.

The tool would not be too difficult to make and a pattern is shown at right. If you do not have a gutter adze there are other ways of doing its work, but these require more time and effort. You could remove waste from the saddled area with a heave

gouge and mallet. You could also use a sculptor's one-handed adze. This is not as heavy as the gutter adze and will not work as quickly. You could also do all of the saddling with the scorp. If you opt for any of these other tools you will want to work with the seat secured to the bench top.

The business end of the gutter adze is curved and can take a thick, narrow chip in a relatively small but deeply concave area. An adze with a wider, less curved blade would be awkward to use, because it would not get into the curves of the saddle. The length of the adze handle is important. The saddled area is no more than 1½ sq. ft., and I stand on the seat while using the adze. For both the sake of safety and the job it is essential to use the gutter adze as accurately as possible. I have hafted my adze with an oak handle that is only 17" long, which allows me to swing the tool with my wrists, and keep the tool close to the work. If the handle were longer, I could not achieve the unfailing accuracy needed to chop out a seat. Even so, I wear steel-toed shoes.

CLEAN UP TORN END GRAIN *and make transitions from one profile to another flow smoothly together with a spokeshave.*

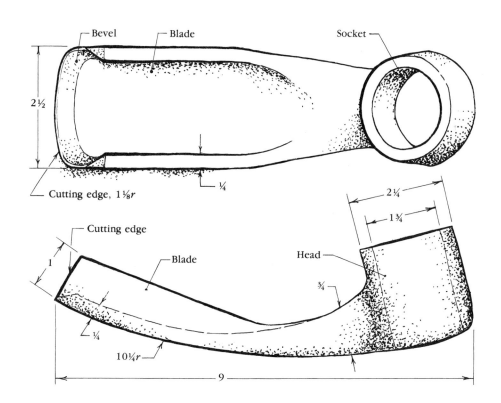

STAND ON THE SEAT TO *hold it when using the adze. Swing the adze with your wrists and follow through the stroke to sever the chip. Work with the grain, from each end of the seat into the center, where the saddling is the deepest. If you are confident, you can use the adze close to the outline of the saddled area (lower left). Reverse the seat to hew along the front (lower right).*

Place the seat on the floor. I like to stand on it rather than hold it with the sides of my feet or ankles - my weight holds the seat immobile and I do not have to worry about the adze missing and hitting a part of me that is not well protected. Work the adze with the grain using short strokes. As with most hand tools it is important to follow through with these strokes and completely separate the chip from the seat. This leaves no digs to be removed with finishing tools.

Resist the temptation to break a chip loose by lifting it rather than cutting it away, because the chip might tear and run right out the other end of the piece. You might practice on a piece of scrap until you are comfortable with the adze. Used incorrectly it can ruin your seat.

Work about half the saddled area beginning at one end of the seat and moving toward the center. Then start at the opposite end, again chopping toward the center. Remove any high spots left in the center by chopping in from both directions with the grain.

The purpose of the gutter adze is to remove a lot of waste very quickly. No real shaping is done with

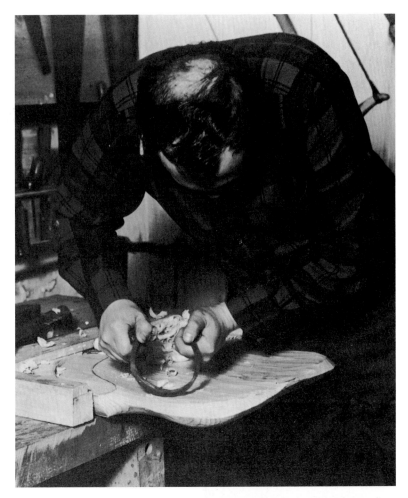

THE SMOOTH SURFACE AT THE *back of the seat (below) has been worked with the scorp, after the entire saddle has been adzed roughly to shape. When smoothing, work the scorp from the back to the center of the saddle.*

the adze and the seat surface will be very rough. Where the saddle is deepest – the dished area in the center of the seat – I remove at least ⅝" from a 2"-thick seat. The more waste that can be removed with the adze the less there will be to remove with light-weight tools. The next step will clean up the rugged depression and begin to give some form to the seat. The tool used for this is the scorp.

You will be hesitant using the adze. This is natural. Although quite safe, the tool is intimidating. As a result, you will often not work deeply enough. To help achieve the desired depth, set a circular saw blade to ⅝" and make a plunge cut in the center of the saddled area. Use this cut as a guide.

Though the scorp is a hollowing tool it is essentially a bent drawknife. It is a basic instrument in that the only control is in the user's wrists. Because the scorp does not have a mouth to regulate the depth of cut as does a plane or spokeshave, it is not the tool I choose for finishing. This lack of a mouth however, allows the scorp to remove a lot of wood very quickly.

The scorp I use has a blade that is bent to a radius. Many scorps, both modern and antique, are U shaped with a flat bottom. This flat bottomed

THE FINAL SHAPING TOOL FOR *the saddle is the miniature compass plane, which has a curved sole. The cutting edge is ground slightly convex so that it will not dig in. Nest the compass plane in both hands and work in the direction of the grain.*

FINISH THE GENTLY ROLLED EDGE *of the front corners with a small spokeshave.*

type seems to have been designed for coopers. It is nearly useless for chairmaking, because that shape does not allow you to get down into the saddle.

To use the scorp, I secure the seat to the bench with the hold-down frame. As with a drawknife a scorp is pulled and performs best when the cutting edge is skewed to the grain direction. Control the tool with your wrists to take either heavy chips or light shavings. Follow through each cut with an upward flick of the wrists to separate the chip completely and prevent the edge from digging in.

First, cut away large pieces of wood to clean up the work done by the adze. Then use the scorp to bring the saddled area to almost its finished depth. Hold the ends of the handles about 1" above the seat to remove wood aggressively and efficiently. Cut from the rear to the center of the seat. If you go any farther, you will dig into the rising grain.

Work also from the front to the center. I do this by sitting on the bench so that I do not have to reverse the hold down frame. Be careful not to remove too much wood from the areas where the leg sockets are to be bored.

When working the edge of the seat some shap-

THE TRAVISHER SMOOTHES THE FURROWS *left on the saddle by the compass plane. It has a curved, wooden body and a curved blade that cuts like a spokeshave. Push the travisher with rigid wrists. Work with or skewed to the grain into the center of the seat.*

ing was done on the concave area in front of where the stumps will be. Now use the scorp to blend this area into the saddle.

On the oval seat the pommel can be shaped with the scorp, because the grain runs from side to side and you can cut with the grain. The pommel of a shield seat is worked across the grain and as a result this has to be done with the small spokeshave. To perform best, the spokeshave should be skewed to the growth rings, forming an X with them if possible. Cut mostly away from the pommel, working from the center to the sides of the seat. This creates a sharp peak that is a distraction on a seat that is otherwise made up of gentle curves. I soften the peak by running the spokeshave right over it, turning it into a swelling. While working in this area, flow the curve of the corners into the edge on either side of the pommel.

The surface left by the scorp will still be rough and will require further work. I use a miniature compass plane first to take out any unevenness left by the scorp. Like the larger compass plane used earlier the sole of this little plane is also curved from end to end which allows it to work in an indentation. The one I use is wooden and only 5" long and 1½" wide. It is small enough to get down into the deepest part of the seat. As with the foreplane, I grind a convex cutting edge on the blade so that it can take a heavy chip without digging into the wood. The

compass plane's depth of cut is regulated - the plane will cut only as deep as the blade is set, no matter how much force or pressure is used.

The operation of this plane is fairly simple. Nest it in both hands, holding your wrists rigid. The secret of its successful use is to follow through with each cut. A short choppy motion will dig into the wood rather than smooth it. I clean up the dished area first, working back to center and front to center as with the scorp. Then I blend the saddle into the seat's outline.

The seat has now taken its final form and needs only to be smoothed. The surface is still somewhat rough because the convex cutting edge of the compass plane leaves a distinctly furrowed track which should be removed. The tool that does this work is, as far as I know, unique to chairmaking. It is called a travisher and it looks like a bent spokeshave. Indeed the travisher works in the same manner as a spoke shave. The curve allows it to clean up hollowed surfaces.

Hold your wrists rigid when using the travisher. It is a light tool set to take a very light cut. Its own weight is insufficient to keep it from wobbling or chattering. If you push it you can put more weight over the tool which will help it cut cleanly. Once again follow the strokes through and end each stroke with an upward flick of the wrists. This completely separates the shaving and eliminates the digs caused by an incomplete stroke.

THE SHAPING OF THE SEAT *is complete when the furrows have been smoothed out and the curves flow into each other.*

Work the travisher with the grain from the front and back of the seat, moving toward the center. In the middle of the seat at the bottom of the depression the travisher sometimes tears. This is because it is cutting into the grain that runs up the opposite slope of the saddle. This problem can usually be taken care of with very short, light strokes. If the tearing persists however, you can eliminate it by working across the grain. This will create some roughness that will need to be sanded away.

My compass plane is an antique and I made my travisher. I cut the travisher's curved wooden body out of a piece of maple and had a blacksmith make a bent spokeshave blade to match. Until I discovered these tools, I finished the saddling with the scorp. You can too. To do this lower the handles until their ends almost drag on the surface of the wood. The scorp will now scrape rather than cut.

Work it skewed to the grain for a more acceptable surface. A seat that has been finished with the scorp will require more sanding than one finished with a compass plane and travisher.

Some areas of the seat are flat enough to be smoothed with the travisher's cousin, the spokeshave. The pronounced dip along the edges of the seat between the stumps and the front corners is more easily worked with the spokeshave than the travisher. I also prefer to finish the gently rolled edge of the front corners with the spokeshave using the part of the blade that is set to take a fine cut. The shaping of the seat is now complete. The curves should be crisp and flow gracefully from one side to the other. If they do the seat will echo the bold curves of the back.

Next, carve the channel that outlines the dished area along the back of the seat. This detail separates

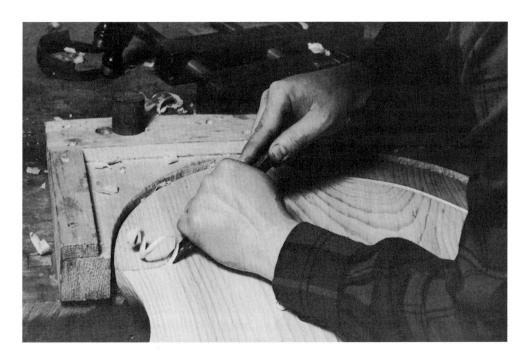

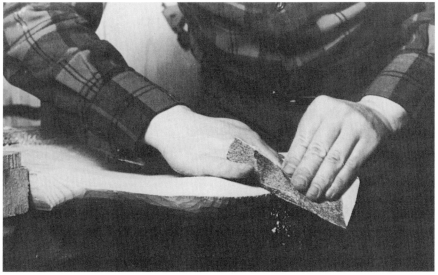

CARVE THE CHANNEL THAT SEPARATES *the excavated saddle from the flat surface at the back of the seat with a ¼" veiner (top). Sand the seat with #50-grit sandpaper. Don not lose the shapr arris on the edge.*

the two distinct areas of the top surface - the saddle and the platform where the sockets are bored. It also makes the transition between them smoother. I use a #11 sweep 7mm veiner. A veiner is a gouge that is deeper than it is wide. You can extend the channel around the arris of the rear edge of the seat if you wish. I prefer to bevel it with a spokeshave. Run the channel or bevel around the tailpiece as well.

I sand the seat with only a quarter sheet of #60- grit sandpaper. This removes any roughness that might remain after smoothing with the travisher. I do not spend a lot of time sanding now because the seat will be bumped and banged and have glue spilled on it as the chair is put together. After the chair is completed I moisten the saddled area with a sponge. This raises the grain as well as any scratches made by the #60-grit paper. When the saddle has dried I sand with #120-grit paper.

Chapter Three

Making the Oval Seat

The oval seat is a much simpler shape than the shield seat and consequently it is easier to make. Select the wood for the oval seat using the same criteria as for the shield seat. The blank should be at least 21" long and 15¾" wide; the grain runs from side to side of the chair. Make a pattern for the seat by scaling up the drawing. Clean off one face of the blank with the foreplane and smooth it with a smoothing plane, then trace around the pattern.

Mark the carved channel that separates the sculpted part of the seat from the flat area (called the platform) that wraps around about three quarters of the edge. The ends of the platform are straight and are indicated by the line running from side to side across the seat as in the photo. Mark the exact middle of the front curve which is the location of the pommel and extend the line of the carved channel out to meet this point. These lines indicate ridges that delineate the extent of the dished area in the center of the seat, and from them the seat will slope gently down to the front edge.

Cut out the seat; then rough out the shape of the edge with the drawknife. The edge profile is a quarter round to the middle of the front edge where it breaks gently into an incline of about 60 degrees with little or no curve. Both shapes are easily roughed out with the drawknife as shown in the drawings shown earlier. I prefer to do most of the finish shaping of the oval seat edge with the smoothing plane.

While I still rough a seat edge with a drawknife, I smooth it with a spokeshave, rather than a plane.

The quarter round edge is faceted by the drawknife, and the plane can bring it to the desired contour more quickly than even the large spokeshave. With the small spokeshave clean up any spots where the plane blade has dug into the end grain. The incline along the front can also be finished with the smoothing plane, and then make the transition from the quarter round to the incline with the spokeshave. The transition occurs beneath where the sitter's legs extend over the seat. All the edge shaping so far can be done with the seat held vertically in a vise.

After shaping the edge, place the seat on the floor and hew out the top surface with the gutter adze. This is done in the same manner as for the shield seat, except that you should swing the adze from each side of the seat toward the center because the grain runs side to side. Hew up to the curved ridge lines drawn between the pommel and the corners of the channel. This gentle ridge will remain after the saddle is complete. If you feel confident of your ability, you can rough out some of the slope that runs down from the ridge to the seat edge. If not, wait and remove this wood with the scorp.

When you are finished with the adze secure the seat to the bench with a hold down frame similar to that used for the shield seat, or clamps. If you clamp, place the seat over a corner so you will have access to more of the seat's circumference.

Work the dished area with the scorp. Cut aggressively and take out heavy chips - clean up the adze marks as quickly as you can. While working in this fashion, rough out the slopes of the ridge if you did not do this with the adze. The ridge serves two functions. The two front leg sockets are bored near it, so the ridge assures ample thickness for a strong joint. The ridge also creates an edge on the dished

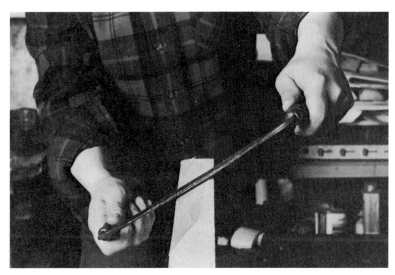

ROUGH OUT THE QUARTER ROUND *profile of the edge with the drawknife. The front edge of the seat beneath the pommel is an incline, which can be roughed out quickly with four or five drawknife cuts at about a 60 degree angle.*

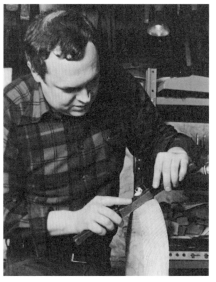

FINISH THE QUARTER ROUND CURVE *along the back edge of the seat with a smoothing plane or large spoke shave. The soles of these tools have worn slightly hollow, which helps them track on the edge.*

THE ROUGH QUARTER ROUND PROFILE *on the left side of the photo is planed and spokeshaved to an even, uniform curve, as remains to be done at right.*

ROUGH OUT THE TOP SURFACE *with a gutter adze, working into the middle. Sever a chip with each swing – don't pry it up.*

area. A sitter can sense this and does not feel that it is possible to slide forward and out of the chair.

The three areas on the top surface - the dished area and the slopes down from the ridges on either side of the pommel - should be worked more carefully with the scorp to bring them to their final shape and depth. I finish the surfaces with the compass plane, travisher, and small spokeshave as described for the shield seat. You can scrape with the scorp if you do not have one or more of these tools to bring them to their final shape.

Take some care with the final shaping of the ridges and the surfaces that slope from them. If the ridges are too sharp or too pronounced, they risk cutting off the circulation of blood to the sitter's legs. I gently round the ridges with the small spokeshave.

Shape the pommel by working away from it toward both sides with the spokeshave. The tool will cut cleanly with the grain. I soften the peak of the pommel by running the shave over it. Later, I round it some more with #60-grit sandpaper. Finish the shaping of the oval seat by carving the channel with a veiner. You can continue the channel around the back edge of the seat or simply bevel that arris with a spokeshave, as I do.

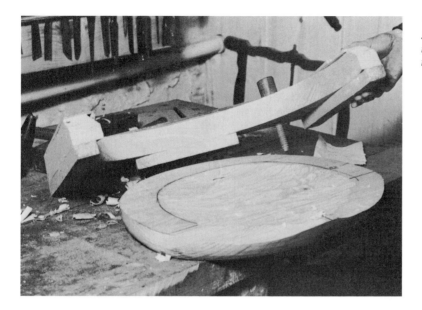

THE HOLD DOWN FRAME IS *shaped to fit the oval seat and is fixed to the bench top with threaded wooden screws.*

WORK THE DISHED AREA AND *the areas around the ridges to their final shape and depth with the scorp as shown below.*

FINISH SHAPING THE EDGE WITH *spokeshaves and planes. The Finish dishing with a compass plane and travisher, or scrape with a scorp.surfaces and the compass plane is useful for the incline along the front of the seat.*

WORK A SMALL SPOKESHAVE WITH *the grain to shape the pommel.*

THE COMPLETED OVAL SEAT HAS *a distinct arris along the front edge, sharply defining the top and bottom surfaces of the seat. A ridge on either side of the pommel separates the dished area from a gentle slope down to the front arris.*

Chapter Four

Windsor Chair Joints

Windsor chairs are held together by socket construction: cylindrical tenons fit into cylindrical holes or sockets. Chairmakers have long relied on socket joints because they can be made very quickly and easily. The holes can be made with a brace and bit or an electric drill. The bit makes a hole of exactly the same diameter each time it is used, and by scribing a line on the bit each socket can be made to the same depth. Tenons can be easily whittled or turned on a lathe.

The speed and ease with which socket joints – round hole, round tenon – can be made is a real advantage. However, socket joints have a dirty little secret. They are the second worst joint known to woodworking. The worst is gluing end grain to end grain. To understand why a socket joint is so impermanent, imagine opening a box of soda straws. You see a cluster of closely spaced openings but little surface. Under magnification, end grain is the same – closely spaced tubes. If you took two handfuls of soda straws and smeared glue on the ends, you would not have a lot of luck getting them to adhere permanently; most of the ends are tiny voids. It's the same problem you encounter when gluing end gain to end grain.

Now, consider a hole drilled into wood. Almost all of its inside surface is end grain, inhibiting a good glue bond. That's why socket joints fail. You know this from experience. What's the first question you're asked when friends and family learn you're trying your hand at chairmaking? "Can you glue my kitchen chairs?" Why this ubiquitous inquiry? Because chair factories glue their socket joints and it does not work over the long haul. Higher end factories try esoteric solutions such as compressing an oversized tenon before inserting it into the socket. Low end factories drive a screw into their joint. Neither work.

This is the lesson for us is. If we wish to take advantage of socket construction's speed and ease, we cannot rely on glue alone. For that reason, every joint in a handmade Windsor chair incorporates some mechanical feature that holds the joint together after the glue has failed. Below, you will learn these mechanical features and how they are

A SIMPLE THROUGH JOINT, LIKE *those used in the backs of both the sack back and the continuous arm are flared at the top by the wedge.*

accomplished. The ways Windsor chairmakers overcame socket construction's inherent weakness are truly remarkable. Like me, you will hold the old guys in high regard.

There are two types of socket joints, blind and through, and I use both in my chairs. The names of these joints are self-explanatory - the blind socket does not go all the way through the piece, the through socket does. In the sack back and continuous arm there are two types of blind socket joints and two types of through joints.

THROUGH SOCKET JOINTS
STRAIGHT WEDGED JOINTS The simplest of the through joints are used in the backs of the continuous arm and the sack back chairs where the short and long spindles are fixed to the bow and/or arm. The ends of the spindles are split with a chisel and a wedge is driven into the split. Glue is smeared on the inside of the hole and on the wedge. The glue on the wedge is important, as an unglued wedge will work its way back out of the split, and loose its effectiveness.

The purpose of the wedge is to flare the end of the spindle so the part cannot pull off the end after

A LOCKING TAPER JOINT CUT *in half shows the tapered tenon and the tapered hole.*

the glue in the joint fails. You can see this flaring in the adjacent picture. To show how the wedge works, two joints have been cut in half.

LOCKING TAPER JOINTS The joints used to secure the legs and stumps into the seats and the top of the stumps into the arm are truly clever. They are locking tapers. The tenon is a truncated cone and fits into a hole with the same degree of taper. If the degree of taper is within a certain range of angles the friction between the parts will lock them together.

This lock is powerful. I demonstrate this for students by clamping a piece of wood with a tapered hole in it to a corner of a workbench. I then tap a leg with a tapered tenon into the hole. Finally, I lift the corner of a 300 pound bench top by pulling upward on the leg.

This is the principle of the self-holding, or locking taper systems that machinists know by such names as Morse, Jacobs, and Brown and Sharps. You are likely to have encountered the locking taper in the drive center of a wood turning lathe. You know how effectively these parts are held in place if you have ever had to remove the center. This friction bond is so strong that to break it and loosen the center you must insert a drift pin into the rear of the spindle and give the pin a sharp rap.

Although the tapered sockets and tenons that join the legs and the seat of a Windsor lock in the same way, nothing will spare them from inevitably loosening as the wood swells and shrinks with changes in humidity. However, each time someone sits in the chair the tenons are driven back into the tapered sockets and relocked. The beauty of this joint is that use, which wears out all other types of chairs, works to hold a Windsor together.

Tapered tenons and sockets are easy to make. The tenons are turned to shape in the lathe. The

sockets are bored with a brace and spoon bit then tapered with a tool called a reamer. A reamer resembles a steel cone that has been sliced in half along its axis; the two exposed edges are sharpened by beveling them toward the inside of the cone. My reamer tapers a socket at about 7 degrees. (Wood has different properties than steel so the angle of the taper is not as critical as for tapers used by machinists.) I generally turn the tenons so that their taper is slightly shallower than those of the sockets. Wedging the tenon at assembly spreads the tenon and makes it conform to the socket. This allows a considerable margin of error when turning the tenons, so gauging the size and taper by eye is quite feasible. (I discuss making this joint in later chapters.)

Of course, you can use a straight, through socket joint to fix the legs to the seat. When doing this, I make a shoulder on a straight tenon, so that only the tenon can enter the socket. Undercutting the socket opening to house this shoulder will make a more presentable joint. At assembly, I wedge the tenon, just as for the tapered joint. The wedge prevents the tenon from retracting. Even when the joint eventually loosens the tenon is permanently trapped between the shoulder and the flared top created by the wedge. At worst a loose, wedged through tenon will rattle and twist in its socket. You can minimize the potential for twisting by using a wedge that is wider than the diameter of the tenon. The edges of the wedge will key into the soft pine of the seat and prevent the shaft from turning. I will explain this technique in greater detail later.

BLIND SOCKET JOINTS

A blind socket is simply a hole bored partway into, but not through the chair part. The tenon, which is turned or whittled to the diameter of the bit used to bore the socket, is glued into the socket. However,

THESE TWO SECTIONS OF DRIVE *fit tenons show how effectively they distort the holes in the pine seat to their individual shapes.*

glue cannot be the only thing that secures the joint, as when the glue bond fails, so does the joint.

DRIVE FIT TENONS This joint is used on the sack back and continuous arm to secure the short and long spindles to the seat. The principal is the same as square peg in round hole. The holding power is from a series of flat facets and sharp corners biting into the pine seat and distorting the hole to the shape of the tenon. I start by making the ends of my tenons ⅝" and drilling 9/16" holes in the seat. Then, with a gouge, as shown in a later chapter, I make pronounced facets. They create relief, while the corners remain ⅝" across. When I am ready, I swab the holes with glue and then drive the tenons into the seat with a hammer, like I was driving nails.

TENONS IN COMPRESSION The stretchers of many types of chairs are blind-socketed into the legs and here is where most of these chairs usually first come apart. Manufacturers have devised super glues, liquids that swell wood, and tenon compressors in an effort to find a way to overcome the tendency of wooden chairs to fail at the leg/stretcher joints. These joints have long baffled anyone who has tried to keep them from loosening. Eighteenth century Windsors tell a different story. The old chairmakers overcame this problem, and obviously knew something that

is not general knowledge today. I wish I could show you the joint in a photograph, but you cannot see the technique. I have to describe it.

Like the old guys, I put these joints in compression by making each of the three stretchers a bit over long. In other words the stretchers push the legs apart. Factories use their stretchers to hold the legs together, so their joints are in tension. Because the glue will fail, these joints continually come apart. The compression technique works because the legs are anchored in the solid wood seat and because the locking tapered joints renew each time someone sits in the chair. Pretty neat, huh? I will explain how to do this as we get into assembling the undercarriage.

I know that the four joints described above work. Why? They were used in making 18th century chairs, and after more than 200 years most of these chairs are still as tight as the day they were made. We can say they have been tested in the ultimate laboratory – daily use.

There are numerous other clever joints used in Windsor chairmaking, such as the one used to secure a footrest to a youth chair, the applied arm to the Nantucket fan back. Since they are not part of either the sack back or continuous arm, they are not included here.

Chapter Five

Turning the Legs

The undercarriage of a Windsor chair consists of the legs and stretchers. These parts are split from unseasoned logs and are turned on the lathe while they are still green. I will discuss how to split the wood first then how to turn the parts.

I am a fast turner, (I do a baluster leg in six minutes) but I could never turn the quantity of parts we require for classes. Today, I buy from a job turner. I turned the original patterns that he copies. This practice is consistent with traditional Windsor chairmaking. The old guys purchased their turnings in large quantities from wood turners, very much the way The Institute does.

RIVING I suggest that you split or rive all the turning stock for the chair. Most people have split wood for the stove, but riving differs from making stove wood in that the placement and direction of the split are controlled. Strength is one reason why I recommend riving. In a riven turning blank the split follows the direction of the grain, so all the wood fibers in the blank run from one end of the piece to the other. Riven wood is therefore tough and capable of flexing.

Had the turning blank been sawn, the cut would have run in a straight line, ignoring the direction of the grain. A turning made from sawn wood risks having its grain run out at a narrow point, as shown below. When the leg is under stress, the wood may break along the grain at that point. Repair of such a break is nearly impossible. A riven turning will not fail in this way. If abused beyond what it can tolerate a piece of riven stock will shear perpendicular to the grain. All its fibers will be severed, and the break will be at a right angle to the length of the turning.

I do not ignore the importance of straight grain and direct my turner to be very selective of the stock he uses for our orders.

Another reason why I recommend riving is economy. Riving is an ancient technique (the word is of archaic Scandinavian origin) and it is a wasteful one when judged by industrial standards. Although it is very efficient in its labor requirement, it is very inefficient in its consumption of materials. It would never be an acceptable general method in today's woodworking industry. However, when purchased in the log, wood is so cheap that people who are not mass-producing chairs can afford to rive stock and still come out ahead. Given the price of hardwood, why pay this kind of money to a lumber dealer when superior stock is readily available in most unseasoned cord wood? I purchase the green wood I need for the undercarriage and backs of my chairs in logs from the same fellow who brings me my firewood. A lot of my riven wood is unusable for chair parts, but because I heat with wood nothing is wasted. What comes into the shop on Monday goes out on Friday as a chair or in a bucket of ashes.

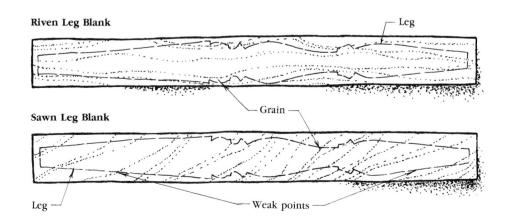

Riven Leg Blank

Leg

Grain

Sawn Leg Blank

Leg

Weak points

FOR MAKING CHAIR LEGS, FIRST *cut the log into billets about 20" long.*

WOOD SELECTION A good baluster leg of the design I make has sharp, crisp details and the wood I choose to turn must be able to render such results. I am fortunate to live in northern New England, an area that is still covered with hardwood forests. Obtaining wood is no problem for me and I have been able to experiment with most of the common species. Through a process of elimination, I have selected two kinds of wood, red maple and paper birch for chair legs and stretchers. (Red maple is a soft maple; paper birch is also called white birch.)

I have several reasons for preferring these woods. Both are common and easily obtained. Both split quickly and cleanly. They are not coarse and open grained as are some other woods used in chairmaking, such as oak, ash, or hickory. They are dense, diffuse-porous woods, so they will cut cleanly in the lathe and allow me to make good, crisp details. Maple and birch have a creamy color and smooth, clear consistency, so legs turned from them will not have pronounced figure that competes with the shape I turn for the viewer's attention. Depending on your location, you may or may not be able to obtain birch or maple. If not, you will have to experiment with species that are native to your region to find one that has these same properties.

I order wood in logs that I cut to 5 ft. lengths. The longest turnings I make are chair legs which are turned from 19"-long blanks. If I allow for two chainsaw cuts a 5 ft. log will render three sections of turning stock for legs and stretchers. Five feet is also a good length for the oak logs from which I rive chair backs. The longest pieces needed are 58" for the continuous-arm chair.

Today, I buy oak logs from a veneer concentration yard. They are usually 10 ft. to 14 ft. long. I go the yard and select logs suitable for bending and have them delivered by a log truck with a cherry picker arm.

I like to work with logs from trees that grew in the forest and not by themselves. I also want them to be no less than 12" in diameter. Trees that grow in the open do not have to compete for sunlight with surrounding trees. Such trees do not usually produce good, straight trunks, free of low limbs that form knots. To understand why forest grown trees less than 12" in diameter are also unacceptable it is necessary to know a bit about how trees grow.

Most of our forests are second growth; trees that have reclaimed land that was originally forested, but was cleared for cultivation generations ago. If you look at photographs of the New England countryside taken in the late 19th century, you will be struck by the lack of trees. As the region became industrially developed, however, the farmers went to work in factories, abandoning the fields. The

HALVE THE BILLETS. SET ONE *or two wedges in the center, and drive them to open the billet. Sometimes, a solid blow will spilt a billet cleanly.*

untilled land was very quickly reclaimed by the forests.

Maples and birches are called invading species because they are among the first to grow when an open space is left fallow. There are no adult trees for the first saplings to compete with. Consequently, these saplings are not forced to grow straight and tall to find sunlight in the openings of the forest canopy. Instead they branch early. As the trees increase in size, however, they must compete with each other for sunlight. The trunk and upper branches shoot up. The lower limbs die and what remains of these branches is encased deep in the trunk near the heart. Wood that grows over the remains of the young tree is deflected. This early growth near the heart is too twisted to rive and turn cleanly. Later growth, however, is less disturbed by the remains of the old branches and this growth is eventually laid on smooth and straight. Several inches of growth out from the heart is necessary before this outer, superior wood can develop. I split turning blanks from this outer wood and toss the heart into the stove. A log larger than 12" in diameter usually contains more usable wood.

A log for chairmaking should therefore have nearly perfectly straight grain, free of knots and twists. Such flaws make a log difficult to rive and parts made from its wood tend to be weak.

An acceptable log will split cleanly in two with a wedge and maul. It takes practice to determine whether a log is worth buying for chairmaking. Here are some outward signs that I look for. You can obtain a pretty good idea of the surprises that a log may contain inside by first examining its bark. Any bumps indicate an encased knot that is fairly close to the surface. I pass such logs by. Clear logs are easy enough to get that I don't mess with any with possible defects. Detecting deeper knots requires closer observation. Paper birch takes its name from the characteristics of its bark, which is as smooth and as white as writing paper. Where the tree has healed over a knot or other blemish a black or dark grey whorl will appear on the bark. This whorl indicates that the log contains a defect that will make the wood useless for riving into turning blanks.

The bark of red maple is a little more difficult to describe, because it can vary so much from tree to tree. On younger trees, it can be grey and as smooth as birch. Any encased knots or other internal problems make themselves known by the pronounced effects they have on this smooth bark. The effects are similar to those described earlier for birch. On old trees the bark is very coarse and a grey brown color. When the tree is felled, skidded, and loaded the bark is abraded. Any high spots that indicate the presence of an encased knot will be rubbed

MARK THE 2" SQUARE TURNING blanks on the end of a section. A wooden maul and a Kent hatchet are ideal for riving pieces of this size.

until they are a distinctive brown, about the color of a pair of undyed leather shoes. The coarse bark also contains fissures that normally run vertically on the standing tree. If these fissures display any pronounced irregularities, there is probably a knot or some other blemish lurking inside.

RIVING AND PREPARING THE BLANKS
Examine the log for the characteristics mentioned, and if you find that it is worth working, lay a tape measure on it and score the bark at 20" and 40" Then buck the log into three sections, which are called billets. One of these 12" diameter billets usually contains just enough wood for two chairs. Halve the billet on the spot using a maul and wedges.

I use a splitting maul with a short, 22" long handle, which increases my control. You can use a sledge hammer, but the wedge on the maul sometimes comes in handy on a reluctant billet. I also use iron wedges rather than wooden gluts. I split a lot of firewood as well as chair parts, and the iron wedges hold up forever. You should wear safety glasses when striking metal on metal. (You will notice I have forgotten mine in the pictures. Do as I say, not as I do.) Place one wedge on either side of the pith and work them down in tandem. This placement of wedges helps ensure a straight, even split that bisects the billet. The halves may be small enough to be carried into the shop for riving into turning blanks. If not, quarter them.

You want to obtain as many 2" square blanks as possible from each halved or quartered section. Sketch these out on the end of the sections. I use a splitting hatchet and a wooden maul to rive the

WHEN RIVING, ALWAYS TRY TO place the split so there is an equal mass of wood on both sides.

CUT THE LEG BLANKS TO *length. A Swedish brush saw works well for this.*

blanks. A Kent hatchet is best for splitting. It has a wide blade, so it can control a split that extends completely across the end grain of a large section. The head of a Kent hatchet also has a long gradual taper from the cutting edge to the poll (the surface on which the hatchet is struck). When driven, the thin wedge of the hatchet head bites into the wood and does not bounce back, as a fatter wedge is prone to do. A splitting hatchet does not need to be kept as sharp as one that is used for cutting. However, if you want yours to do double duty, keeping it sharpened will not affect its ability to split.

A Kent hatchet has a heavy poll which can withstand indefinitely the blows of the wooden maul. The maul is a heavy wooden club about 6" in diameter and 18" long. I turn mine on the lathe from green oak or hickory. A maul has a short life span. It will be gradually knocked apart until it has lost so much weight that it can no longer drive the hatchet with authority. When this happens, I run the old maul through the stove and turn a new one to take its place.

When riving the turning blanks from the sections, it is always best to split pieces of equal mass. This does not mean that the outline of the end of the section has to be perfectly bisected. The sections are too irregular. Instead, the amount of surface area should be about equal on either side of the hatchet head. The resulting two pieces should weigh about the same, even though they may have two very different cross sections. If you do not rive pieces of equal mass, the split will run out toward the side

with less mass, as it is weaker. Birch is much more susceptible to this run out than is maple. If a split begins to run out there is not much you can do to prevent it. However, in addition to legs and stretchers the chair requires stumps and short spindles that are turned from shorter blanks. Use blanks that have been ruined by run out for these parts.

Whether you are making a continuous arm or a sack back chair, rive enough blanks for four legs and three stretchers. Plan the sequence of splits so that you are always riving blanks of equal mass. Rive 1¼" square blanks for the two stumps and ¾"-square blanks for the four short spindles now, too. Next, cut the leg stump and short spindle blanks to the lengths needed for turning. (The distance between the legs determines the lengths of the stretchers, so they are turned after the legs and the sockets in the seat are made. I will discuss the stretchers in another chapter.) I make my leg blanks 19½" long, the stump blanks 14" and the short spindle blanks 12". Each of these lengths includes ½"for waste where the blank is attached to the spur drive center of my lathe. Depending on your lathe, you may need to allow more for waste. Each blank also includes a little extra length so that the through tenons will protrude beyond the sockets, making wedging easier.

The rest of the extra length on each leg blank will occur at the foot. This will have to be trimmed after the chair base is assembled for the final time. I like about 1" extra on the foot end. That gives me plenty of latitude so that I do not have to make the

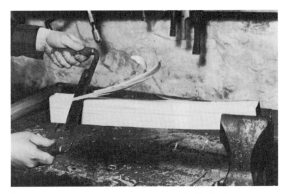

PREPARE THE TURNING BLANK FOR *the lathe by removing the high spots with a draw knife.*

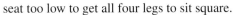

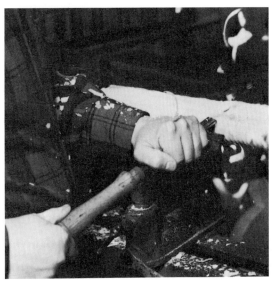

seat too low to get all four legs to sit square.

I cut the blanks to length with a brush saw. I like these inexpensive, tubular metal frame saws because they cut green wood so quickly. Their needle sharp teeth have a heavy set and cut a wide kerf that does not allow the wet wood to bind on the blade. The blades are inexpensive and can be simply discarded when dull. These saws are available in most hardware stores. I use one with a 21" blade.

When all the blanks are the desired length, I remove the high spots and square edges with the drawknife. It is much easier to do this than turn down the high spots. The drawknife easily slices off long, heavy shavings. These dry quickly and make excellent kindling. I generally set the roughly rounded turning blanks aside rather than turn them right away. In as little time as overnight in a heated shop, they will lose a lot of moisture. In the summer I set them out in the sun for an entire day. Freshly riven wood is so wet that it spits water and does not turn as nicely as it will only 24 hours later.

TURNING Green wood is a joy to turn. Once you have tried it you will regret any time you have spent in combat with dry hardwood turning squares. After the green wood blank is completely round the chips come off in unbroken lengths like ticker tape. They pile up on your hands like spaghetti until the tool is obscured and the chips need to be dumped off.

I prefer to turn at the slowest speed possible, which on my lathe is about 1000 rpm. Green wood is soft and a high rpm is not needed to drive it against the tools. On the other hand the turning tools need to be kept razor sharp. The additional pressure needed to make a dull tool cut unseasoned wood will cause the blank to vibrate, which can easily knock the blank out of round because it is so soft. Once it is out of round the blank is good only for firewood. I cannot place enough stress on the

ROUGH THE LEG BLANKS TO *the diameters of the major and minor vases on the legs. While the blank is spinning, mark the position of the bead and cove above the major vase, and the wafer above the minor vase with a pair of dividers. If you do not have a model leg, determine these points by measuring from a full scale pattern.*

need for razor sharp lathe tools when turning green wood.

When mounting a dry wood turning square in the lathe you can find the center on each end by drawing the diagonals from corner to corner. That is not possible with irregularly shaped riven turning blanks. I mount them in the lathe by eye. If the blank is obviously off center and causes the lathe to vibrate dangerously, I will reposition one or both of the ends on the lathe centers. When the blank is centered, turn on the lathe again and watch the blank. The stroboscopic effect of the spinning blank makes the center mass appear solid and the edges read as a translucent blur. The center mass indicates the largest possible diameter to which the blank can be turned.

I use the baluster leg that is shown in the plans for both the continuous arm and sack back chairs. My general production consists of these two chairs and a side chair. These are often purchased in sets - two of either style of armchair, and six side chairs. As a result, one leg pattern makes it easier to match the set. I occasionally use the double bobbin leg, shown in the sack back drawings for a chair or set of chairs. The double-bobbin leg is simple to turn, so I will describe the turning of a baluster leg here. I will also assume that you are familiar with basic wood turning techniques.

I do not work from a drawing or template of the baluster leg. Instead I transfer measurements with calipers directly from a model leg that I have used for years. For your first leg you will have to work from the drawing, or an existing chair. Scale up the drawing to full size and transfer the full size measurements to the leg blank using calipers. When you have finished your first leg, use it as the model for the remaining legs. Do not worry if all the legs are not identical. When you have made a chair or two,

you will probably have produced a leg that seems just right. Keep that leg for your permanent model. I also use a model when turning double bobbin legs. If I make a chair on special order that has different legs, I make a model and store it for future reference.

I use only four tools when turning: a ¾" gouge; a ¼" gouge; a ¾" skew; and a ½" skew. I rough down the blank with the ¾" gouge and make the larger shapes with it and the ¾" skew. The smaller gouge and skew produce the finer details. I cut with both the gouges and skews but scrape only with the skews. Scraping must be done carefully with sharp tools, or you will just raise fuzz. I wear a face shield to protect my face and eyes when I work at the lathe.

First, turn the irregularly shaped blank down to a cylinder with the large gouge. The baluster leg has a major and a minor diameter, corresponding to the widest points on the upper and lower vases. (The vases are the two softly rounded swellings on the leg that look just like their namesake.) Set two pair of calipers to these diameters on the model leg or full scale drawing, and rough the blank to those diameters, checking with the calipers. The minor diameter, at the top of the leg extends about two-fifths the length of the blank. It is best worked on the end of the blank that is fixed to the tailstock center. The foot is fixed to the drive center. The waste attached to the drive center will be trimmed off later when the leg is cut to length.

Next, locate the three points A, B, and C shown on the leg pattern drawing. I do this by holding the model leg parallel to the spinning blank. Line up the end of the tenon with the tailstock end of the blank. If the lengths of the legs vary, I want the variation to occur at the foot of each where any extra length can be trimmed off without affecting the tenon. (If you are setting out the leg from a pattern drawing, start

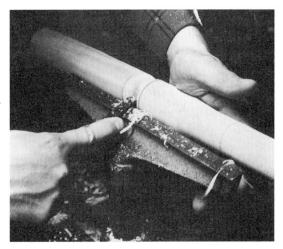

CUT THE COVE WITH A *small gouge, working down to the bottom from both sides. Use a skew to clean the fillet between the cove and bead with a scraping cut.*

at the tenon end.) Lightly scribe each point by laying one leg of a sharp pair of dividers on the model and touching the point of the leg to the spinning blank. I complete the turning by eye, having done it thousands of times before. You will probably want to work more slowly and compare the turning to the model or pattern more often.

Scribe marks A and B indicate the bead and cove that separate the tapered foot from the major vase. The bead takes up about two fifths of the distance between these two lines. The remaining three fifths are needed for the cove. I eyeball this division. I make the bead with a skew, pushing in on each side with the tool cutting, not scraping. Round the bead by gently scraping with the skew.

Make the cove with a small gouge. Cut (don't scrape) from both sides down to the lowest point. Allow room for the fillet that divides the bead and cove. The fillet makes the transition from the convex to the concave shape sharp and distinct. As you deepen the cove you will expose end grain on its sides. If one of the cuts should move beyond the lowest point the gouge will grab in the end grain and will be sent spiraling up the leg. This will usually ruin the turning. Once the cove is made, clean the fillet with the heel or toe of a skew.

Next shape the bottom of the major vase and cut the sharp, wafer-like ring that divides the vase from the cove. Allowing room for the wafer, start the vase by making successive angled cuts with the heel of the large skew. The vase should have a round bottom, so be careful that your cuts produce a curved profile not a straight one.

Reduce the diameter of the wafer with the skew. If you leave the wafer the same diameter as the major vase and the bead it will be more exposed

FORM THE BOTTOM OF THE *major vase with the heel of the skew. Remember to allow for the wafer beneath the cove. Reduce the wafer's diameter by cutting gently with the skew. Then cut the wafer's radius with the skew's heel. Shape the major vase with a large gouge.*

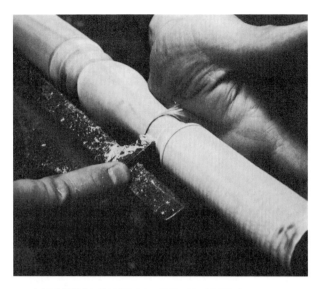

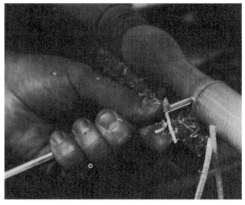

USE A SMALL GOUGE TO *cut the cove that ends the major vase. Make the cove's stop with a small skew; use your free hand to control vibration. Shape the bottom of the vase and its wafer with a skew.*

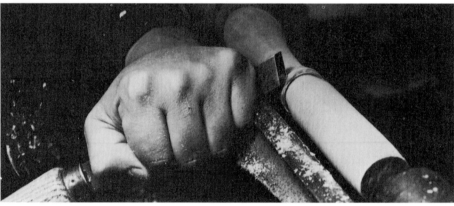

and in greater danger of being damaged. One side of the wafer is formed by a side of the cove. Cut the other side to a radius with a skew making the edge of the wafer sharp.

Move up the blank and shape the rest of the major vase. I do this with the ¾" gouge. Cut the neck of the vase so that it will be thinner than the largest diameter of the minor vase as shown on the pattern drawing. The neck slopes and finishes with a cove. When shaping the neck you will have reduced considerably the diameter of the blank and it may vibrate or buzz under the pressure of the tool. You can eliminate this vibration by using one hand as a steady rest. Hook the handle of the tool under your right elbow, pinching it against your ribs. Grip the turning tool with your right hand close to the tool's cutting edge and lock your wrist. Control the tool by turning your torso. Support the turning from behind with your left hand. Do not push too hard with the left hand. Push enough to duplicate the pressure of the tool on other side of the turning. Keep palm open. You do not want to catch your skin between

the spinning wood and the tool rest.

I have sufficient calluses on my left hand so that the heat caused by the friction does not bother me. If it is uncomfortable for you, wear a thin glove. Cut the cove that ends the major vase with the small gouge. Cut the right angled stop that separates the cove from the neck with a skew. This stop should be good and sharp, without any jaggedness at the transition.

Move to the right of the cove and cut the bottom of the minor vase with a skew. This cut should form a radius, to give the vase a round bottom. A wafer separates the bottom of the minor vase from the cove. Reduce it in diameter and round it to a sharp edge with a skew, as was done for the wafer under the major vase.

Now move to the other end of the blank and shape the tapered foot.

I am always careful in making any turning to do the center first, and then work in both directions away from the center to the ends. This is contrary to the natural tendency of a right-handed person

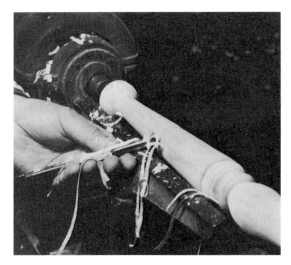

MAKE THE TAPERED FOOT WITH *a large gouge. Complete the end of the foot with a large skew. Clean up the taper with a planning cut. Only one edge of the skew should touch the rest.*

to begin at the left-hand end of a turning and work along the blank to the other end. If you cut one or both of the ends before the middle, however, you weaken the blank considerably and increase the amount it will vibrate on the lathe.

I have noticed a tendency of a tapered cone to appear to have a convex, slightly bulging profile, sort of like a carrot. To compensate for this tendency, I make the taper just slightly concave along its length. The classical Greeks made their temple columns slightly convex along their length to compensate for the tendency of a straight column to appear concave. This convexity is called entasis. Perhaps the slight concavity of the leg taper could be called reverse entasis.

Shape the taper with the large gouge. When the shape is completely developed, clean up the last inch or so of the foot with a skew. I do this by holding the large skew with its wide side flat on the rest, as I would if I were about to scrape. I raise the cutting edge slightly above center and feed the skew straight into the wood. This leaves a wafer of waste on the end that can be knocked off later with a drawknife.

Next, clean up any gouge marks on the tapered foot. I do this with the ¾" skew as well. Start at the top, or right hand end of the taper, just below the bead. Lay the wide side of the skew on the rest as when cleaning up the foot. I lift the right edge of the skew so that it is rotated about 45 degrees. In this position, the skew is in contact with the rest only on one corner of its left edge. Support the turning with your left hand to prevent it from vibrating, and slowly move the skew along the taper. The chip cuts loose in more of a clump than the ribbon that you usually obtain when cutting. The surface is cut perfectly clean and should require no sanding.

I call this a planing cut. It is a difficult tech-

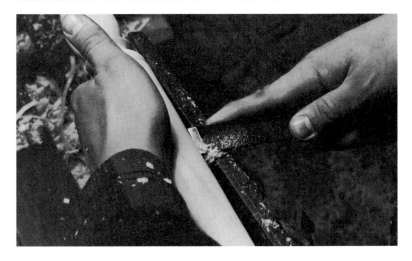

CLEAN UP THE TAPER WITH *a planing cut. Only one edge of the skew should touch the rest.*

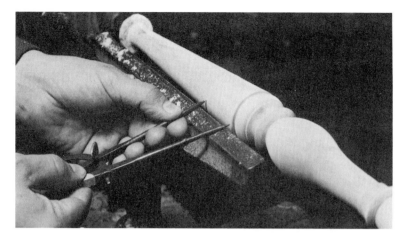

SCRIBE A RING ON THE *tapered foot to locate the stretcher socket.*

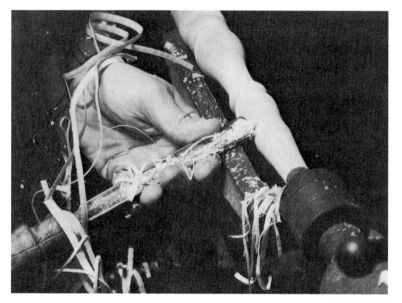

TRUN THE NECK OF THE *minor vase and the tapered tenon with a large gouge. For a slight swelling where the neck meets the tenon.*

THE STUMP IS A MINIATURE *leg, and the same techniques are used to turn it. The tapered tenon on the lower end of the armpost is the same size as the tenon for the legs. The tenon at its upper end fits into a 7/16" taperd socket.*

nique to refine, but once mastered you will be able to use the skew for cleaning up any straight faces, as on the taper or any gradually concave or convex surfaces. I use this planing cut on the bobbins of stretchers, on the entire double-bobbin leg, and on the taper and vase of the baluster leg and stump.

Before leaving the tapered foot, scribe a ring on it to locate the stretcher socket. Set a pair of dividers from the model leg or pattern by placing one leg on the scribe line and the other at the point where the bead meets the taper. Place the dividers in the same position on the spinning blank and push the pointed leg into the taper to scribe the ring.

Slide the tool rest to the other end of the blank to shape the last details there. Relieve the neck of the minor vase with the large gouge. I turn a slight

swelling on the neck where it meets the tenon. This swelling allows the diameter of the vase's neck to be less than that of the base of the tapered tenon. The swelling looks something like a shoulder, but it has no mechanical function. The point at which the leg disappears under the edge of the seat occurs along the neck of the vase. It appears to the viewer that the leg continues to taper down to a very small diameter. Actually, the vase swells to form a strong, robust tenon. The swelling contributes to the illusion of delicacy that is also seen in the shaping of the seat.

Shape the tapered tenon with the large gouge. I determine the amount of taper by eye, but you may want to make a gauge. Bore a ⅝" hole in a piece of 2"-thick pine scrap. Ream this hole with a tapered

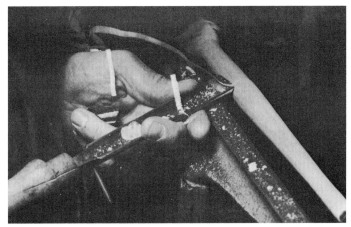

SHAPE THE SHORT SPINDLES WITH *a large gouge to a continuous sweep from end to end.*

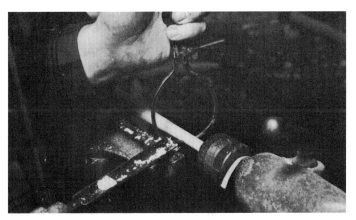

THE NECK FORMS THE TOP *tenon; check its diameter with a pair of calipers.*

reamer as described later. To use the gauge, you will have to remove the leg from the lathe. To re-center the leg perfectly after gauging the tenon, you must relocate the end on the drive center exactly as it was. This can be difficult to do. I grind a small notch in the beveled edge of one of the spurs on the drive center. This notch creates a dimple in one of the marks left by the spurs in the end grain of the turning. Aligning the dimpled mark with the notched spur should re-center the leg perfectly.

If you are using a straight tenon on the leg, measure its diameter with a pair of calipers. Set the calipers from the bit you will use to bore the seat sockets rather than setting it with a ruler. This pre-vents mistakes in measuring. The swelling at the top of the neck decreases suddenly in diameter to form the tenon's shoulder.

The two stumps are turned in the same sequence and manner as the legs. I turn tapered tenons at both ends. The tenon on the lower end is the same size as that on the legs and it can be tested using the same

gauge. You can make another gauge for the upper tenon which fits into the arm. Bore a $\frac{7}{16}$" hole in a piece of scrap and taper the hole with the reamer.

Both the sack back and the continuous-arm chairs have two short spindles behind each stump. These spindles are also turned. They are at the limit of the ratio of length to thickness that can be turned without intolerable vibration. Be careful when turn-ing them and use your hand as a steady rest. Turn the spindle blanks to shape with the large gouge. The outline is a clean, continuous sweep from the shoulder of the lower tenon up over a gentle swell-ing and down to a $\frac{7}{16}$" neck. The neck also forms the upper tenon. To achieve a smooth outline, make a final clean up pass, planing gently with a sharp skew. This finishing technique is only mastered with considerable practice. If it is too difficult at first, let the spindle dry, and then sand the surface smooth. Be sure to sand in the direction of the grain

Rather than spending time trying to make the lower shouldered tenon a perfect fit for a $\frac{9}{16}$"

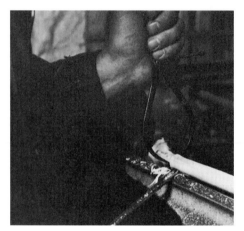

CLEAN UP THE SURFACE WITH *a planing cut of the skew chisel (left). Use a small gouge and skew to make the lower, egg shaped tenon (bottom, left). The neck below the tenon's shoulder should be a little narrower than the socket, and the egg should be a little wider (bottom, right).*

socket, I turn the tenon slightly egg-shaped and oversized. Next to the shoulder, I make the neck a little narrower than the bit that will be used to bore the socket when I assemble the chair. I can shave the egg with a chisel to fit perfectly in the socket. Also the chisel produces a faceted surface that bites into the soft pine walls of the socket. These facets help resist torque that might otherwise weaken the joint.

I never sand turnings on the lathe. Green wood does not sand well. And on any wood, green or dry, sanding on the spinning lathe will create concentric scratches that are almost impossible to remove, no matter how fine the paper. Also, sanding softens the crisp details that I have taken so much care to make. Good control of sharp tools will eliminate the need for almost all sanding. Between turning and assembly, the parts will have been bumped and will have

had glue spilled on them. Some grain will rise as the parts dry. Therefore, I find it most efficient to sand with #220-grit paper after the chair is assembled, just before applying the first coat of paint. Anything I miss will be abraded away by steel wool when I smooth the first coat of paint.

In 1984 I suggested making a gauge in a piece of pine to test your tapered tenons. That technique required you remove the leg from the lathe to test the tenon's fit. Instead, cut the gauge in half along the tapered hole's length. Now, you can hold a half against the tenon while the leg remains in the lathe. It's a lot easier.

Chapter Six

Socketing the Seat

You have completed the seat, the legs, the two stumps, and the short spindles. Before the stretchers can be turned the sockets for the legs must be bored in the seat. The legs and sockets are angled to the seat and it is worthwhile to take a look at why this is so.

Vertical legs are ideal for supporting downward pressure. However, we do not use chairs in an ideal manner. We do not sit bolt upright like West Point cadets at mealtime. We recline and shift and squirm. These forces are transmitted throughout the chair in other directions than just downward. For example, as we shift in the chair to find a comfortable position we create torque, a twisting motion of the seat against the legs. The same force is exerted in a wrestling match. A wrestler does not throw his opponent by pushing downward on his shoulders. He does so by wrenching him sideways. To resist this wrenching torque, the other wrestler braces himself by spreading his legs and arms apart and throwing his shoulders forward. His legs and arms are now splayed in two planes very much like those of a Windsor chair.

It may seem strange to compare a chair and sitter to a pair of wrestlers, but the relationship often seems no less adversarial. When we approach a chair, we turn and flop ourselves into it. The chair is suddenly and violently stressed by the 150 lb. to 250 lb. of humanity landing in it. We then, twist and turn until we have found a comfortable position. This strains the legs and the stretcher system as well as the back. We shift our weight by sliding our buttocks forward or backward, or by crossing and uncrossing our legs. When we stretch, we prop our shoulders against the chair back and our bottoms against the front of the seat. In spite of Mother's warnings, we still rock back on the legs. When we finally get out of the chair we put yet another strain on it. Instead of lifting our own weight with our legs, we put our hands on the arms of the chair and push ourselves up.

To better resist these assaults, each leg of a Windsor is canted in two planes, away from both its adjacent partners. This widens the base of the chair (the points formed by the intersection of the

legs with the floor). This wider base makes a chair more resistant to the stresses and strains put upon it. It also makes the chair less likely to roll out from underneath the sitter should he lean too far forward backward or to the side.

To discuss the specific leg-to-seat angles, it is necessary to define two terms - splay and rake. In normal use both words mean the same thing, but I define them differently for Windsors. Splay refers to the way that the two front legs (and the two rear legs) are canted away from each other. When looking at a chair from the front or back you see the splay of the legs. Rake refers to the way that the two legs on a single side are canted away from each other. Rake is seen by regarding the chair from either side.

Splay and rake combine to resist the compression and torque caused by the sitter's movements and to stabilize and prevent the chair from tipping. However, it is possible to have too much of a good thing, and a chair is weakened if the legs are splayed or raked excessive. I consider between 105 and 110 degrees good splay for front and back legs. A chair is weakened if these angles exceed about 115 degrees. Also, front legs that splay too much continually get in the way. They make it difficult to get in and out of the chair, and people passing by the chair trip over them. Other chairs cannot be placed close to a chair with excessively splayed legs, which makes such a chair awkward to have around a table.

It is not necessary to splay the rear legs to the same angles as the front legs. However, if they are not splayed enough, or are placed too close together, they cease to stabilize the chair. In the extreme, rear legs placed too upright act as a single point, and the chair becomes like a three-legged stool. When a chair with upright rear legs is rocked back, there is little to prevent it from rolling sideways.

Rear legs should have a distinct rake, because the majority of the sitter's weight will be supported by these legs. The backs of all Windsors recline; those designed for relaxing or reading have a more distinct recline. The greater the slope of the back, the farther the sitter's weight is carried backward. If the rake of the back legs is insufficient, the chair has

a precarious balance when in use. The rake should increase with the slope of the back. I am most comfortable with a chair whose back legs are raked about 110 to 113 degrees. A rake of less than 107 degrees is insufficient.

This much rake is unnecessary for the front legs, because there is relatively less weight placed over them. When the sitter leans forward he has his own legs under him for additional support; when he leans back he has only the chair. To rake the front legs as much as the rear would only encumber people walking by the chair, or make it more difficult for the sitter to get out of it. Too much rake, like too much splay, can also weaken the chair. However no rake at all is dangerous. When the sitter leans forward on front legs with no rake, the chair pivots on the legs and it can kick out backward from underneath its occupant. I prefer a rake of about 95 to 100 degrees for the front legs.

Before boring the sockets you should know about spoon bits. You are not uninformed if you do not know what these bits are. They were dropped from toolmakers' product lines early in this century, and were considered obsolete. They were revived when I began using them to make chairs and talked about them to anyone who would listen. Spoon bits are one of the most ancient tools. They were known to the Romans and have been excavated from Viking sites. By the eighteenth century they were known as chair bits. Spoon bits have a number of properties that make them ideal for chairmaking: The speed of cut can be regulated; the angle of a socket can be altered as you bore, and sockets can be bored at very shallow angles to the work.

To understand a spoon bit and how it works, imagine a test tube sliced in half along its length. Each half would closely resemble a spoon bit. The semicircular end of the bit is the business end and does all the cutting. If the end is pushed into the surface of a piece of wood, it will score a half round line similar to what could be made by a carving gouge. Unlike the cutting edge of a gouge, however, the upturned nose of the spoon will also undercut. As the bit is turned by the brace this scoring becomes a complete circle. If only one turn is made, a little round undercut plug can be popped loose.

You may have guessed from the comparison with a gouge that pressure is what makes the spoon bit cut. The more weight placed behind the bit, the deeper its nose will score. The chairmaker's weight on the brace provides the pressure. There is no lead screw on a spoon bit to regulate the speed of the cut - you have total control. By controlling the amount of weight on the brace you can easily regulate the speed. You can bore a ⅝" socket in a 1½" thick birch leg with only 15 to 20 turns of the brace. By applying less weight you can cut as slowly as desired. This is very useful when boring holes in slender parts such as bows and arms.

Without a lead screw the round nose of a spoon bit allows the user to alter the angle of the socket, even after it is halfway completed. When assembling chairs by eye, this ability to adjust the angle after you have begun to bore the socket is essential. It is also possible when using a spoon bit to bore sockets whose angles are as shallow as 30 degrees, such as where the outermost long spindles meet the bow of the sack back and the arm of the continu-

MARK THE POSITIONS OF THE *seat sockets through holes drilled in the pattern.*

PLACE A BACKING BOARD BENEATH *the seat, so that you do not bore into the bench top.*

ous arm. Antique spoon bits are seldom perfectly symmetrical so they wobble slightly when turned. This is not a problem when using a hand brace but you must never use a spoon bit in a drill press or an electric drill.

BORING THE SOCKETS

Now that you have been introduced to splay and rake and the spoon bit, you ready to bore the sockets. The procedure is the same for both seats, so I will demonstrate using the shield seat. First, position the seat pattern on the top of the seat and transfer the locations of the leg sockets as well as those for the stumps and the short and long spindles. I mark them by pressing a pencil point through small holes that have been made at the proper locations. I am not a slave to the pattern. It merely gives me an idea of where the sockets should be. The seats are handmade, so they will not be exactly perfect in either shape or outline. If the seat is not precisely symmetrical for example, some adjustments may be required in the placement of some or all the sockets to balance their positions on the seat.

When you are satisfied with the socket placements, fasten the seat to the bench with the hold-down frame or hand screw clamps. Put a backing piece under the seat so that you do not bore into the bench when the bit exits the bottom of the seat. If you use clamps, place the seat on a corner of the bench so that you have access to it from the front and both sides.

The sockets are ⅝" in diameter and are bored from the top of the seat. Boring them from below would ruin the top surface when the bit breaks through. Clamping a waste block to the top of the

seat to prevent break out would be difficult, if not impossible because of the contour of the surface. It would be equally difficult to bore the holes from the bottom before shaping the seat. Imagine trying to work a concave surface that has four holes in it. Every time the tool ran into one of these it would dive, creating a depression around the hole.

Before making the first socket it is not a bad idea to practice using the spoon bit. When using a spoon bit always start the socket by holding the brace and bit perpendicular to the work. To prevent the nose from wandering, gently push it into the wood's surface. Now, turn slowly. The first couple of turns will produce a distinct volute shaving. The scored circumference will quickly increase to the bit's diameter. A full width, unbroken shaving will began to rise up the hollow shaft of the spoon, like a cork being withdrawn from a bottle. After the nose is buried in the wood, the brace can be gradually pulled to the desired angle. Be sure to keep turning the bit as you maneuver it into position.

To bore the first socket in the seat you will need to establish the splay and rake angles for it. I use measurements and angles from model chairs that we use in our kitchen - when they are not in the shop. (After all these years I still do not have either a complete or a matching set of chairs, just the shop models.) I work by eye, referring to the model chair before boring. I have done this so often that I have a feel for the correct angles. For your first chair, however, you might feel a bit more secure with some assistance from a protractor or an adjustable bevel square. I will describe and show how to use bevel squares. If you are not copying an existing chair, take the angles from the drawings.

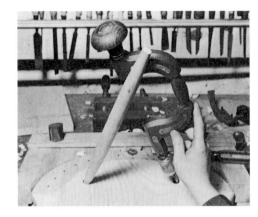

YOU CAN USE AN ADJUSTABLE *bevel square to determine the splay (shown here) and rake angles while boring the sockets. Sight along the axis of the brace and bit to the blade of the bevel square and adjust accordingly (above). Establish the rake and splay angles of the second sockets with a dummy leg inserted in the first socket. The axes of the dummy leg and the brace should intersect to create an isosceles triangle. Notice how the intersections differ for the shield seat (top, right) and the oval seat (bottom, right) – yet both form an isosceles triangle.*

It does not matter which leg socket is bored first. Out of habit I generally start with the left rear. The first socket is easy because it need not duplicate angles already existing in the seat. But this is a mixed blessing because an existing angle could be used for reference. So, when boring the first socket you're on your own. You need be concerned only that its angles are reasonably close to the same splay and rake as the plan drawings, the model, or the rest of the chairs in a set. A chair is not generally viewed from the rear, so the tolerances for splay and rake are greater here than for the front legs. Set the blade of the bevel square to the splay angle and place its stock on the flat surface at the back of the seat. Establish the rake by eye or set another bevel square or protractor from the drawings, or a model chair. Although you cannot measure the bit directly against the angled blades, you can sight along the bit to each blade to estimate the desired angle.

Start the socket with the bit perpendicular. As you turn the brace, gradually pull down to the final angles. Refer to bevel squares as you make this adjustment. You can gain a better vantage for judging the splay be squatting down in front of the seat, still holding the top of the brace. When the angles are right, bore about halfway through the seat. Then stop and check the splay and rake against the bevel squares. Correct if necessary and finish boring the sockets.

The completed socket supplies a reference for establishing the splay and rake of the second rear leg. For this reference, I use a dummy leg which is no more than a dowel with a shouldered tenon turned to the same diameter as the spoon bit for the socket. I keep four of these dummy legs on hand. Insert a dummy leg into the first socket, from the top of the seat. To bore the second socket at the correct splay and rake angles, the brace and bit need to mirror the position of the dummy leg. (The axis of the brace and bit forms an isosceles triangle with the axis of the dummy leg and the bottom of the seat. You remember from high school geometry that this triangle has identical base angles.) Start the second socket perpendicular. As you turn the bit move the brace into position to complete the isosceles triangle.

When you are happy with the splay adjustment, pull the brace toward the front of the seat until the axes of the bit and the dummy leg create an imaginary plane. This plane establishes the rake. These relationships – the identical base angles and the two axes in the same plane - geometrically produce both rake and splay angles for the second rear leg socket.

When the brace is finally in position, remove

GAUGE THE SPLAY OF THE *front leg against a bevel square. You can estimate the shallow rake of the leg (left). Use a dummy leg to find the rake and splay angles of the second front-leg socket (above).*

the dummy leg and start to bore. About halfway through stop and verify the setting of the brace to make sure it has not wandered. Do this by reinserting the dummy leg and squatting again in front of the seat to view the triangle. Also check that the axes are still in the same plane. Adjust the angles of the brace and bit if necessary and complete the socket.

The first front leg socket poses the same problems as the first rear leg socket. Again, the splay can be gauged by sighting along the brace and bit to a bevel square resting on the flat back of the seat. If the front of the seat overhangs the bench you will have to make an educated guess as to the rake. There is no way to put a gauge on line behind the brace. The angle of rake for a front leg is not easily noticed by an observer because a chair is usually viewed from the front and rake is only visible from the side. In addition the rake is quite small - the leg is very near perpendicular. These two factors allow for a considerable margin of error.

Begin the socket and establish the angle. Bore about halfway through, check for accuracy, and then complete the socket. The second front leg socket is bored just like the second rear leg socket, using a dummy leg to establish an imaginary Isosceles triangle and plane with the brace and bit.

STUMP SOCKETS The stumps are also set at two angles to the seat. They lean forward and outward. I use two more terms to define these angles. The spindles and stumps radiate away from each other like the fingers on an open hand. I call this outward lean "flare." These parts also lean either toward the front or the back of the seat and I call these "slope." Therefore the stumps flare outward from each other and slope forward.

The stump sockets are also ⅝" diameter and the procedure for boring them is the same as that for the leg sockets. Begin by starting the hole with the spoon bit held perpendicular to the seat. Once the nose of the bit is set, hold a bevel square against the bit to establish the flare. Then, as you turn the brace, pull it forward and measure it against another bevel square set for slope. When you are sure of the angles, bore halfway through the seat, check the angles again, make corrections, then finish the socket.

Insert one of the dummy legs into the socket, then stand back and take a look at the seat. The stumps flare outward, so they cannot form an isosceles triangle with the seat as base. I establish the angles of the second stump by eye, placing the brace so its axis is a mirror image of the dummy leg. If you do not trust your eye, you can always rely

ESTABLISH THE FLARE AND SLOPE *angles of the second stump socket by eye, positioning the brace and bit to mirror a dummy leg inserted in the first stump socket.*

on bevel squares. Start the hole and then bring the brace into the flare position. Use the plane formed by the axes of the dummy and brace to find the forward slope. Bore about halfway through, check the angles, and then complete the hole. (I also bore the sockets for the spindles now. A beginner should probably wait and do this after assembling the seat, legs, and stretchers, so I will discuss these sockets later.)

Before removing the seat from the bench, insert another dummy leg into second stump socket. Back away the seat and squat down to judge the angles. If there is a discrepancy, make a mental note of it so you can correct later with the tapered reamer.

Unclamp the seat, insert all four dummy legs, and set them upright on the bench top to check the accuracy of the leg sockets. Mark on the bottom of seat or make a mental note of any that are out of line for correction with the reamer.

TAPERING THE SOCKETS

If you are using simple through tenons, no more need be done to the sockets. For tapered joints, however, the sockets still need to be reamed. The reamer, as mentioned earlier, resembles a steel cone that has been sliced in half along its axis. It is a scraping tool, so the two beveled edges can be sharpened with a file and honed with a medium grit stone. The bevels should be flat, and you must be sure not to round them or to turn a burr on them. Either will prevent the reamer from cutting

Remove the dummy legs from the seat and clamp it on edge in a bench vise with the bottom

facing out toward the work area. Secure the tapered reamer in the chuck of a brace and insert the reamer's business end into one of the sockets. As you turn the brace feed the reamer slowly into the socket. If you feed the reamer too quickly it will ride over the end grain and make the socket oval. Let the tool scrape its way into the socket. You cannot speed up the action by applying pressure to the reamer. The harder the wood you are working the more time required to ream the sockets.

Use the reamer to make adjustments in the angles of the sockets. For example, if a front leg has insufficient splay, you can increase the angle by pulling the brace out toward the seat edge as you ream the hole. Set an adjustable bevel square to indicate how much correction is needed.

Crank the brace and feed the reamer until you think the socket has been opened enough to receive its leg tenon. The entire tapered tenon, but no more, should fit into the socket. Some of the tenon should protrude above the seat to make wedging easier. Test by inserting the tenon into the socket, and ream further if necessary. I have turned so many legs that the tenons are all nearly identical. Yours may not be. Therefore, it would be best if you fitted each tenon to a particular socket and marked the matching pairs. As you continue to make chairs, you will eventually be able to skip this step.

Ream all the leg sockets. The angles of the second front or rear socket to be reamed can be judged against a leg inserted in the first reamed socket. A bevel square will also help. Reverse the seat and ream the stump sockets, correcting the slope and

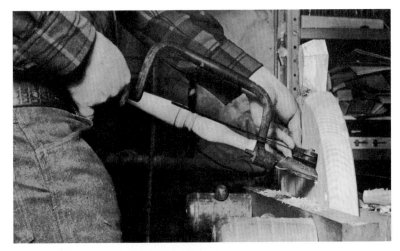

THE SOCKETS MUST BE REAMED *to take the tapered tenons. The socket angles can be corrected at the same time. Here the splay is checked against a bevel square. When reaming the second socket of a front or back pair, the brace and reamer should mirror a leg inserted in the already reamed socket. A bevel square can help check the splay. Taper the stump sockets with the reamer. The flare and slope angles can be corrected by gauging each stump against the other, and against a bevel square.*

flare angles if necessary. The stump and sockets should also be test fitted and marked in pairs. The stump tenons should protrude beneath the seat so they can be wedged at assembly. When all the sockets have been bored and reamed you can insert the legs and stumps into the seat and see the chair taking shape.

The old guys called the process of constructing the under carriage "Legging up." Having taught thousands of people how to leg up I have refined this process and made it a lot more sure and easy. The method just described is worth reading because it includes all the same concerns and objectives we address today.

Our new template has a center line that we transfer to the seat and work from. By drawing a sight line from the leg hole to a location on the center line, we create a vectored angle that incorporates both splay and rake, allowing us to work with one angle and one bevel square. You can see the sight lines on the photos of our current c-arm and sack back templates.

Each sight line has a number next to it. This is the angle. Today, we use what we call "chair-maker angles." Like the guys who drill for oil, we assume the perpendicular is zero, not 90 degrees. This allows us to work with the smallest possible numbers. This is not only easier, it helps avoid mistakes, as most people can envision 16 degrees, but not 106 degrees.

We still drill from the top of the seat, but today use a cordless drill with brad points. We have changed the size bit to %₁₆" This too is easier, as all the holes in the seat are the same diameter.

My habit has changed and I now consistently begin with the left front leg hole. This is my left, not the chair's. We stress the importance of working in front of the chair, and call this the "chair-maker's position." Therefore, the left of the chair corresponds to our left.

Using the sightlines and angles on the template, drill the six through holes, four legs and two stumps.

We use a reamer that we designed to fit into a cordless. It has a %₁₆" pilot, so it will follow the hole.

We divide reaming into four steps. The first step is to accomplish front splay and rake for one

THE CHAIR TAKES SHAPE.

front leg (15 degrees splay and 8 degrees rake on c-arm, and 14 degrees and 10 degrees for sack back.) Rake and splay differ from the vectored angle we used drilling the holes. We ream enough to insert a dummy leg with a locking taper and check against this. Make corrections as necessary and be sure that the end of the tenon projects above the seat surface (for wedging).

With the first front leg established we move on to the other. We need it too to have 14 degrees of splay, and will once again check a dummy leg with a bevel square. However, we establish rake for this second leg by making it coplaner with the first. We do this with a pair of winding sticks. Winding sticks are easy to use and read, and are very accurate. Place the dark one on the tenon ends of the legs against the seat. Place the lighter one on the ends of the leg tapers. Sighting across them tells you whether you have to increase or decrease the second leg's rake to arrive at coplaner.

With the two front legs at 14 degrees of splay and coplaner at 10 degrees of rake, move on to the rear legs. In class we tell students that there are no rear leg angles. Obviously there are, but we do not know the number of degrees, and don't need to know. This is because your focus has shifted. In this step you are seeking to acheive the same distance between a front leg and its adjacent rear leg at the height of the scribe lines.

This will result in the side stretchers being the same length (and interchangeable). You are using applied Geometry to accomplish the rear rake. If the front legs are indentical (coplaner), and the distance between the front and rear legs is identical, the rear rake angles are identical. While there is no fixed number for the distance, the most typical length is 12¼" For stability and strength the length should not be less than 12" or more than 13" Any other length within those extremes works, as long as it the same on both sides.

Because you are going to compare one side to the other, ream both rear leg holes and insert all four legs. Place the assembly upright on the bench so you can measure your result. The distance is inside to inside at the location of the scribes. You are measuring where the stretchers will be placed.

The last step is to check your rear splay. This is also the least important step. Because your chair is not viewed from behind, you have latitude in the rear splay. You are checking for gross error. Remember, when it comes to rear legs, there are no angles. Place the foot ends of the front legs so they align with the edge of your bench top. Place straight edges against each side pair of legs. The benchtop and the straight edge form an angle. On one side, set a bevel square to this angle. Compare this angle to the other side.

You now know how you need to adjust the rear legs to achieve the same distance between the scribes with similiar rear leg splay. When done, place all four legs in the chair and set it upright on the bench. You will next calculate your stretcher lengths and turn those parts. So I do not have to remember the distance between the legs (this length will become X in the equation we use next chapter) I write it in pencil on the seat top. Since 12¼" is the most typical length, I will use it as an example. In the example I would write X = 12¼".

Today, I ream the stump holes after legging up, although I still drill them while doing the leg holes. Sit on a stool next to the chair (our shop stools are 19" tall and place me just above the seat.) Place a foot on a stretcher to hold the chair steady. From here on, the process is identical to reaming the front legs. Use a dummy leg to get one stump to the desired slope and flare angles (10 degrees of flare and 14 degrees of slope.) Ream the second hole and adjust using the 10 degree flare bevel and winding sticks to make the stumps coplanar. Continues arm stumps have 22 degress of slope and 15 degrees of flare.

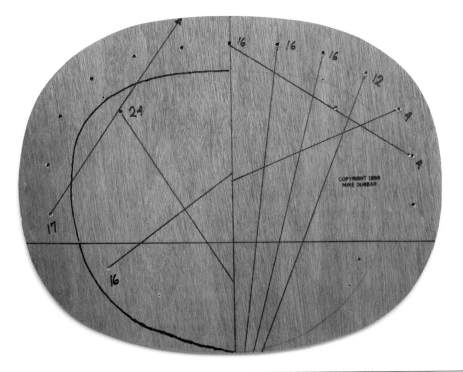

THIS IS MY NEW SACK *back seat template. It is 16¼" deep and 21" wide. We call it the "DNA of the Chair" because it contains almost all the information needed to recreate the chair. The angles are vectored to make one bevel square possible. Each sight line connects to a location on the center line (some of those intersections occur in front of or behind the seat.) Each sight line has a number of degrees. These are Chairmaker Angles, the amount of variance from the perpendicular along the sight line. To prevent confusion, lines and angles are shown on only one side of the template. The distance between spindle holes is 2⅜"*

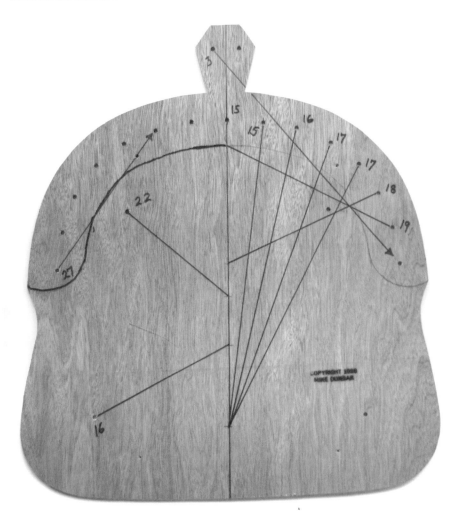

THE NEW C-ARM TEMPLATE IS *17⅞" deep without the tail piece and 21" with. It is 18½" wide at the rounded corners. The distance between spindle holes is approximately 1⅝" Walk it off with a pair of dividers, tweaking as necessary.*

Chapter Seven

Turning the Stretchers & Assembling the Undercarriage

In this chapter, I will describe how to measure and make the stretchers, bore the sockets for the stretcher tenons, and assemble the legs, stretchers, and seat. The procedure is exactly the same for both the sack back and continuous-arm chairs, and it is the same whether you use baluster or double-bobbin turnings, locking tapered tenons for the legs or straight through tenons. I will use the sack back as an example.

In hand work the distances between the legs varies slightly from chair to chair. For this reason, it is best to determine the lengths of the stretchers from the particular chair you are making, rather than from a drawing. I will discuss the side stretchers, the ones that extend between the front and back legs first.

SIDE STRETCHERS

Insert the leg tenons into the seat sockets. I usually tap the foot of each leg with a hammer to make the joint self-lock. Set the chair upright on a bench to measure the stretcher lengths. First measure the inside dimension between a pair of front and back legs at the height of the scribe marks on the tapered feet. The typical measurement for my sack back Windsor is 12¼" I will use it as the example for what follows. Caution: This is just an example. You must use the number from your chair.

You will remember that the stretchers are meant to push the legs apart, not hold them together. To ensure that this critical compression is created, I add ¼" to X, the distance between the front and back legs. You must also add the lengths of the stretcher's two tenons. I turn my Windsor legs to a diameter of 1½" at the scribe marks so I make each stretcher tenon 1¼" long.

Thus, the total length of a side stretcher is the sum of the following: the inside distance between the front and back legs, ¼" of extra length to create compression, and the combined lengths of the stretcher's two tenons. Consistent with my exam-

ple, the length of one side stretcher would be:

$$12 \frac{1}{4} + \frac{1}{4} + 2 \frac{1}{2} = 15$$

When I trim the turning blank to length I also include ½" for waste at the drive center end of the turning. You may want to add more for waste, depending on your lathe.

TURNING The blanks for the stretchers were rived at the same time as the leg. Trim them to length, as described above, and then remove their corners with a drawknife. Secure one of the side stretcher blanks in the lathe and turn it down to a 1¼" diameter cylinder - the largest diameter of the finished stretcher. I use a ¾" gouge for this. I take this diameter directly from my model chair with calipers. (Drawings for the stretchers are shown with the plans.)

The tenons in the drawings show the grooves for the Lily Tomlin joints. Ignore these and turn uniform, cylindrical tenons.

To layout the stretcher, set a pair of dividers one-half the visible length of the side stretcher. The visible length is the inside distance between the legs plus ¼" For the example stretcher, visible length is 12½", so the dividers would be set at 6¼" (Remember, to calculate from your own chair.) To locate the scribe line measure in from the tailstock end of the blank the length of a tenon (1¼"). Turn on the lathe, and lay the right leg of the dividers, against the wood at this point. Push the point of the left leg into the spinning blank. The scribed mark locates the center of the stretcher. Later, you will use this mark to locate the socket for the center stretcher.

Rough out the simple bobbin shape of the stretcher. The techniques are similar to those described for turning the major vase on the baluster leg. Start several inches from one end and make a single pass, cutting out to that end. Begin the next pass about ½" closer to the center of the blank.

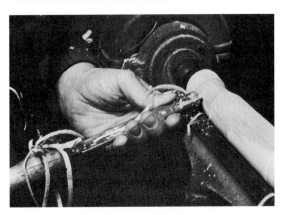

INSERT THE LEGS AND MEASURE *the distance between each pair of front and back legs. Turn the side stretcher blanks to a 1½" diameter cylinder. To mark the center of a side stretcher, set a pair of dividers to one-half the stretcher's visible length. Place the right leg a tenon length from the blank's tailstock end and push the left leg into the spinning wood.*

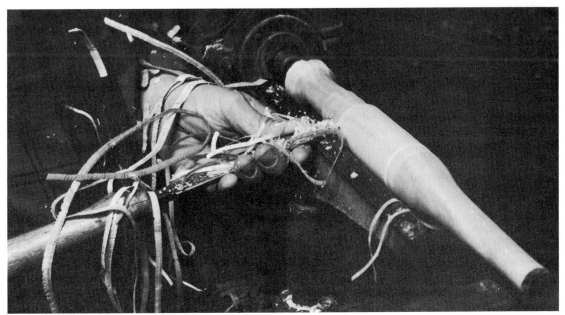

ROUGH OUT THE BOBBIN-SHAPED STRETCHER *with a large gouge. Start from the ends and work in toward the middle to form the swelling.*

Repeating this process a number of times reduces the diameter of the end of the stretcher and automatically starts the development of the bobbin.

With practice, you will learn to make the cuts of a certain length and thickness so that the swelling for the bobbin occurs right where you want it. Rough out the last 1¼" of the blank to ⅝" diameter for the tenon. Move the tool rest and rough out the other half of the stretcher in the same way.

Next, place one leg of the dividers (still set to one half the stretcher's visible length) on the center scribe. Reach out with the free leg and scribe the shoulders of the tenons on each end of the blank. I bore all the sockets in the undercarriage using the same ⅝" spoon bit used for the leg and stump sockets. The thickness of the tenon should allow an easy friction fit into the socket. You can check for the proper fit by drilling a ⅝" hole in a piece of hardwood scrap. The tenon should not rattle.

While we now drill all holes in the seat at ⁹⁄₁₆", all stretcher holes remain ⅝".

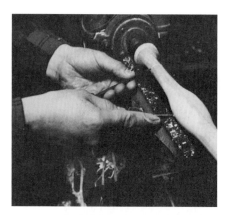
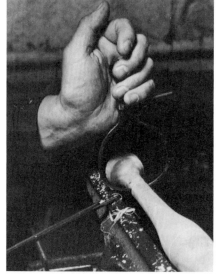
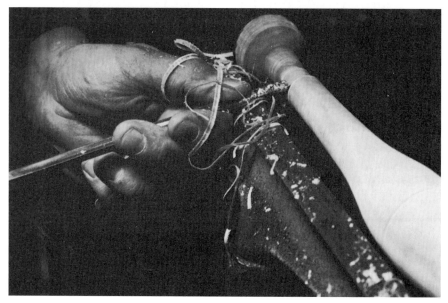

SCRIBE A MARK FOR THE *tenon shoulder with a pair of dividers. Turn the ⅝" tenon diameter with a small gouge. Finish the profile by making a planing cut with a skew chisel.*

When the tenon is the correct diameter, round its end with a ½" skew. This conforms the tenon end to the round bottom of the socket. Also, the tenon will fit more easily and not require a lot of pressure to assemble, as the rounded ends will not get hung up on the walls of the socket during assembly.

Make a planing cut with the ¾" skew over the entire profile to clean it up. When the stretcher is complete remove it from the lathe and cut the waste from the drive center end. Turn the other side stretcher in the same way.

CENTER STRETCHER

It is easy to calculate the lengths of the side stretchers because the distance between the legs can be measured directly. It is not possible to measure for the center stretcher directly because I turn all three stretchers before boring the sockets and assembling the chair. I determine its length in two steps.

The first step is to calculate the length of the center stretcher excluding the tenons. This is the visible length of the stretcher (L) and it can be found with the formula:

$$\left(\frac{x+y}{2} - d\right) + ¼ = L$$

In the formula, x is the measured center-to-center distance between the front legs at the height of the scribe; y is the measured center-to-center distance between the rear legs at the height of the scribe. (It is easy to get the center-to-center distance by measuring from the inside of one leg to the outside of its mate.) Dividing the sum of these measurements by 2 gives the center-to-center length at the position of the stretcher, midway between the front and back legs. Subtracting two radii of the side stretchers at their scribe marks gives the visible length of the center stretcher. Two radii equal one diameter - d in the equation. I simply measure with calipers the thickness of one side stretcher at

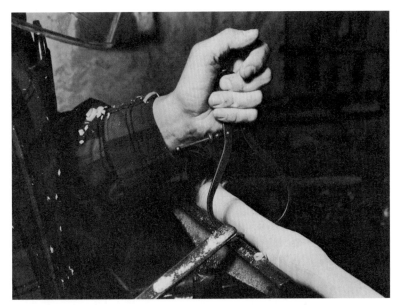

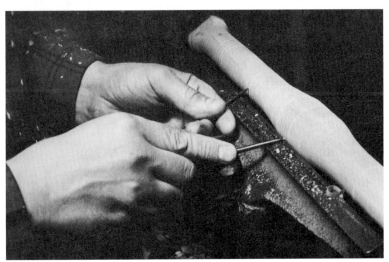

FIND THE CENTER OF THE *stretcher, then turn the blank on either side of the bobbin down to the diameter of the arrow-shaped details). Scribe the position of the arrows.*

the scribe mark. The extra ¼" ensures that the center stretcher also pushes the side stretchers apart, putting the joints in compression.

The center-to-center distance between the front legs of my sack-back chair usually measures between 16½" and 17" Let's take a 17" measurement as the example. So, x = 17" For the rear legs let's call the center-to-center distance 14½" So, y = 14½" The diameter of the side stretchers at the scribe mark (d) is always 1½" So the visible length of the center stretcher is 14½":

$$\left(\frac{17+14\frac{1}{2}}{2} - 1\frac{1}{2}\right) + \frac{1}{4} = 14\frac{1}{2}$$

The second step is to add the length of the tenons and an allowance for the waste to the visible length. This gives the length of the turning blank that you will need for the center stretcher. Each tenon is again 1¼" long and I allow ½" for waste, so for the example given above, I would cut the turning blank 17½" long:

$$14\frac{1}{2} + 2\frac{1}{2} + \frac{1}{2} = 17\frac{1}{2}$$

TURNING Begin the center stretcher by turning a cylinder of the diameter of the stretcher at its thickest point, (which is the center of the bobbin.) Make a scribe mark at the center with dividers as described for side stretchers. Remember to allow 1¼" for the tenon. The center bobbin slopes down to meet tapered arrow-shaped turnings at each end. Set calipers to the largest diameter of the arrows and

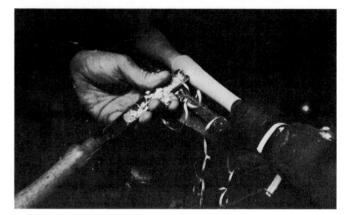

SHAPE THE BOBBIN WITH A *large gouge. Clean up the surface with a planing cut. Cut a cove at the beginning of each arrow with a small gouge. Turn the arrows with a large gouge; make the tapers slightly concave.*

reduce the blank on either side of the center scribe to diameter using a large gouge. This will begin to create the bobbin.

Next, set a second pair of dividers to the distance from the center scribe to the beginning of the arrows. (Keep the first pair of dividers set to one half the stretcher's visible length - you will need this pair to mark the tenons.) Scribe these points on the blank with the dividers. Shape the bobbin with a large gouge using the same method as for the side stretchers. Here, however, you work only to the scribes for the arrows. Set calipers to check the diameter of the bobbin where it meets the arrows. Square up the right-angled stops that separate each arrow and the bobbin with a skew. Use the same cut as for cleaning up the last inch or so of the foot of the baluster leg. Clean up the bobbin by making a planing cut with the large skew.

Soften each stop by making a small cove cut with a ¼" gouge. Then, shape each tapered arrow from the cove to the end of the turning blank. The taper is very slightly concave, another example of reverse entasis. The arrows should reduce to a ¾" diameter at each end. Scribe the tenon shoulders with the dividers, and cut the tenons in the same

manner as for the side stretchers.

The seven parts that will be used below the seat are now complete. If you turned the stumps and short spindles while making the legs, you will not need to return to the lathe. If you dried your turning stock you are ready to go. If not, set the wet parts aside to dry. Remember, you never want to put unseasoned parts into a chair.

In classes at The Institute we use stretchers that were produced by my job turner. We still calculate and layout our side stretcher's the same way as I described in 1983. However, today we make the tenons with a ⅝" tenon maker, rather than turning them in the lathe.

The major difference between now and 1984 is the way that we calculate and layout the center stretcher. We have made this process much easier and eliminated a lot of risk of math errors. After we have laid out our side stretchers we secure one to each pair of front and rear legs with rubber bands looped around the stretchers and legs. We locate the stretchers so their center lines lay across the leg scribe lines. The important tip to remember is while one stretcher is mounted on the outside of one pair of legs, the other stretcher

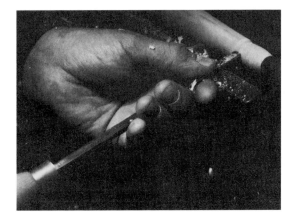

SCRIBE THE TENON SHOULDERS AND *turn the tenon.*

DETERMINE THE ANGLE AT WHICH *the center stretcher meets the side stretchers with two straight edges.*

is on the inside of the other pair of legs. This is similar to find stud centers by measuring inside to outside. The distance between the side stretchers is now the same as it will be in the completed chair and can be directly measured. Remember to measure inside to inside at the location of the stretchers' scribe marks. In other words, measure where the center stretcher will be in the finished chair.

The measurement you obtain is the center stretcher X. On today's sack backs the typical number is 15½" I will use that as my example, but once again, use the measurement from the chair you are making. We plug X into a simple formula: S/to/S = X + ¼. S/to/S stands for shoulder-to-shoulder. In 1984 I called this visible length. We find S/to/S by adding ¼" to X. In my example S/to/S = 15¾"

If you are turning your stretchers, calculate your turning blank's length by add the length of two tenons, plus some waste.

Because I am working with a stretcher that has already been turned, I divide 15¾" by 2 and arrive at 8⅞" I set my dividers to this measure-

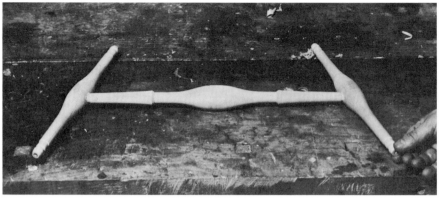

ROTATE THE FIRST SIDE STRETCHER *as you push it onto the center stretcher. The assembled stretchers should all lie in the same plane.*

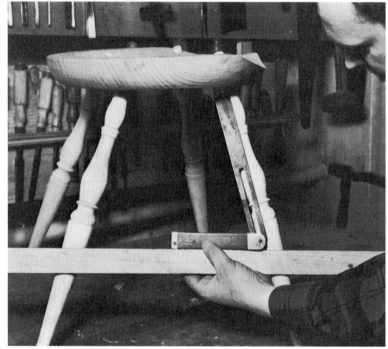

PLACE A STRAIGHTEDGE BETWEEN A *front and back leg at the height of the scribe marks to determine the angle of the side stretcher to each of the legs.*

ment. Placing one leg of the dividers on the center stretcher's scribe line, I use the other divider leg to locate the shoulders on both ends. Hence, shoulder-to-shoulder.

Next, we add in the tenons. Today, these are 1⅛" long. The math for my example chair is: 8⅞" + 1⅛" = 10" Reset the divider to this amount and layout the ends of the tenons. Cut the stretcher at these points and make the tenons with the tenon maker. This device has a depth stop so it makes a tenon 1⅛" long.

ASSEMBLY

The undercarriage is ready for assembly. It is my habit to bore the sockets for the stretcher tenons as I assemble. I judge the angles of the sockets by eye.

In the beginning, you may feel more comfortable using adjustable bevel squares. I will describe how to do this as I go along. Insert the four legs into the seat. Set the partially assembled chair upright on a bench top and find two straight edges. Yardsticks are good. Set one stick flat on the bench with one edge against the two front feet. Place the second against the front and rear feet on one side. The sticks intersect at the same angle at which the center stretcher is joined to the side stretchers. Set a bevel square to this angle.

Put one side stretcher in a vise so that its length is vertical. The socket is bored on the scribe mark that indicates the center of the bobbin. The location of the socket in relation to the grain is not important. Bore the hole using the bevel square to check

ESTABLISH THE CORRECT ANGLE FOR *boring the stretcher socket by holding a bevel square against the legs and the brace and bit. Insert the leg into the seat and pull the stretcher assembly into position. The center stretcher should be parallel to the seat.*

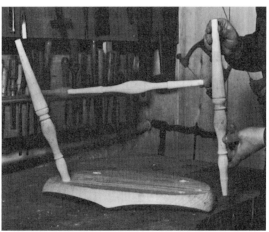

the angle. Hold the head of the brace against your stomach to steady it. Start the spoon bit at a right angle to the stretcher. Then set the blade of the bevel square against the stretcher, parallel to an imaginary centerline. Raise the brace until its centerline corresponds to the stock of the bevel square and bore the socket. I have filed a mark on the back of the spoon bit used to make the leg sockets. The mark, 1¼" from the nose of the bit, tells me when I have bored as deeply as I can without coming through the other side.

The socket is angled only to the length of the stretcher and bisects the thickness. You might want to check with the bevel square before completing the socket to make sure that the bit has not wandered: you can easily remember the location of the head of the brace against your belly. This reference point makes it easy to maintain the correct angle.

Remove the side stretcher from the vise and assemble it with the center stretcher. Squirt some glue into the socket and smear the glue uniformly over the sides of the socket with a small stick. Insert one of the center stretcher tenons into the socket. It should fit smoothly. Rotate the side stretcher as you press it onto the tenon.

Bore the socket in the second side stretcher and mount it on the other end of the center stretcher in the same way. Twist the side stretchers so that the three pieces form a plane. Place them on the bench top to test this.

Next, you need to find the angles at which the legs are mounted on the side stretchers. Place a straightedge against one front leg and its corresponding rear leg at the height of the scribe marks. Set bevel squares to the angles formed by the

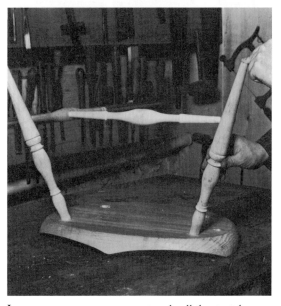

INSERT THE LEG INTO THE *seat and pull the stretcher assembly into position. The center stretcher should be parallell to the seat (top). Bore the socket into the second leg and add the leg to the stretcher assembly. Then insert the first leg in the seat and twist the second leg until its tenon can be inserted in its socket.*

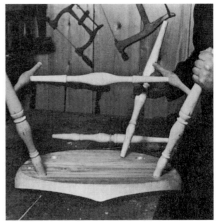

Twist the first rear leg *onto its stretcher tenon. Then rotate the leg into its socket (top left and right). The legs will not line up with their sockets because of the extra lenght of the stretchers. When the tenons are forced into their sockets during final assembly, each leg will be stressed equally. After inserting the legs, rap their ends sharply with a hammer to set the tenons firmly in the seat sockets.*

straightedge and the legs. Using two bevel squares will save you from having to reset a single bevel after boring the front leg sockets.

Armed with this information put one of the front legs in the vise. Start the socket at a right angle to the leg. Place the blade of the bevel square parallel to an imaginary center line of the leg and bring the brace up to match the stock. Bore the socket. You may want to check for wandering before completing the hole. Put glue in the socket and mount the leg onto the appropriate side stretcher tenon with the same twisting and pressing motion as was used in joining the stretchers.

The angle of the leg in relation to the plane of the stretchers is critical. Put the leg tenon into its socket in the seat (don't glue this joint) and pull the stretcher assembly down until the center stretcher is parallel to the plane of the seat. The tenon of the side stretcher should twist in the leg socket to

allow this movement. Note: the side stretchers may or may not be parallel to the seat depending on the rake of the leg.

Remove the assembly from the seat and bore, glue, and mount the second leg on the appropriate side stretcher tenon. Put the tenon of the first leg back in its socket and twist the second leg until its tenon can be inserted into its socket in the seat.

Next, bore the socket for the first rear leg. If you are using only one bevel square, remember to reset its angle for the rear legs. Put glue in the socket in the leg and mount it on the side stretcher tenon. Insert the two front legs in their sockets and rotate the rear leg until its tenon fits into the corresponding seat socket.

Do the same operations on the last leg. However, when it is twisted into its location do not be surprised if it will not fall readily into its socket. Instead, it will meet the seat at a point slightly

SHAPE A WEDGE ON THE *end of a dry, riven hardwood stick. The wedge should be slightly wider than the socket, and it should taper slightly in its width, as well as its thickness. Make a split for the wedge in the end of the tenon with a chisel. The split should be down the axis of the leg. It should also be at about a right angle to the grain of the seat.*

behind that socket. This is because the stretchers were made ¼" overlong, which spreads the legs apart. If the assembled legs and stretchers are lowered onto the seat together, each tenon will be just slightly off the mark. Forcing the tenons home will create the compression in the undercarriage that makes the chair durable.

Remove the undercarriage from the seat. You want to work quickly and assuredly at this point. Remember that glue will be setting up in the joints. There is, however, no reason to hurry and risk a mistake. Squirt glue into the sockets for the legs in the seat and spread it evenly on the socket walls before it has a chance to run out. Place the seat top-down on the bench. Hold the front pair of legs near the joints. Draw the legs together; this will stress the stretcher-to-leg joints slightly. When the tenons are at the same locations as the sockets, insert them with a snap of the wrists. This locks them in place. Do the same to the back pair of legs. These legs must be squeezed together and pulled toward the front legs to fit their sockets. Because of the extra length of the stretchers all the undercarriage joints are in compression.

Lift up the seat to check that the top ends of all four tenons are exposed above the surface of the seat. The legs are now ready to be set a final time. Sharply rap the foot end of each leg with a hammer. You want the joint to be tight, but do not risk split-

ting the seat. Be cautious - if driven with too much force a tapered tenon can act as a wedge.

When the tenons have been set, place the chair upright. You need to wedge the tenons before the glue begins to set. A wedge performs several tasks. It spreads the tenon so that a good tight glue bond is achieved. It produces a flare at the top of the tenon so that when the joint does loosen the tenon will not fall out of the socket. The wedge should also completely close the joint on the top surface of the seat so that no visible gap remains between tenon and socket.

Some people make a separate individual wedge for each joint. I have never understood why. I cut a wedge on one end of a stick, drive the wedge in, cut the stick off, and then make another wedge on the same end. There is little wasted wood or effort. The stick is steadily whittled down to a stub like a pencil and it is run through the stove when it becomes too short to hold. I keep a supply of riven oak sticks for wedges stored over a heat duct. These are leftovers from riving spindles. If a riven piece is too thin or otherwise unacceptable for spindles, I place on the duct where it can dry. By doing this I always have dry wood on hand to use for wedges

I cut wedges with a drawknife. One end of the stick is held in my tin knocker's vise while I shape the wedge on the other. The wedges should be slightly wider than the sockets. The edges of the

wedge will bite into the soft pine, producing a keying effect. A keyed wedge will prevent the tenon from slipping due to torque. Taper the width of the wedge as well as its thickness. This taper makes the end of the wedge narrower than the tenon, so it is easier to start in the split. As the wedge enters the split it becomes wider and will gradually bite into the softer pine.

Make a split for the wedge in the end the tenon. I make the split with a chisel driven by my cobbler's hammer. You must be ever conscious when wedging that it is possible to split the seat. For this reason you must wedge at a right angle to the grain. However, this placement does not always close gaps on the surface of the seat between the tenon and the socket. You can rotate the chisel on the end grain of the leg tenon to position the split so the wedge will close these gaps. There is a possibility of too much of a good thing. A slight gap is better than a seat that has broken into two pieces. (If the joint will not close by repositioning the split, it can be double wedged. Drive in the first wedge at about 45 degrees to the grain, then a second wedge at a right angle to first to close the gap.)

Drive the wedge by rapping the end of the stick with a hammer. The joint will supply its own sig-nal when the wedge is driven home. As the wedge is driven, it vibrates and gives off a short hum like a plucked guitar string. Each blow of the hammer shortens the stick and lowers the pitch of the sound. The pitch decreases until suddenly, a blow produces only a dead knock. This sound indicates that the wedge is not moving anymore. Stop driving now, because any further hammering may split the seat! Cut the stick loose with a saw and form a new wedge on its end. Wedge the remaining joints in the same way.

TRIMMING THE LEGS The undercarriage and seat are assembled, but the legs do not yet sit squarely on the bench. They must be cut to length. This recalls the old vaudeville routine in which a poor fellow tries to cut all the legs of a chair to the same length and ends up with a seat sitting on stubs only a couple of inches high. If he had used the following method, he would have got it right the first time. I cut the legs of both chairs so that the seats are ½" lower at back than the front. This slope adds to the chair's comfort, and I like the way a sloped seat feels.

Start by measuring the height of the seat pommel above the bench. For example, let's say that this measurement is 18¼" Next, measure the height of

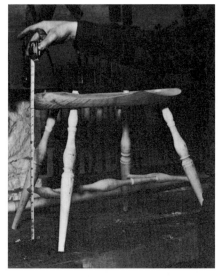

To TRIM THE FRONT LEGS, *measure the height of the seat at the pommel and at each stump. Calculate how much to cut off and mark the legs. Trim with a backsaw, holding it parallel to the bench top. Hang the last leg over the bench top to determine its correct length. You can use the bench top as a guide for sawing.*

the seat in front of each stump. Let's say the right side is 17¾" and the left is 18¼" I like the pommel of all my chairs to be 17" above the floor, so the leg on the highest side must be lowered 1¼". Measure 1¼" up from the bench top on the taper of the left leg and make a mark.

If you also cut 1¼" off the leg on the other lower side, however, the front edge of the seat will not be level. Cutting ¾" off the right leg and 1¼" off the left should bring the pommel down to about 17", and make the front of the seat level. Measure up from the bench for the right leg and cut the excess length off each leg with a back saw. Be careful to keep the blade of the saw parallel with the surface of the bench.

At this point, only one of the back legs usually touches the bench. This can occur for a variety of reasons. One rear socket may have been reamed more deeply than the other. One tenon may have been formed slightly further up the minor vase. Or, one rake angle may be slightly greater than the

other. It doesn't matter anyway, as the rear legs also get trimmed.

If the pommel is 17" high, height of the seat at the back should about 16½" high. Let's say that the right leg as you face the back surface is longer than the left, and the back surface of the seat is currently 17½" above the bench. Mark up 1" on the taper of the right leg and cut off the excess. The chair now rests on the left leg, which is still too long.

To cut off the correct amount on the last leg, hang it over the edge of the bench. The seat now rests on the three legs that have been measured and cut to correct length. The edge of the bench top intersects the fourth leg at precisely the correct location for the final cut. Mark this point and cut it with the backsaw or cut using the bench top as a guide.

Only one more detail remains. The ends of the leg tenons need to be shaved flush with the surface of the seat. I don't do this earlier because the seat will not sit squarely before the legs are trimmed to length; uneven legs make the seat difficult to hold

A WIDE, SHALLOW CARVING GOUGE *(#3 sweep 35mm) works well to trim the tenon ends flush with the surface of the seat.*

still. I use a wide, shallow carving gouge (#3 sweep 35 mm) to trim the tenons flush. I drive it with a mallet, cutting across the end grain. You know what happens when you plane end grain - the last little bit tears or breaks off. The same danger exists when flushing the tenons. Therefore, chop through only about two thirds of the tenon from one direction. Then work back toward the middle from the other side. After most of the waste has been removed, put down the mallet and trim the tenon flush with a slicing cut, holding the blade at an extreme skew to the direction of the cut.

Trim all four tenons the same way.

It is likely the ends of the tenons will eventually rise above the surface of the seat. This occurs for a number of reasons. During the first year the hardwood tenons may be driven by use further into the softwood sockets pushing, the ends slightly above the seat. Throughout the life of the chair, expansion and contraction of the seat and legs with seasonal humidity changes may sometimes cause the ends to pop up more. It's futile to try to trim the tenons so that they will always be flush. If you trim them flush when the seat has shrunk they will just be recessed when the seat has swollen again. Therefore, I think it is best to trim the ends at assembly then leave them alone. The exposed top of the leg tenon is part of the nature of the beast.

I can only add information to this process, as it has not changed significantly in 30 years. We have Record 53 vises at each work station so now we drill stretcher and leg holes into parts secured horizontally, rather than vertically. We do check to make sure the part is parallel with the vise jaw, as when drilling, that is where we rest the bevel's stock. In this position it is possible to flip the leg end for end and drill in the wrong direction so the hole is upside down. We check ourself with this mnemonic, "Top of leg to top of leg." This means the leg's tenon is poking you in the thigh and is in the right direction.

I urge you to leg up doing what we call a "wet fit". I used the wet fit in 1984 legging up the chairs for this book and illustrate it in the photos. However, I did not stress it as I do today in a class. Because a wet fit is so contrary to the way we usually make furniture the very idea of it will make you hyperventilate; your palms will sweat. When legging up a Windsor there is no dry assembly and test fit. Doing a wet fit, you drill a hole, glue that hole, test it, and confirm it before drilling another hole. If the joint passes the test, leave it assembled and in place and keep moving forward. (The test is that the tenon on the other of the end of the stretcher should be pointing at the location of the adjacent leg's scribe line.) If the joint fails this test, disassemble and correct it.

By finding the mistake immediately, you can ensure that you do not repeat it. To illustrate the problem I have hanging on the shop wall four legs, all drilled in the wrong direction. Not only did the student not use the mnemonic "Top of leg to top of leg," he couldn't bring himself to do a wet fit. He repeated the same mistake four times and didn't realize it until he began the assembly. If he had been doing a wet fit he would have discovered the mistake after drilling the first hole and not ruined a complete set of legs. In brief, a wet fit is a far safer way to leg up.

A wet fit is also a more expeditious way of working. Barring a mistake, you are done after the last hole, and ready to move on with an assembled undercarriage that is sure to fit your seat.

Use a slow set glue in all chair assembly. We prefer white glue. Yellow glue can seize a joint

THE ASSEMBLED SEAT AND UNDERCARRIAGE.

before you have rotated the leg or stretcher to the desired orientation. If this happens, there is not solution but to saw the turning in half and start over. Remember, these undercarriage joints are in compression. That is their strength, you don't need a stronger glue. You need more open time.

We trim the legs with a new technique that is easier to understand than the one I used in 1984. Begin by leveling the chair. Place a straight edge across the seat at the groove in front of the stumps and measure its height from the bench top. Shim the leg on the low side until the seat is level.

The next step is similar to taking a trip and finding the distance between two places using a computer map program. The computer asks two questions. "Where are you?" and "Where do you want to go?" To proceed with your chair, you need the same information. Our new seat heights are 17½" at the pommel and 17" at the rear center. That's where you want to go.

To find out where you are, measure the pommel's height. Don't measure to the bottom of the seat. We use this mnemonic, "Chairmakers measure top to top." As an example, let's say the pommel is 19¼"

On an outstretched tape measure place the point of a pencil compass on 17½" and extend the pencil point to 19¼" This is the amount that needs to be trimmed from the front legs. Use the compass to scribe a line around the bottom of the leg taper on both sides. Repeat the process for the rear. Here, your destination is 17" If one leg is hanging in the air, leave it elevated as you scribe. Trim with a back saw following the scribed lines.

Chapter Eight

Bending the Back

With the base of the chair finished, you are ready to make the back. It is the bent back that distinguishes one Windsor from another, as is reflected in the nomenclature – low back, high back, sack back, bow back, continuous arm, and so on. Most types of Windsors have at least one piece of bent wood in their backs. The sack back chair has a bent arm and a bent bow. The bow is joined to the arm, and both parts are connected by spindles to the seat. Both are U-shaped and are bent on the same form. The continuous arm chair has a single back piece bent in two planes. Because of its compound shape, this piece is more difficult to bend than those for the sack back. In this chapter, I will describe how to bend all three of these pieces.

Wood Selection

Perhaps no single aspect of Windsor chairmaking is as challenging as is bending the pieces for the back. The most important factor in bending is wood selection. Bending is alien to the nature of wood. Being heated and then suddenly contorted are assaults that wood does not accept without some reluctance. The bending process creates tremendous strains that only the best pieces of wood can be expected to survive. Therefore, do not waste your time working wood that does not meet the standards I am going to describe.

I regularly receive telephone calls from people who are having trouble bending the back for a Windsor chair. The caller will explain that he has selected the best piece of wood he can find, and his bows still break. When I ask where the wood is coming from, the answer is invariably a local lumber dealer. I have learned not to speak in absolutes, but on this matter I come very close: Do not try to bend sawn wood from a lumberyard. It is a waste of time. The best blanks for bending are riven directly from the log. A saw pays no attention to the direction of the wood fibers - the grain of a sawn piece will not run uninterrupted from end to end. Furthermore, wood purchased from a lumberyard has usually been kiln dried. I have noticed that kiln dried wood feels more brittle when working it than air dried wood. I know of no one who is regularly

able to bend the stuff successfully.

Although many species of wood can be rived, steamed, and bent successfully, my preferred wood is red oak. I can perhaps most easily explain why I prefer this wood by first describing the problems I have had with other species.

HICKORY While still green, hickory is a delight to work. Billets that do not contain any knots and that have straight grain split with ease. The fresh wood is as soft as butter; it cuts cleanly and shaves easily. When steamed, hickory does not soften or plasticize as much as do some other species. However, the wood is so tough when green that it can actually be bent without first being steamed. In other words unseasoned hickory will bend cold. This process requires mechanical assistance. After a piece of cold bent hickory has cured, it will retain its shape, but I caution against being in the way if a cold bent hickory bow should slip loose from its bending form before curing. It will give you a good knock.

Once hickory has seasoned it is difficult to work, it takes on an almost metallic hardness, and a great deal of effort is required just to bore a hole through it. The bent parts of Windsor backs require a lot of holes to house the spindles, so this characteristic is undesirable. Seasoned hickory is also less flexible than red oak and it tends to be more brittle.

Fresh-cut hickory billets dry quickly, and their ends develop large checks even if painted. Therefore, hickory has a short shelf life. If kept on hand more than a couple of weeks, it either spoils due to checking or dries to a point where it is unworkable.

WHITE ASH While green, white ash also splits cleanly and easily and it whittles and planes easily. Steamed, it plasticizes and bends without too much effort. However, it dries to a metallic hardness, too, and is difficult to work.

Ash does not check as badly as hickory when drying. However, when left in the log, ash is attacked by a fungus that breaks down the wood so that it shears easily across the grain when stressed. The fungus is indicated by a spotted, light blue stain in the sapwood. To prevent this fungus attack it is necessary to quarter the log and remove the bark.

To split a 5-ft. long *red oak log for chair backs begin the split by driving a wedge into the edge of one end. Add a second wedge near the heart.*

Of course the smaller pieces of wood will season more rapidly.

I have observed a curious phenomenon in ash. I once set aside some ash quarters that became quite workable a year or so later. They split well, worked with reasonable ease, and bent nicely. I don't know what caused this.

WHITE OAK Second growth white oak trees tend to branch fairly low. The result is a short trunk in which the layers of annual growth are deflected near the stump and lower limbs. Such trees do not contain as much serviceable bending stock, which must be straight grained, as do taller trees.

Of the woods discussed thus far white oak is often the most difficult to split. Unlike hickory and ash, it does not usually pop open cleanly under the force of a wedge. Instead, wood fibers pull loose from both sides of the split. Dozens of these fibers, each the thickness of a pencil, hold the halves together and must be snipped with a hatchet to separate the pieces. These torn fibers ruin the surrounding wood that could otherwise be made into backs.

White oak also becomes difficult to work as it hardens. It is a great fire wood, but I pass on white oak when it comes to making chair backs.

RED OAK The troubles I have described above can be avoided by using red oak for bending. This species often grows 20 ft. to 30 ft. before branching. A good forest tree is as straight as an arrow, and its trunk will render several logs suitable for chair backs. There is enough stock in one good red oak tree to keep me busy for as long as two years (in practice, I do not use wood that old. I reorder fresh logs twice a year. Last season's oak is next winter's firewood.)

A good red oak log will split open as easily as hickory or ash. After several blows of the maul the log signals its surrender with a resounding pop. When the two halves fall apart, I have to skip quickly to protect my ankles. Another nice feature of red oak is its bark. It has a texture that is a portrait of the log's interior. Any deflection or distortion in the grain around an enclosed blemish will show up on the bark.

As soon as the oak is brought into the shop, it begins to dry. As the year progresses, the wood contains less and less moisture. This is not a problem with red oak - when bending you just steam it longer to bring up the moisture content. It does harden somewhat as it seasons, but it never takes on the almost metallic hardness of hickory, ash, or

HALVE, THEN QUARTER THE LOG (above and right). Notice the deflected grain near the heartwood. The seccussive annual growth toward the outside of the log becomes straighter. This is why logs at least 12" in diameter are best for chairmaking.

FOR A LOG THIS SIZE, eighths are about the smallest parts that need to be split with the maul and wedges (above).

white oak. When a bent part is hung up to dry, it will not become too hard to plane, scrape, saw, or bore easily.

There is only one problem with red oak. It contains tannic acid which causes the wood to stain a purple color when it comes in contact with a ferrous metal. This stain is never very deep and it is easily removed with a cabinet scraper. Red oak also takes on a slight grayish cast after it has been steamed. This color is permanent, but most people will not notice if it is not pointed out. I always recommend paint as the appropriate finish for a Windsor and if this advice is followed, this slight discoloration is nothing to worry about.

Red oak grows nearly everywhere east of the Mississippi. If it is not native to your region, you will have to experiment until you find a species with the same qualities.

Riving and Shaping

Whether you use red oak or a comparable species, it is important to select a good log. The grain of the blanks you rive from it must be sound and run uninterrupted from one end to the other. A blank should be straight with no distortion. A slight curve is acceptable, but the grain cannot be deflected anywhere along its length. Curly grain, pin knots, ingrown bark, or any other blemishes are unacceptable.

When you have selected the log saw it to length. Sack back bows and arms can be got out of 4 ft. long sections, continuous arms from sections 5 ft.

AFTER RIVING, STRIP THE BARK *off the red oak billets with a drawknife.*

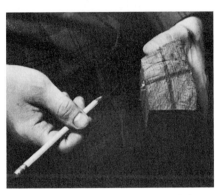

AFTER REMOVING THE BARK AND *pith from a billet, sketch out the blanks on an end for riving. Hold the billet vertically and rive the back blanks with a hatchet driven by a wooden maul. Always split so there are pieces of equal mass on each side of the hatchet.*

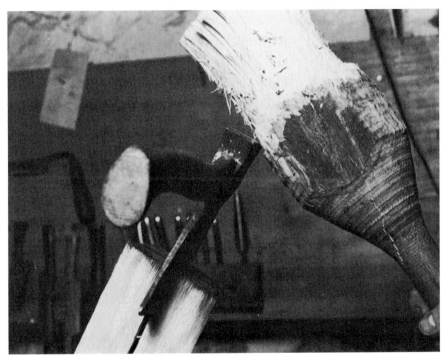

long. Split the log into billets that are small enough to be easily handled and transported. I often split a log into eighths. At this point, I cease working outside and go into the shop. One of the eighths should yield enough material for at least one, but probably two or more chair backs. Remove the bark from the billet with a drawknife. The bark must be taken off before any further work is done. If left on the wood it will sometimes cause a split to run where you do not want it to go. Also, the bark can hide the split and you will not be able to watch it. (If you are storing the remaining billets for future chairs, remember to drawknife the bark off them to prevent fungus from forming.) Next, remove the pith, as well as a couple of inches of surrounding wood by riving it from the billet. There are usually pin knots and deflected grain in this area.

With a pencil, sketch on the end grain the number of back blanks that you can obtain from this billet. I rive blanks for the sack back bow and for the continuous arm about 1⅛" square. A blank for a sack back arm is about 1⅛" x ¾". I want each piece of riven stock to be close to the final dimensions of the back piece. Riving is not as accurate as sawing and can be difficult to control when working to close tolerances. The nearer you try to size each blank to its finished dimensions, the more you risk making it too small. I am happy if 75% of the blanks that I sketch out are usable.

The rule for splitting bending blanks is the same as for splitting turning stock. Always split pieces of equal mass. If you try to rive a thin piece from a large billet, the split will run out in the direction of the smaller and weaker side.

A FROE IS HANDY FOR *splitting long pieces. Using the handle as a lever, work the blade back and forth to control the split as it opens. The wedge-shaped blade can also be driven into the end grain to start a split. You can try to redirect a split that is running out by driving the edge of a hatchet into the billet in the direction the split should go.*

I use a Kent hatchet, wooden maul, and a froe to rive the backs. Place the oak vertically. I hold it upright in my bench vise. Start the split with the hatchet and maul. The hatchet head may become buried until it can no longer be driven with the maul. When this happens, I insert a froe below the hatchet to complete the split. This simple tool has a long metal blade that is wedge shaped in cross section. Its wooden handle is set into an eye on one end of the blade and at a right angle to the blade's length. The handle functions as a lever, and allows you to work the blade back and forth when opening a split.

The first split in a 4" x 4" billet is usually easy. Any trouble will occur riving the final pieces. I find it easier to control the split in a narrow piece if I take the piece in hand and drop its lower end on the floor. The resulting shock opens the split more gently and with more control than can be obtained by striking the hatchet with the maul. If the split begins to run out, turn the piece around and split from the other end. If this does not work you can try to reestablish the split from the middle of the billet. Rest the billet on a chopping block. Set the cutting edge of the hatchet on it in the direction that the split should be

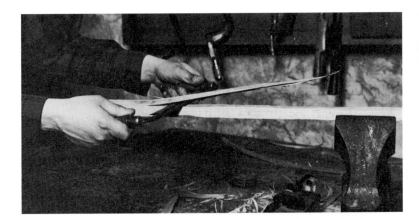

To shape the sack back *arm, remove the bulk of the waste from the blank with a draw-knife. Then, plane the blank to its finished dimensions.*

going. Give the hatchet a sharp rap with a maul to drive the edge into the grain. If you are lucky, the hatchet's edge will pick up the split and redirect it.

It may sound like you will have to struggle with the wood. I have described the worst case run-out and its remedy. Most pieces open just as nicely as could please and split to size with no trouble at all.

A question that I am invariably asked is "Why can't I cut the blanks on a table saw?" The problem with sawing is that the saw ignores the direction of grain. If there is a long, gentle bow in the oak billet, riving will follow that bow and still render a serviceable back blank. A table saw is oblivious to grain direction and cuts a straight line that severs the grain along the way. You will not even save time by sawing. I can split out back blanks as fast as they could be sawn, and I am assured of their quality.

SHAPING THE SACK BACK Once you have split the blanks near to size, trim the bow blank 45" long and the arm blank 44" long. Then begin to shape them. The first tool I use is a drawknife. The drawknife is a roughing tool, and I only rely on it to hew off the bulk of the waste. I can easily take off shavings that are the full width of the piece and as thick as a pencil.

Drawknife the arm blank until is it is roughly rectangular in section. Once you have removed most of the waste, clamp the blank on a workbench

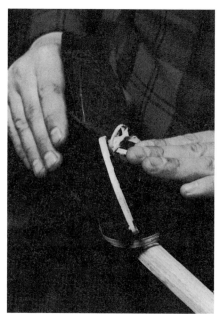

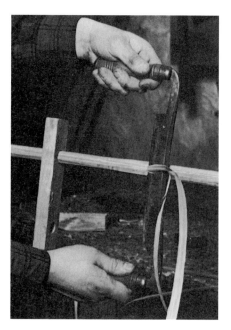

ROUND THE BOW BLANK WITH *a drawknife.*
*Make a simple gauge to check the diameter
of the bow as you go along. A forkstaff
plane, which is a smoothing plane with
a concave sole, is useful for finishing the
round bow. Taper the ends of the bow from
¾" to ⅜" in diameter with a drawknife.*

and finish up the four sides with a smoothing plane to the final ½" x ¾" cross section. The unseasoned oak blank will plane cleanly and easily.

The bow can also be rounded roughly with the drawknife. I maintain a consistent ¾" diameter by passing the bow through a gauge. The gauge is no more than a small block of wood with a ⅞" hole bored through it. (If the bow passes through this larger hole, it is the desired ¾") Move the gauge along the developing bow to find the high spots. It will not pass over these places, and they must be trimmed down. I do this with a forkstaff plane. This plane looks like a smoothing plane, but has a concave sole that makes it very useful for rounding parts, such as bows. You can also round the bow with a spokeshave.

When the entire length of the bow will travel through the gauge, place the bow in a vise and taper both ends with the drawknife. The last 6" of the bow decrease in diameter from to ¾" to ⅜". This is the size of the socket for joining the bow to the arm. Leave the ends slightly oversized and do not do any finish smoothing or scraping at this time. The bow still must be bent, and there is always a risk that it will break. If it breaks, you will throw away all the extra finishing work.

Finally, locate and mark the center of the lengths of the arm and bow. You will need these marks later to position the pieces on the bending form.

SHAPING THE CONTINUOUS ARM The continuous arm is a more complex shape. The arm is bent in two planes. The center of the arm is in one plane that is more or less vertical and is supported above the seat by the long spindles. The arm curves at each end into a horizontal plane. These end segments, which support the sitter's arms, are fixed to the seat by the stumps and short spindles. In each plane, the arm has a distinct cross section. The center segment in the vertical plane is a square of about ¾" on a side. Its back surface is slightly rounded, as shown in the drawing at the end of this book. The end segments, those in the horizontal plane are about ⁷⁄₁₆" thick. They also become wider, enlarging from ¾ in. to about 1⅛" wide at each end.

Next, lay out marks on the back surface of the blank to help when developing the changing cross sections of the arm. Locate and mark the center of the blank 28 in. from either end. Mark a line 14 in. on each side of the center. This divides the blank into the center and two end segments.

Place the blank, face down, in a vise and then pare the two end segments to ⁷⁄₁₆" thick with the drawknife. The transition from middle to end segments is a short taper. When this waste is removed, the blank will approximate its finished shape. There is now no doubt which of the surfaces is the face and which is the back.

Clamp the blank on the bench and plane one edge square to the face. (If the blank has flared ends, plane the edge opposite the flared edge now.)

This will be the inside edge of the vertical center segment. It will be placed against the curved form when bending. Next, plane the back surface to make the center segment ¾" thick.

The remaining edge will be flat along the length

AFTER RIVING, SELECT THE FACE *of the continuous arm blank and plane it flat. With the blank held face down in a vise, drawknife the ends 7/16" thick.*

Shaping the Continuous Arm

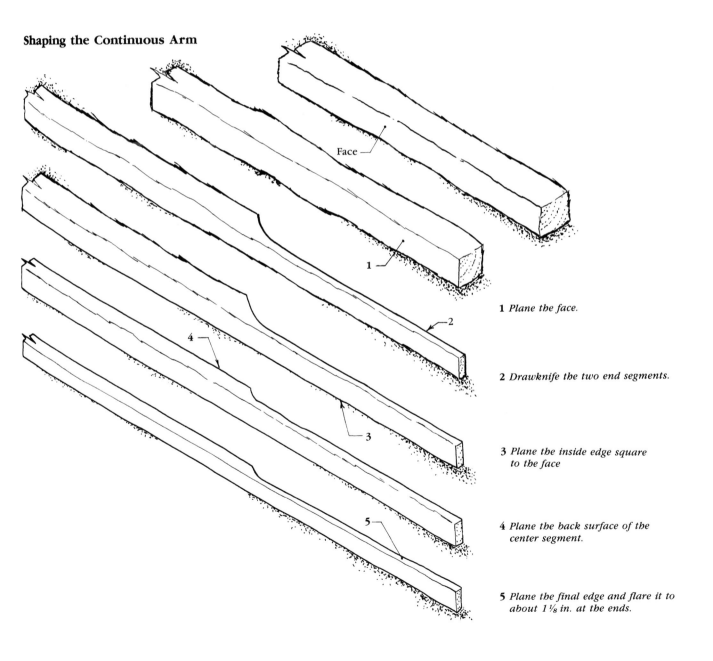

Face

1

2

3

4

5

1 *Plane the face.*

2 *Drawknife the two end segments.*

3 *Plane the inside edge square to the face*

4 *Plane the back surface of the center segment.*

5 *Plane the final edge and flare it to about 1 1/8 in. at the ends.*

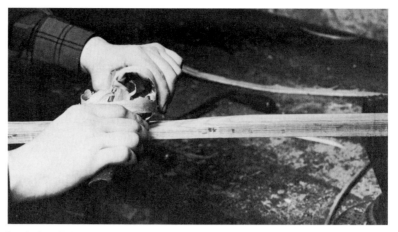

ROUND THE ARRISES OF THE *center segment with a forkstaff plane, followed by a spokeshave or smoothing plane. Soften the transition from the center segment to each end with a with a spoke shave.*

of the center segment and flare out so the blank is wider at both ends. Plane this final edge to make the center segment of the blank ¾ in. square, and taper the end segments into the center. To do this you will need a plane that has a short sole such as a smoothing plane. A plane with a longer sole will not allow you to shape the flared ends.

The square center segment does not have four sharp arrises. The two on the back surface are gently rounded. I do this with the forkstaff plane. You could use a smoothing plane or a spokeshave. Next, clean up the transition on the back surface from the center segment to the thinner ends. Make the tran-

sition taper gradually over a couple of inches. This is a short area and it is end grain, so I use a spokeshave. Locate and mark with a pencil the exact center of the arm. (Your original marks were probably removed during shaping.) Mark also the inside edge of the arm. These marks will position the piece on the bending form.

Steaming and Bending

Almost every procedure in making a chair relies on skill to ensure success. For example, when I start a seat, I am almost certain that when I am done I will have an acceptable part. The only possibility for failure is an unnoticed flaw in the wood itself. Bending, however, is not as certain. In spite of the knowledge gained from having made countless bends, I still occasionally lose a bow or an arm. The sickening sound of rending wood is in my mind's ear as I state that bending requires as much intuition as skill.

Two elements are necessary for successful steam bending: moisture and heat. If both are present in sufficient amounts the wood is said to be plasticized. If either moisture or heat is absent, the wood will not bend regardless of how much of the other is applied. The wood could be soaked until waterlogged, but it would break if not sufficiently hot. It could be heated to nearly the flash point, but without the required amount of moisture it would not tolerate the stresses of bending.

To bend the parts for the chair backs the wood must have about 20% to 25% moisture content and be heated to about 180 degrees F. Unseasoned oak or other suitable and unseasoned species should already contain sufficient water; the problem is to raise the temperature. This could be done by boiling the wood in some sort of container, but you would have to find a suitable tub. This method would also require boiling a relatively large amount of water. I prefer to steam the wood in a small pipe that is only somewhat airtight and that requires you to heat only a small amount of water.

THE STEAM BOX My setup requires a metal utility can, either two or five gallon. The water in the can is heated on a propane fired burner. The

Steam box is 6 ft. long and is 4 in. diameter schedule 80 PVC pipe, used for drain, waste and vent plumbing. Schedule 40 will not withstand the heat, and will sag. A PVC cap is placed over each end of the pipe to contain the steam.

A PVC pipe steam box is lightweight, easily stored, and impervious to rot and mold. PVC is a good insulator. When my steam box is perking at full tilt I can easily hold my hand on its surface without discomfort. PVC pipe is expensive but is available at most plumbing suppliers.

The steam generated in the utility can is carried a short distance up to the pipe through an automotive radiator hose. One end of each hose is attached to the spout of the utility can. The other end is inserted into a PVC T/Y connection in the center of the pipe.

The chair parts are supported in the upper half of the pipe on four stainless steel bolts that pierce the pipe. The steam will condense and water will gather at the bottom of the pipe, so if the parts were laid on the bottom they would be resting in condensate that is considerably cooler

A SIMPLE SACK-BACK BENDING FORM *with dowles and wedges for holding the piece in place.*

than the steam.

The pipe is suspended above the utility can by a sawbuck. The condensed steam runs out ½" diameter vent holes bored in the bottom of each end of the pipe. Once you have obtained the parts for a steam box, the whole setup can be assembled in about a half hour.

The other piece of equipment that you will need to bend the back of each chair is a bending form.

THE SACK BACK FORM Both the sack back arm and bow can be bent on the same simple form made of 2"-thick pine or other inexpensive softwood, attached to a backboard of ¾"-thick plywood. Cut the pine to the outline of the curve shown below. You can make a pattern by plotting the points and connecting them to form a smooth curve. After cutting the curve, screw the pine securely to the plywood. At the apex of the curve, about 1¼" from the pine block, attach a stop made of a small rectangular piece of hardwood. The stop should be at least 1" thick and securely fastened, because it must endure a lot of strain.

After bending, each end of an arm or bow is held in place by a dowel near the bottom of each side of the pine block. Bore ½" holes for these dowels in the plywood about 1¼" from the edge of the block. Make a distinct, easily located mark on the block at the apex of the curve. When a hot, plasticized arm or bow is placed on the form for bending, its centerline should correspond to this mark. To complete the form, cut two ½" dowels about 4" long, and make three hardwood wedges, 5" to 6" long. Taper the edges from a cross section of about 1 in. square to a thin end.

THE CONTINUOUS-ARM FORM This form has some similarities to the sack back form. It, too, has a 2"-thick pine block attached to a plywood backboard.

Sack-Back Bending Form

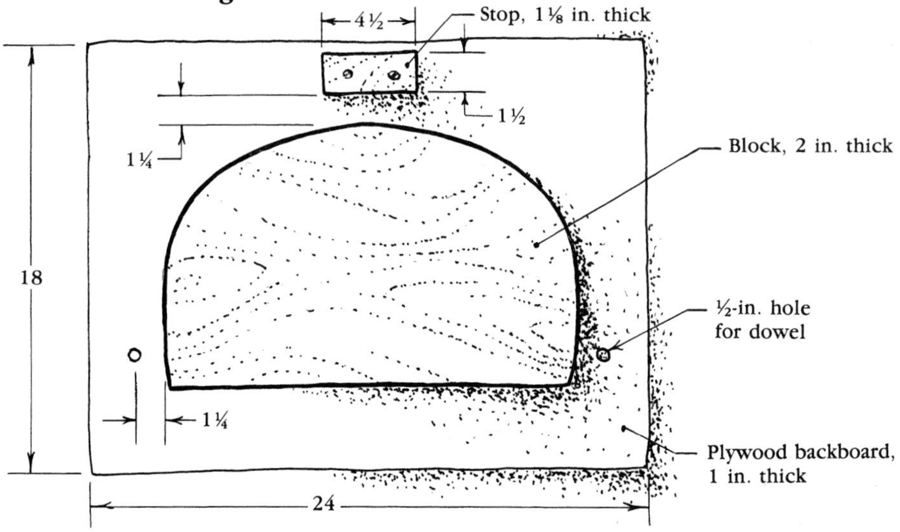

4½
Stop, 1⅛ in. thick
1½
1¼
Block, 2 in. thick
18
½-in. hole
for dowel
1¼
Plywood backboard,
1 in. thick
24

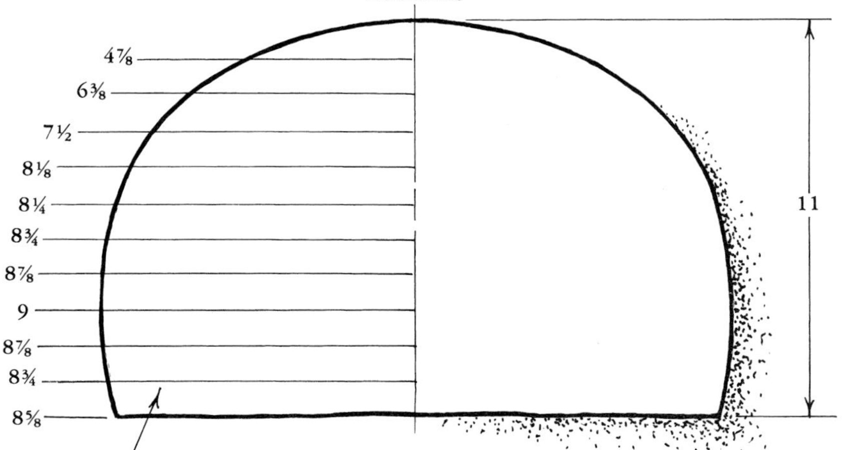

Centerline
4⅞
6⅜
7½
8⅛
8¼
8¾
8⅞
9
8⅞
8¾
8⅝
11
Dimensions, taken at 1-in. intervals, indicate distance from centerline.

Continuous-Arm Bending Form

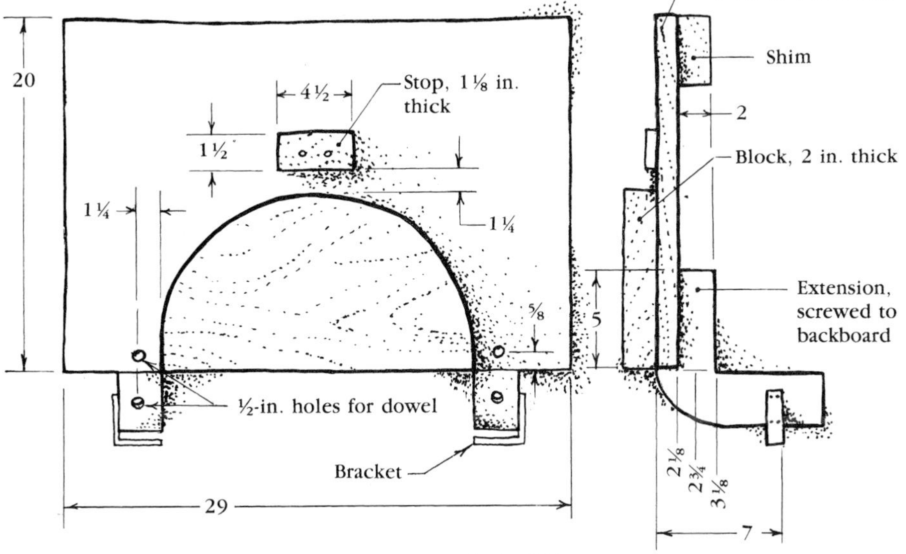

Plywood backboard,
¾ in. to 1 in. thick
Shim
20
4½
Stop, 1⅛ in.
thick
2
1½
Block, 2 in. thick
1¼
1¼
Extension,
screwed to
backboard
⅝
5
½-in. holes for dowel
Bracket
2⅛
2¾
3⅛
29
7

Pattern

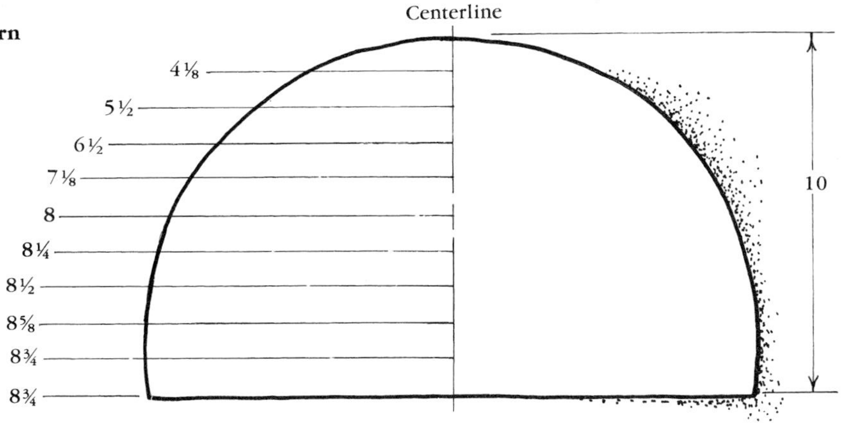

Centerline
4⅛
5½
6½
7⅛
8
8¼
8½
8⅝
8¾
8¾
10

To BEND A STEAMED SACK *back arm, first align its center mark with that of the form. Wedge the arm between the hardwood stop block and the form. Pull the first half around the form with a slow, steady motion. When it is tight to the end of the form, insert a dowel into the backboard. Drive a wedge between the dowel and the arm so the dowel will not dimple the wood. Pull the second half of the arm around the form and hold it in place against the block with a dowel and wedge.*

This block shapes the curve of the center segment of the continuous arm (the curve that will be in the vertical plane.) Make a pattern to the curve shown on the drawing below and cut the block to the curve. Screw the block flush with the edge of the plywood. At the top of the curve, screw a hardwood stop block to the plywood 1¼" from the curve. Mark the center of the curve on the pine block.

This form has two extensions that are attached to the plywood. These shape the end segments of the continuous arm (they will be in the horizontal plane). I cut the extensions from "-thick pine. The drawing shows a pattern for the extensions, too. The top of each one is cut to a radius and notched to take the plywood backboard. Make sure that the radius will finish flush with the top surface of the plywood. Screw the extensions securely to the plywood.

Bore ½" holes in the plywood near the base of the block in each extension and near the edge of the plywood and the outside surface of the extension. Dowels placed in these holes during bending hold the center segment in place on the form. The ends

of the piece being bent are held down by two angled pieces of iron attached to the extensions. I use angle brackets available in any hardware store. You will also need two dowels and three wedges the same size as those for the sack back bending form.

BENDING THE SACK-BACK PARTS To use the steam box, pour a gallon of water into the utility can. This amount will last a long time and there is no need to boil a full five gallons for one chair. The pipe soon fills with a cloud of steam that cannot escape around the tight fitting end caps. Its only egress is the small drain holes. When steam begins to blow out the holes in a plume that is 6" to 8" long, you are ready to insert the pieces. I will describe how to bend the sack back parts first.

(In the photos I am using a bending form made of a thin strap of wood attached to dowels. I made it about 12 years ago as an experiment, and have used it ever since. At the time I thought it was a better solution to making a form than what I have just described, although it was so long ago that I have forgotten why. This form does not work any better or worse than one made of a solid block of wood and it is more work to make.)

Place the arm and bow in the steam box resting on the bolts and put the cap on the open end. The chamber is so tight that the parts will heat quickly. They will be ready in as little as 15 minutes, but I always give them more time. If the stock from which the backs are made has dried out, steam them for as much as 45 minutes to raise the moisture content back to 25%. While the parts are steaming, clamp the form securely to the bench.

Before removing a plasticized arm or bow from the steam box, I have one word of caution. When you open the pipe, the escaping steam can severely burn your skin. I was careless only once and lost the skin on my thumb because of a scald. When you take a part out of the pipe, do not use your bare hands. I prefer to seize the end of the part with a pair of tongs. Once the piece is safely away from the open end, I take it in my bare hands. I do not recommend wearing gloves because they decrease sensitivity. Bending is not an exact science. It relies on intuition. You will need every possible bit of sensory data to achieve a successful bend. That data will be transmitted through sight, sound, and feel. I would not wear gloves while bending any more than I would wear dark glasses while bending.

If you look closely before pulling a part from the pipe, you might notice a curious phenomenon. The wood becomes so hot that sometimes the sap can be seen boiling out the end grain.

Pull a part out of the pipe with the tongs. Let's say it's the arm. The wood is so hot that you will have to pass it back and forth from hand to hand as you rush it to the bench. The discomfort is about as much as you can tolerate, but it forces you to work quickly. And quickly you must. You have about 45 seconds in which to bend. By that time the piece will have cooled too much and will no longer be plastic.

Lay the arm between the pine block and the hardwood stop. Place one of the wide faces down and an edge against the pine block. Be careful to line up the center mark on the arm with the mark on the pine block that indicates the apex of the curve. Insert a wedge between the arm and the hardwood block and give it a light rap with a hammer. This locks the wedge and tightly pinches the arm against the pine block.

Bend the first half of the arm by grasping it near the end with both hands and pulling it with a steady motion. As I said earlier, bending is as much an intuition as a skill. It is very difficult to describe the process. As you bend the part you can watch the wood move. The outside edge will stretch, while

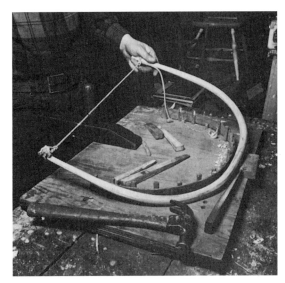

WHEN THE ARM OR BOW *is cool to the touch, tie its ends together with string. The part will retain the shape, and you can use the form to bend the other part.*

the edge against the block compresses. Listen for any faint wrenching sounds that might indicate that the fibers are shearing either across or along the grain. Sometimes you can feel this shearing just as it begins to happen. If you hear or feel shearing you may be pulling too fast for the wood to accept the stresses. Pull more slowly. On the other hand, if you pull too slowly the part will cool and lose its plasticity before the bend is completed.

If a small shear does begin you can sometimes push with one hand against the area that is shearing while continuing the bend with the other. Just that little bit of extra support may make the difference between losing the piece and saving it. For your first several bends, you might find it helpful to have an assistant help push where necessary.

The wood will only accept the bend if pulled with a steady, continuous motion. Do not jerk the end. When the first half is flush against the pine block, insert a dowel into the hole and slide a wedge between the dowel and the arm or bow. The wedge prevents the soft, hot wood from pressing against the dowel and developing a dimple.

The first half is always the easiest to bend. When the outside edge of the first half stretches, it steals some of its expansion from the outside edge of the other half. You can see this – the unbent half will move as the first bend is made. When you bend the second half, you will feel that it is stiffer. It has lost some flexibility to the first half, and the wood is cooler than it was during the first bend.

Pull the second half steadily, and a little slower than for the first half. Usually, if a part is going to

POSITION THE CONTINUOUS ARM FACE *down on the back board and wedge it in place. Pull the first bend around the form and hold it in place with a wedge. Support the grain at the transition as you make the second bend.*

break it will do so during the second bend. Listen and feel for shearing and apply pressure to any suspect areas. When the second half is against the block, hold it in place with the same dowel and wedge arrangement used previously.

I usually make two chairs at a time. If I waited until an arm or bow was dry to take it off the form, I would need four bending jigs to make two sack backs. However, wood is only plastic when both heat and moisture are present. About 20 minutes after bending, the part will have cooled so that it is still wet, but no longer plastic. At this point I can tie its ends together to hold the curve, remove it from the form, and bend the next arm or bow. Working this way, I can bend the arms and bows for a pair of sack back chairs on one form in less than two hours.

In the winter, I hang the tied arms and bows over the stove in my shop to dry. In the summer I set them outside in the sunshine. In a couple of days, when the chair backs are ready to assemble, I remove the string. The bent pieces will be dry enough to retain their shape permanently.

Bending the continuous arm

Pull the steamed arm from the steam box with tongs and place it face down on the form. Make sure that the inside edge (the straight edge, not the flared one) is against the block and the center lines are aligned. Insert a wedge between the hardwood block and the arm. The first bend forms half of the curve of the center segment. It is made in exactly the same manner as the first bend of a sack back arm or bow. Pull the arm steadily around the pine block and hold it in place against the block with a dowel and wedge.

The second bend is made down over the curve of the form's extension. The short tapered transition between the thick center segment and the thinner end segment will be at about the end of the pine block. Support the transition by pressing against it with one hand while bending with the other. The end gain exposed on the taper may lift loose rather than bend. This will happen to a certain extent every time that you bend a continuous arm. Pressing against the transition should keep the grain from lifting too much. The grain that does lift can be shaved away with a spokeshave after the part has dried.

There are four bends to be made on the continuous arm and only about 45 seconds in which to make them. To save time I usually hold the second bend in place with my knee, rather taking the time

HOLD THE SECOND BEND IN place with your knee while you make the remaining bends. Bend the arm against the block, and then over the extension. Then slip both ends under the brackets.

to slip it under the bracket. I slip the two ends under the brackets after all the bends have been completed.

The second half of the arm will be stiffer than the first. Pull the third bend against the block and secure it with a dowel and wedge. Make the fourth and final bend while applying pressure to the transition to prevent the grain from lifting. Finally, slip the second end, then the first under the brackets.

While the arm is wet and on the form, it is difficult to judge whether any torn or twisted grain has occurred during bending that will ruin it. (This is also true of the sack back arm and bow.) When the arm has dried you can examine it. Small flaws such as a short section of wood that has sheared along the grain can usually be trimmed flush with a spokeshave. Sheared grain up to ¼ in. thick can sometimes be glued and clamped back down in place. Of course, sometimes an arm cannot be saved. I do not lose many of now, but when my bending intu-

ition was still developing, the failure rate was much higher.

Because the continuous arm is bent in two planes its ends cannot be tied so that it can be taken off the form. Still, I have not bothered to make two forms. I produce two of these chairs a week. I bend one arm on Monday and place it and the form near the stove or out in the sun, depending on the season. It will be dry by Wednesday and can be removed to free the form for the second arm. This arm will be dry by Friday, when I put the chairs together.

Finishing Up

When the bent parts are dry they are in no condition to be used on the chair.

The hands need to be made and the rough surfaces smoothed. The hands of a Windsor are at the ends of its arm, where the sitter places his hands. Hands are generally any one of a number of scrolled

To MAKE HANDS FOR EITHER *chair, joint the mating edges of the blocks and the arm. Size the edges, then glue and clamp the pieces together. Plane the blocks flush with the arm after the glue has dried.*

shapes. The hands of the sack back and continuous arm are wider than the ends of the arms, so pieces have to be glued on to form them.

There are several reasons why these pieces are glued on to make the hands, rather than making them from the same piece of wood as the arm. To get the wider hand out of one piece, you would have to start with a larger blank. This means more work and more waste. If the arm breaks while being bent, the work that goes into making the hand is lost. To shape the hand from one piece, you would have to saw into the back edge of the arm. This sawing would actually increase the odds of the arm breaking during bending.

There is another consideration for the sack back. Its scrolled hand has delicate details. If cut in oak or some other ring porous wood suitable for bending, these details would be very fragile. A blow to the middle of the hand could easily break the point off.

To overcome these problems, I glue pieces of birch to the edges of the arm after bending. I prefer birch because it is less fragile than oak and finishes smoothly, even on end grain. It planes and saws well, and it is easy to clean up the edges of the scroll with a chisel after the shape has been cut out. There are always a lot of birch scraps from turning stock lying around the shop. I split these into short blocks about 1 in. thick, 6" long, and 2" wide, and

then set them aside to dry. If the birch blocks are the same thickness as the arm before gluing up, you will have a devil of a time aligning the surfaces. It is a lot easier to glue on a block that is thicker than the arm and then plane the surfaces flush.

The hands of a Windsor endure a lot of stress and strain. People are forever putting their weight on them as they get in an out of the chair. It is essential that the joint of the block to the arm not fail. A good joint requires perfectly mated edges. It would be dangerous to joint these small edges on a machine jointer. So, I clamp my jointer plane upside down in a vise and run the edges over it. The resulting surfaces are as good as any done mechanically.

As insurance for a good joint, I always size the mating edges before gluing and clamping. Sizing is done by wiping a thin film of glue over each edge and allowing it to dry. When the joint is ready to be assembled, a second layer of glue is applied. The first application prevents the second from being forced into the wood by the pressure of the clamps.

After the glue has dried, clamp the arm to the bench and plane the block flush with the arm. Next, trace the pattern onto the hand and saw out the shape with a coping saw. The edge of the scroll on the sack back is at a right angle to the upper surface of the arm. The edge of the hand for the continuous arm is cut at a bevel. I clean up the saw marks on the sack back hand with a chisel and gouge that fits the

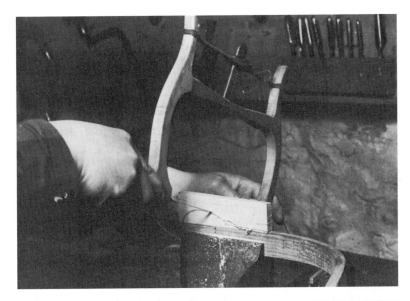

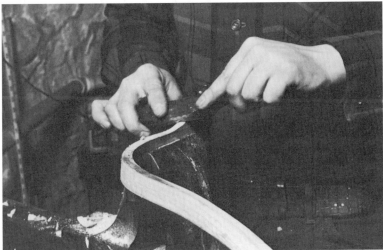

To SHAPE A CONTINUOUS ARM, *angle the coping saw as you cut to produce a beveled edge. Clean up with a spokeshave, working with the grain. Cut the scroll of the sack back hand perpendicular to the face of the arm. The concave curve of the scroll is best cleaned up with a gouge.*

curve of the scroll. On the continuous arm the clean up can be done with a spokeshave.

The hands are now finished, but the rest of the bent part remains rough. I secure the part in my tin knocker's vise and clean it up with a cabinet scraper. A curved block of wood helps hold the curves of the parts in place in the vise. The scraper removes the grain raised by steaming, and it also eliminates any remaining tool marks. Purple spots that result from the tannic acid in the oak coming in contact with ferrous metal can be scraped off as well. A light sanding with #220-grit paper is all that is required to finish the surfaces. The arm and bow for the sack back and the continuous arm are all scraped and sanded in the same way.

My continuous arm has a bead molding on the top and bottom arrises of the face. This molding could have been worked on the arm before it was bent. I did not do it then because the work would have been wasted if the part did not survive bending. Instead, I work the molding after scraping the arm. I made a simple scratch tool for this. The scratch tool appears primitive, but its action is really rather complicated. To make the tool, cut a small hardwood block about 1 in. by ¾"x 3½". Drive a 1" wood screw (No. 10 or No. 12) into the 1 in. wide face, about ⅞" from the end. Gently round the face from which the head of the screw protrudes. This will allow tool to track on even very tight curves.

The edge of the slot in the screw head cuts the groove that forms the bead. The slot acts like the throat in a molding plane. A thin chip curls

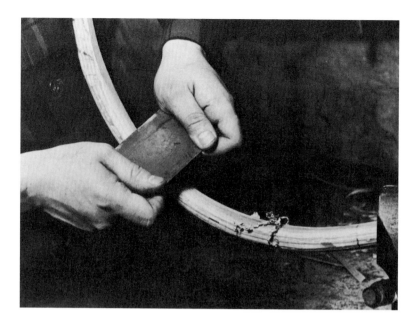

CLEAN UP THE ROUGH SUR-FACES *on a continuous arm and the sack back arm and bow with a cabinet scraper.*

upward as the groove is formed. Acting as a fence, the hardwood block maintains the cut at a uniform distance from the edge of the arm. You can vary the width of the bead by either backing out the screw or advancing it. After scratching the grooves, round the arrises with a cabinet scraper to produce the beads.

Hang the bent part or parts out of the way until after you have whittled the spindles and are ready to assemble the chair back.

What I wrote in 1983 still applies. We have made some additions to our bending, but no significant changes. Today, we bend the sack back arm and bow with the aid of a bending strap. Because of the double bend, we do not have a strap for the c-arm and do it exactly the same way as 30 years ago. A bending strap is a band of thin, flexible steel with stop blocks bolted to the ends. These stops are 46" apart and fit over the ends of the arm or bow. These blocks create a lot of compression on the part's ends. This compression is sufficient to crush a bow's tapered ends. For that reason, we now make the tapers after the bow has dried.

Because the back strap supports the bend's outer edge, it reduces the number of failures due to delamination and sheer. In a sack back class we bend as many as 30 parts in an afternoon. Each student has a lot of time invested in his or her parts, and a break can send that student into a funk. Because we have the extra hands present, we bend in pairs, one person on each end of the part.

I have changed some dimensions in the bent parts. The new seat pattern requires a 45" arm and bow. Bend both at 46" and trim an inch. The arm is now ⅝" thick, by ⅞" wide. The bow is ⅞" and is tested by passing it through a 1 in. hole in a gauge. I did not change the shape of the sack back bending form.

The inch of trim length allows you to "balance the bow". This step is necessary, as a bent back is seldom perfectly symmetrical. Create a line on your bench top parallel to the edge. The distance from the edge is not critical. Ours is 12". Place the arm (and later the bow) with the ends just overhanging the bench top. Examine the inside space created by the arm and the parallel line. Adjust to make it symmetrical. Now, maintain this relationship as you slide the bow so the amount of over hang on one end, when added to the amount of over hang on the other, equals 1 in. The amount is usually different, but can sometimes be the same (½") Sometimes the full inch has to be trimmed from one end. Mark and trim.

Our new c-arm is 58" long. The area in the center for the vertical bend is ¾" thick by ⅞" deep. The distance from the center line to the drop is 15" When I enlarged my c-arm chair seat I added 1 in. to the height and width of the bending form's block.

A c-arm will dry close to a right angle, too vertical to fit the chair. Correct the angle as needed by placing the bend's apex on your bench top and pushing down on the hand and vertical bend. Simply put, adjust the arm to fit your chair by unbending the wood.

One on the most repeated misconceptions

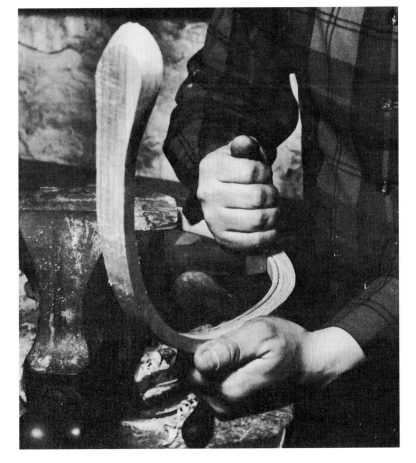

A CURVED BLOCK WILL HELP *hold the bent parts in a vise for scraping. Make a simple scratch tool for beading the continuous arm from a small hardwood block and a flat head screw. Press the block against the edges of the arm and draw the screw over the face until a groove is formed. To form a bead, round the arrises with a scraper.*

in woodworking is "Always over bend to allow for spring back." The opposite happens. When dried, bent wood compresses. This means it takes on even more of a bend. As a result, a string that is taut on a freshly bent bow will droop when the bow is dry. For this reason, avoid bending long in advance of using an arm or bow. You may discover it no longer fits your chair.

Chapter Nine

Whittling the Spindles

The following conversation is typical of many I have had when introduced to a new acquaintance. "What line of work are you in?" "I make Windsor chairs." "Windsors, aren't those the ones with all the spokes at the back?" It is not surprising that this is the recollection most people have of Windsors. The image they retain is of only the most dominant features, and the spindles in the back of a Windsor create a very strong impression. They are pronounced verticals that seize the viewer's attention and draw it upward in the direction of their flare. The role of spindles in the engineering of a Windsor chair back is equally important. They act as thin, vertical springs, absorbing the weight of a sitter rather than resisting it. Thus, the spindles allow the back of a Windsor to be delicate and airy

without being fragile.

It is extremely important to the longevity of the chair that the spindles be capable of flexing without breaking. The only way to ensure this is to make them from riven wood. At no point along the spindle's shaft should the grain run out. If it does, the spindle will be severely weakened. The stock for spindles of modern factory made Windsors is sawn into squares. The saw is oblivious to the direction of the grain and cuts across it as easily as along it. To ensure sufficient strength, therefore, factory-made spindles must be thicker than handmade riven spindles.

Wood for making spindles should have the same qualities as wood for bending. It must be flexible and easily worked. It must also split well. I use

SPLIT 1" SQUARE SPINDLE BLANKS *with a hatchet and wooden maul. Be sure to plan the riving sequence so you are always splitting pieces of equal mass.*

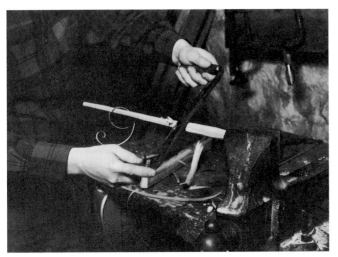

Rough out the long, thin *end of the spindle with a drawknife. Work the last 6" or so of the bottom end with a drawknife. Turn the spindle again and thin the shaft above the swelling.*

red oak for spindles because I always have plenty of it on hand. Unseasoned hickory or white ash is equally good. You need not be concerned about the hardness that develops in ash or hickory as they season, because no holes are bored in a spindle. I still recommend against white oak because it does not usually rive cleanly. However, if it is the only available wood, it will be adequate.

The longest spindle blank you will need for either chair is 22", so first buck a 22" length of oak from a log. I halve and quarter this on the spot, then bring the smaller, more portable billets into the shop. Remove the bark from the quarters with a knife then place them on a chopping block and rive them with a hatchet and maul. Be careful to split pieces of equal mass, and reduce the quarters to as many spindle blanks as you need. The cross section of each blank should be about 1 in. square.

The continuous-arm chair requires eleven whittled spindles, the sack back chair seven. Even red oak requires more effort to work as it becomes drier, so I split only enough spindle blanks for the two chairs that I make in a week. Working freshly split wood saves wear and tear on my tools and me. However, if a billet renders more blanks than I need I am not about to discard good wood – I set the extras aside and use them the following week.

I whittle my spindles with a drawknife and spokeshave. I hold the end of the blank securely in my tin-knocker's vise; I much prefer this vise to a shave horse. Held in the vise the blank projects into my work area and is accessible from three directions: the top and both sides. On a shave horse I cannot work as much surface area, so the spindle needs to be continually released and moved to whit-

tle all surfaces. Using my tin-knocker's vise I need to move the spindle fewer times.

The spindles for the two chairs look much the same, but there are a few differences in the way they are made. I will first discuss continuous arm spindles, which are simpler to make.

Continuous arm spindles

First cut the eleven spindle blanks to length. Blanks for the three center spindles and two brace spindles should be 22". Cut two more blanks 21" long, two blanks 19" long, and a final pair 17" long. All of these lengths are longer than the visible shaft of the spindle. The extra length allows for a 1¼" tenon at the bottom end and a tenon of about ¾" at the top which, fits into a socket in the arm. The rest of the extra length is waste but it is necessary for assembling the back and is trimmed when you are done.

Grasp the bottom end of the blank in a vise. First, rough out the thinner top part with a drawknife. I start my cuts about three fifths of the way down the shaft. When this end has its basic shape, turn the blank around and work the other thicker end. Drawknife up from the end about 6". This leaves a definite swelling below the center of the roughed out shaft. Turn the spindle again and work the long shaft above the swelling.

The swelling is very important. The back of a Windsor should be light and airy. However, as is true of most of other design considerations, there can be too much of a good thing. The spindles would look like wires if they were uninterrupted tapers from the ⁹⁄₁₆" socket in the seat to the ⅜" socket in the arm. The back would look fragile. The spindles flare out from the seat, but because of the swelling in each

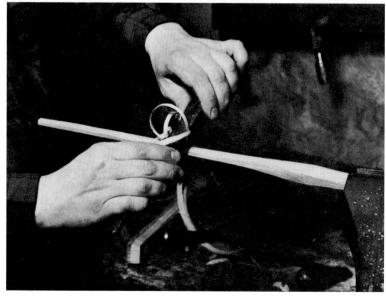

AFTER DRAWKNIFING THE SPINDLE ROUGHLY *to shape, switch to a spokeshave. Rotate the spindle frequently so you maintain its round cross section.*

one, there is no real increase in the distance between them for the first two fifths of their length. The spindles appear to spread only above the level of the arms. The long, thin portions of the spindles create an open, delicate fan, while the swellings restrain this effect.

Next, smooth the roughly shaped spindle with a spokeshave. Because the wood was riven the grain runs only in one direction. The spokeshave will remove long, thin shavings. This work is easy, and my only caution is to not get carried away with it. Be sure to rotate the spindle occasionally and to work all the sides. The tendency for a beginner is to work one area for too long. This results in spindles that are oval in cross section.

The ends of each spindle will be socketed into the seat and the arm and must fit snugly. I gauge the size of the ends by eye while spokeshaving. Until you have more experience and feel confident gauging by eye, you may want to use a simple gauge made from scrap wood. Bore a hole in the scrap

with the same bit you will use to bore the spindle sockets in the arm – I use my ⅜" spoon bit. Gauge the thickness of the spindle's top end with this hole.

Bore a second hole for gauging the bottom ends of the spindles. When assembling the chair you will whittle a shouldered tenon on the bottom of each spindle. So for now, you will want these ends to pass through a hole slightly larger than the sockets. The spindle sockets are %₁₆" in diameter, so the last 1¼" or so of each spindle should fit snugly in a ⅝" hole.

Finally, blend the swelling into the shaft above and below it. The diameter of the swelling on my spindles is about ¾". However, in both the sack back and the continuous arm, the area of the back where the swellings line up is so busy that the eye cannot detect slight variations in them. Because the diameter of the swelling is not critical, do not bother to check it with a gauge. Make sure however, that the swellings are not too pronounced. The vertical lines of the spindles draw the eye up to the curve

SACK BACK SPINDLES ARE MADE *in the same way as those for a continuous arm chair. However, they must fit tightly where they pass through the arm. Make two gauges to ensure that the spindles are the correct diameter at the correct height. After the spindles have dried, remove stains and whittling marks with a cabinet scraper.*

of the arm; if swellings are too heavy, this upward motion is disturbed.

SACK BACK SPINDLES The seven sack back spindles are made in almost the same way as the continuous arm spindles. The sack back spindles, however, have to pass through the arm before being wedged into the through sockets in the bow. The joints at the arm cannot be wedged, so they must be a tighter friction fit. The arm ties the spindles together and strengthens them, but if the spindles are loose in the arm sockets these functions are subverted. Therefore, the diameter of each spindle where it passes through the arm socket is critical.

You will need to gauge the spindles to ensure a tight fit. The sockets in the arm and bow are bored with a ⅜" spoon bit. To make the gauge, bore a hole with that bit in a piece of scrap hardwood. In the time it takes to make and assemble the back, spindles made of freshly riven wood will shrink. To allow for this shrinkage, I enlarge the ⅜" hole about ⅟₃₂" with a rattail file. I occasionally use blanks left over from the previous week's chairs. In the winter these blanks will have dried considerably and will not shrink as much as a freshly riven blank. I fit spindles made of dry wood to the gauge; these, and any others that do not fit properly, will be spokeshaved or scraped to fit during the dry assembly of the back.

The spindles must also tighten in arm at a predetermined height. If a spindle tightens too high up its length, the distance between the arm and the seat will be too great. This would make it impossible to assemble the back. If the spindle tightens too low on the shaft, the joint will be loose. You need another gauge to ensure that the shaft is a tight fit at the correct height. The bottom of the arm should be about

8½" to 8¾" above the surface of the seat, and the bottom tenon of each spindle is 1¾" long, so cut a stick about 10" long for the gauge.

To make the spindles, cut three blanks 22" long, two 21" long, and the remaining pair 19" long. Rough out and do the initial spokeshaving of each spindle as described earlier. As you approach the correct diameter at the top end of the spindle, slip the diameter gauge over the top end. As you work the gauge down the shaft of the spindle, it finds the high spots and shows you how much more wood to shave away. As the gauge approaches the middle of the spindle's length, check its distance from the lower end with the length gauge. Keep shaving, and when the two gauges meet, about 10" from the spindle's bottom end, it is time to stop

Turn the spindle around once again and finish its lower end. Then complete the swelling, as described earlier. The diameters of each spindle at its top and bottom are also ⅜" and ⅝" respectively. I recommend a gauge like the one described for the continuous arm chair to check the bottom end.

When all the spindles are whittled, place them aside to dry. In the winter, I suspend them over the wood stove in my shop. In the summer, I set them out with the bent parts in the sun. In damp weather, you can even dry them in the oven. When dry, the spindles scrape very well. I remove all the whittling marks and any stains with a cabinet scraper. A light sanding with #220-grit sandpaper finishes them.

Spindles are the easiest parts of the chair to make. I do a lot of daydreaming when making them. Spindles for a continuous arm require about three minutes apiece, those for a sack back about five minutes, so it takes me a little over an hour to make spindles for a pair of either type of chair.

*THE ENDS OF A SPINDLE fit into
sockets in the seat and arm.
Check their thicknesses with a
simple wooden gauge as you
work. The top end of a spindle
should pass through a hole ³⁄₈"
in diameter, the bottom end
through a hole ⁵⁄₈" in diameter.*

At some point, you will probably be tempted to
try to make spindles on the lathe. However, you will
quickly become so frustrated that you will return
to whittling them. Spindles are too long and thin
to turn unless you are very experienced and use a
steady rest.

If you want to use a lathe it is feasible to turn
the lower part of the spindle, including the shouldered tenon and the swelling. However the more
flexible, upper length will still have to be whittled. There are some problems with this technique: The turned and whittled segments must be
blended together with a spokeshave. Some vibration will still occur in the lathe, so the surface of the
swelling will contain some nicks that must also be

removed with the shave. The cleanup needed with
this method exceeds the labor required to whittle
the spindles in the first place.

**For my current sack back make your spin-
dles: 3 @ 23", 2 @ 22", and 2 @ 20". I increased
the hole through the arm rail from ³⁄₈" to ⁷⁄₁₆". This
makes the spindle stronger at a stress point. In
class, we make all seven spindles 23" long and cut
them to length before fitting them to the arm rail.**

**The new lengths for our c-arm spindles are: 5
@ 24", 2 @ 23", 2 @ 22", and 2 @ 20".**

Chapter Ten

Assembling the Sack Back

Whittling the spindles completes the making of parts for the chair back, and now you are ready to assemble it. The order in which several of the initial steps are done can vary. I will begin here by boring the stump sockets in the arm, then boring the spindle sockets in the seat. You could reverse this order, as I do in the following chapter when assembling the continuous arm.

STUMP SOCKETS Insert the stumps in the seat and place the arm on top of the tenons. Stand behind the chair and hold the arm roughly parallel to the plane of the seat. Position the hands so they intersect the stumps approximately where the sockets should be. On my chairs this is about 2" from the end of either hand. Sight down from above to see how the arm relates to the curvature of the spindle socket positions marked on the seat. The two curves are not identical, so try to position them symmetrically.

When you are satisfied with the position of the arm, mark where one stump would intersect the top surface of a hand. Because the armrest will pierce the hand at an angle, make sure to place the socket so that it will not be too close to the inside edge of the hand and weaken it. To bore the socket, clamp the arm and a backing board to the bench top. The hole is bored from the top surface for the same rea-

sons that the seat sockets are bored from the top of the seat. Clamp near the hand, being sure to leave enough space to turn the brace without striking the clamp. Before boring the hole I return to the chair and sight down the stump, mentally checking its slope and flare angles. They must be reproduced in the arm socket. I suggest that for your first chair, you set bevel squares to these angles and check the brace against them as you bore the socket. Start the 7⁄16" spoon bit at a right angle to the hand, and then lower it into position as you turn the brace. When you bore this hole do not bore as fast as the spoon bit will allow. The arm is narrow and could split if you press too hard on the brace and bit.

The stump tenon is tapered, so its socket must be reamed. Grip the hand in a vise, bottom surface toward you. The arm is quite thin in comparison to the seat, so ream slowly, allowing the bit to enter the socket at its pace. Periodically, remove the reamer and test fit the corresponding tenon. When the tenon can be inserted so that only the large end of its taper is exposed beneath the arm the socket is complete. (You might want to bore and ream a socket in a piece 7⁄16"-thick scrap wood for practice before trying one in the arm.)

Return to the seat and slip the socket over the stump tenon. The arm will rotate on this sin-

POSITION THE ARM ON THE *stumps and mark one socket on a hand. Bore the first socket carefully; check the angles against bevel squares if necessary.*

REAM THE SOCKET SO THAT *the tenon fits into it up to the base of the taper.*

PUT THE FIRST SOCKET OVER *its stump, and position the arm for marking the second socket. The arm and seat edge should form symmetrical arcs.*

BORE THE SOCKET FOR THE *center spindle first. Viewed from the front, it is perpendicular to the seat.*

gle point. Rest the unsocketed hand on the other stump. Stand behind the chair again and adjust the arm so that it is symmetrical with the spindle sockets marks. You should see something like what is shown in the photo. Make sure that the position of the hand on the stump is correct, and then mark the second socket. (This certainty of adjustment was not possible before boring the first socket.) Clamp the arm to the bench, establish the brace at the correct angles and bore the second socket. Ream and fit it to the armrest tenon.

Slip the arm over both stump tenons, then stand back to examine the chair from a distance. The arm should be nearly parallel to the plane of the seat. You needn't worry if the seat and arm converge slightly, but if they diverge, you may have to correct the angle of the stump sockets in the arm. Test how much the arm will flex; if the error is small, you should be able to pull it down until it is parallel to the seat. If the error is large use the reamer to adjust the angles, but be careful not to enlarge the sockets too much.

When you are satisfied with the relationship of the arm to the seat, measure the height of the hands from the seat on both sides. If there is any discrepancy between them, ream the socket on the higher side again. Before proceeding further, swap the stumps to see if they are interchangeable. If not, mark them left and right.

SPINDLE SOCKETS IN THE SEAT As I mentioned earlier, the beginner should bore the spindle sockets in the seat now, rather than when socketing the seat for the stumps and legs. By placing the arm on the stumps you can get a sense of what the spindle flare and slope angles should be. Then, with the chair standing on the floor, you can sight down the brace very much like what would be done when aiming a rifle to establish these angles when boring each socket.

At first you will probably want to check the brace and bit with bevel squares. (Approximate angles are given on the drawing.) As you gain experience, you will not need the bevel squares. Eventually, you will remember these angles so well that you will be able to bore all the sockets in the seat at the same time. I find this the most efficient method.

I bore the sockets with a 9⁄16" spoon bit that has a scribe mark 1¼" from its nose. This mark indicates when the socket is deep enough. Bore the socket for the center spindle first. This spindle slopes back, but it is perpendicular to the seat when viewed from the

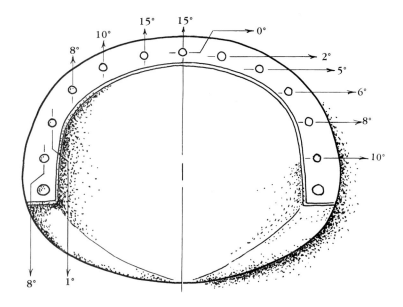

YOU CAN SIGHT DOWN THE *brace and bit to establish the slope and flare angles for the remaining spindle sockets. The axis of the brace and bit should correspond to the position of the spindle. You can use bevel squares to check the angles until you gain confidence in sighting.*

SPINDLE ANGLES FOR SACK BACK *Slope is indicated on the left half of the drawing. Flare is shown on the right. Arrows indicate direction of slope or flare. The spindles are symetrical around the center spindle.*

front. You could say that it has zero flare. You can use a try square to establish this angle, or gauge it by eye.

The remaining spindles have both slope and flare. Corresponding spindles on either side of the center are mirror images. I bore one of the sockets adjacent to the center spindle, then the adjacent socket on the other side. I repeat this process for each pair. This helps because I have the slope and flare of the first spindle in mind and need only reverse the direction of the flare for the second. If you are checking the angle with bevel squares you can use the same settings for each pair of spindles.

When all the sockets are bored in the seat, I like to whittle the tenons on the ends of the long spindles and insert them in the appropriate holes. I whittle the tenons by holding a wide, shallow carving gouge (#3 sweep 35 mm) against my sternum and pulling the tenon against it. The tenons should be about 1¼" long. They should fit the sockets tightly and have pronounced facets. These facets key the joint, much like the oversized wedges do for the leg

tenons. The facets bite into the walls of the sockets, minimizing the ability of the spindle to twist. You do not need to round the bottoms of the tenons to conform to the socket bottoms - the hard oak tenon will make the socket conform to it. At the same time, facet the tenons of the short spindles to fit their seat sockets.

Once all the spindles are in place, step back to view the chair. You can now spot any discrepancies in the angles of the spindles. The spindles are flexible and consequently very forgiving of error. If one appears incorrect, see if you can pull it into place. If it is too far out of kilter, you can adjust the flare of the surrounding spindles when you bore the sockets in the arm and bow, so that the spindles appear even and symmetrical. At the worst, you might have to plug the socket in the seat and bore a new one. At this time you will notice that the project is beginning to look like a chair. Even after all the Windsors I have made, I still appreciate this moment and I find it a satisfying time to take a coffee break.

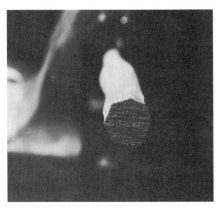

TRIM THE SPINDLE TENONS TO *fit the sockets. Facet the tenons with a wide, shallow gouge. The facets will bite into the socket walls so the tenon will not twist.*

CHECK THE SOCKET LOCATIONS ON *the arm against the spindles. Small adjustments to align a spindle and a socket will not be noticeable.*

SPINDLE SOCKETS IN THE ARM With the arm attached to the two stumps; place the center spindle in its socket. It should rest against the arm at the middle of the curve. However, bent wood is never perfectly symmetrical. Some adjustment of the spindle from side to side may be necessary. A couple of degrees of movement either way are possible without being obvious.

When you are satisfied with the position, mark the intersection of the spindle and the arm. Next, set a pair of dividers and walk off the sockets for the remaining spindles. On my sack backs there is 2⅞" between all the long spindles. When the positions are marked insert all the spindles in the seat and check them against the socket locations on the arm. This is the time to adjust for any discrepancy in the flare of the spindles.

Locate the sockets in the arm for the short spindles by eye rather than with dividers. Because the

arm is not symmetrical it may not be the same length on both sides of the center spindle. You can hide this discrepancy by locating the short spindle sockets so that they divide the length of arm between the outside long spindle and the stump socket into three equal sections.

To bore the sockets in the arm, clamp it to the bench over a backing board to protect the bench top. I make the long spindle sockets with a ⅜" spoon bit, the short spindle sockets with a ⁷⁄₁₆" bit. A small C clamp will prevent the bit from splitting the arm. This sort of accident does not happen often, but when it does it is doubly aggravating - first because it happened at all, and second because a little foresight could have prevented it.

I usually start with the center spindle socket, then I bore pairs of sockets on either side of the center, as described earlier. Remember to position the socket toward the outside edge of the arm, so that

CHECK THE SOCKET LOCATIONS ON *the arm against the spindles. Small adjustments to align a spindle and a socket till not be noticeable (above). Locate the sockets for the short spindles by eye. The sockets should divide the distance between the outside long spindle and the stump socket into three equal sections (top, right).*

the angled hole will not weaken the inside edge. I bore these sockets by eye, but if you are hesitant to try this, use bevel squares set to the same angles as the spindle sockets in the seat. If you decide to try it by eye, here's a word of caution. The slope and flare angles for the long spindles are not extreme, and a beginner will usually exaggerate them. It is difficult to see such a slight angle when sighting down the brace from above. Try holding the brace at the correct angles with one hand while you squat down behind it to check flare, and then move to the side to check the slope. The flexibility of the spindles will forgive a certain amount of error in boring these sockets.

ASSEMBLING THE LOWER BACK When all the sockets are bored in the arm dry assemble the lower back (the spindles, arm, and stumps). First, put the long and short spindles in their arm sockets. Check the long spindles with a tape measure (or the length gauge that you used when whittling them) to make sure that they extend about 10" below the arm. This will ensure that the arm will rest at the correct height on the spindles when the back is assembled. Scrape or shave any spindles that are too thick until they fit correctly.

With all the spindles in their arm sockets, place the arm on the stump tenons. Tap the spindles down one by one until their tenons have begun to enter the seat sockets. You only want to test the fit of the back

BORE THE CENTER SPINDLE SOCKET *in the arm.*

BORE THE CORRESPONDING SOCKETS ON *either side of the center. Judge the slope and flare angles by eye, or with bevel squares.*

INSERT THE SPINDLES IN THE *arm sockets, and check that they extend the correct distance below the arm. Dry fit the spindles and arm. Tap the spindle tenons part of the way into the seat sockets.*

now, so do not drive the tenons home. You want the tenon facets to bite fully into the socket walls only at final assembly. Next, tap the arm down into place on the spindles.

I like the arm to sit about ½" lower at the center of the back than at the stumps. This slight drop counters an undesirable optical illusion - when the arm and the seat are parallel, the arm appears to be higher at the back than at the stumps. By dropping the arm at the stumps, you create the illusion that it is really parallel with the seat. When the back is finally assembled, the distance from the top surface of the arm to the seat at the center spindle should be about 9", at the stumps it should be about 9½" (When measuring at dry assembly, remember to allow for the amount that the tenons will be driven in at final assembly.) These heights can vary from chair to chair because the lengths of the tenons or the size of the reamed sockets for the stumps may be different on one chair than on another.

Before gluing up the lower back you need to bore the sockets that join the bow to the arm. Put the bow in place on the dry assembled chair. Weave the bow through the spindles, one spindle to one side of the bow, the next to the other side, and so on. This holds the bow in the plane it will occupy when the chair is finally assembled. If the bow were merely rested against the fronts of the spindles, it would be too far forward. Behind them, it would be too far back.

Roughly locate the ends of the bow between the two short spindles. Look down on the bow from behind and adjust it so it is symmetrical in relation to the curve of the seat and the curve of the arm. When you are satisfied with the position, mark the location of both sockets on the top surface of the arm. The bow slopes back but has no flare, so you can center the sockets on the arm. The ends of the bow cross the arm at the angle of the sockets. Trace this angle on the inside edge of the arm to serve as a guide when you are boring the socket.

Remove the arm by tapping it off the spindles with a hammer. Strike between all the spindles, alternating the hammer blows to raise the arm evenly and prevent it from kinking. If the arm catches on one of the spindles, the thin walls of the socket could break.

Clamp the arm and a backing board to the bench top so that you can see the angled scribe mark on the inside edge of the arm. I lay the hand parallel to the edge of the bench top. Put a small C clamp on the arm to prevent the bit from splitting it while you bore the socket. Make sure that the clamp does not cover the angled scribe mark. Start the ⅜" spoon bit at a right angle, and then gradually lower it to match the angled mark, and complete the socket. Bore the sockets for both ends of the bow in this way.

There is an alternate method that a beginner might feel more comfortable with. In this method the sockets for the bow are bored after the lower back (the spindles, arm, and stumps) has been glued in place. Go through basically the same procedure

WEAVE THE BOW THROUGH THE *long spindles of the dry-assembled chair. Adjust its position, and then mark the location of the sockets in the arm. Trace the slope angle of the bow on the inside edge of the arm. To bore the sockets for the bow start the bit perpendicular to the arm and gradually lower it to the slope angle traced on the arm.*

as just described. The sockets, however, are made with a ratchet brace while the arm is fixed to the chair. Be sure to use a C clamp here as well, to prevent splitting.

When the sockets for the bow have been bored the lower back is ready for the final assembly. I recommend assembling in the following order to minimize glue spillage and the resulting mess. First, put all the long spindles in the proper arm sockets. Do not glue these joints - glue only bonds well under pressure, and there is no way to wedge these joints.

Next, swab glue into all the spindle sockets in the seat, then put glue into the four short spindle sockets in the arm and insert the short spindles. Spread glue in the stump sockets in the seat and insert the stumps. (Remember to put them into their proper sockets if they have been marked left and right.) Finally, put glue in the stump sockets in the arm and set the arm down onto the stumps.

Line each spindle up with its seat socket and

tap the tenon in. When all the tenons are in their sockets, give each spindle a firm rap to set the tenon facets into the soft pine sides of the sockets. Now, tap the arm down to correct height (½" lower at the back than at the stumps), and measure to check. Be sure not to cock the arm on the spindles by driving it in only one area. Tap around the whole arc, working the arm down uniformly. Do not drive the arm too aggressively. Also, remember that the tapered tenons on both ends of the stumps can act as wedges, and can split the seat or arm if driven with too much force.

When the arm is at the desired height, trim the tops of the short spindles and the stump tenons with a coping saw so that no more than ¼" is left above the arm. These parts are smeared with glue, and when the teeth of the coping saw blade become clogged, the blade can be disposed of. Wedge these tenons in the same manner as the leg tenons. I shape the wedges with a drawknife or a wide, shal-

DURING THE FINAL ASSEMBLY, DRIVE *the spindles into the seat sockets. Then tap between the spindles to set the arm in position, alternating blows from side to side. Measure from the seat to check the arm's height at the center spindle and each stump (above).*

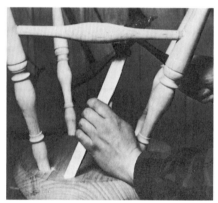

WEDGE THE SHORT SPINDLES AND *stumps in the arm. Make the split for the wedge at a right angle to the grain of the arm. Rest the arm on the bench top and wedge the stump tenons into the seat.*

low gouge, depending on how much wood must be removed. Do not make the wedges wider than the tenons. The arm is thinner than the seat and made of hardwood, so instead of keying the joint an over wide wedge could split the arm. Make the splits with a chisel in the end grain of the tenons. When driving the wedges, listen for the dull tone that indicates when to stop.

After wedging the joints in the arm, invert the chair on a bench top and wedge the stump tenons in the seat. Do not key this wedge either – the distance between the socket and the edge of the seat is short and too much pressure could cause a crack to open in the end grain of the seat. Set the chair upright and shave the protruding tenons and wedges flush with the arm. I do this with the wide, shallow gouge that I use for making wedges and whittling tenons. Then, scrape the arm with a cabinet scraper and lightly sand it with #220-grit

sandpaper.

SPINDLE SOCKETS IN THE BOW Shave the ends of the bow with a spokeshave until they fit into a ⅜" hole bored in a gauge block. Then weave the bow through the spindles and insert the ends of the bow into the sockets in the arm. The center spindle should now cross the bow at the location of its socket. While the spindles hold the bow in place, step in front of the chair and make sure that you are satisfied with the location of the center spindle. Some adjustment may be necessary to center the spindle and ensure that the bow is symmetrical. If when adjusting the bow an end hits a short spindle, just remove the bow and trim the end.

Mark the socket for the center spindle. With the brace and bit at the ready, place your toe on the back of the seat behind the spindles and support the bow with your knee. Keep the chair from moving by pushing it against a workbench or wall. Boring this

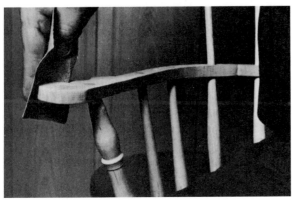

SHAVE THE TENONS AND WEDGES *flush with the arm, then scrape and sand the surfaces.*

first socket is a delicate operation, but your knee should give you all the support you need to prevent shearing the ends of the bow at the arm. Bore gently and slowly, sighting down the axis of the brace and bit as you would down the barrel of a rifle. Aim at the spindle's arm socket. This should also line up in your sight with the spindle's seat socket.

It is difficult and unnecessary to attach a waste block to the bow to prevent break out. The bow is round in cross section, so when the spoon bit exits, a burr is created rather than splinters. I remove the burr with the wide, shallow gouge. If any more breakout than that occurs, it will not be visible because it will be on the underside of the bow.

Once the socket is complete, pull the ends of the bow out of the arm and insert the end of the center spindle in the socket. Weave the bow through the other spindles for support and put the ends of the bow in the arm sockets. With a pair of dividers, walk off the positions of the two sockets adjacent to the center spindle. I set the dividers from my model chair; you can take these measurements from the drawing. (Remember that your chair may

differ from these approximate measurements. You may need to adjust the position of the sockets in the bow slightly to align them with those in the arm and seat.) When the sockets are satisfactorily marked, place your knee against the bow and bore each hole. Repeat the process for the next two spindles. Remember to start the bit perpendicular to the bow, and gradually move it to the correct angle. To establish this angle, sight down the brace as you did previously.

When the bow is placed over these five spindles it will be well enough supported so that you will not need to use your knee when boring the remaining two sockets. It is just as well. Boring these sockets is riskier than anything you have done so far, as they intersect the bow at an extreme angle.

Mark the location of these outside sockets with the dividers. Start the bit at a right angle to the surface of the bow. The bit will be almost parallel to the plane of the seat. As you deepen the hole, sight down the brace and slowly bring the bit up to the correct slope and flare angles. Finish the hole gently - at this angle the burr on the underside of the bow

WEAVE THE BOW THROUGH THE *spindles and adjust its position. The bow should be symmetrical to the curves of the arm and seat. Brace the chair against the bench and support the bow with your knee while boring the socket for the center spindle. Sight down the brace to establish the slope and flare angles.*

INSERT THE CENTER SPINDLE IN *its socket, and reposition the bow. Then walk off the positions of the two adjacent sockets with dividers and bore the holes (above). Start the sockets for the fourth and fifth spindles perpendicular to the bow. Sight down the brace and gradually move the bit to the correct angle (right). Whittle a point on each outside spindle to make assembly easier (below right).*

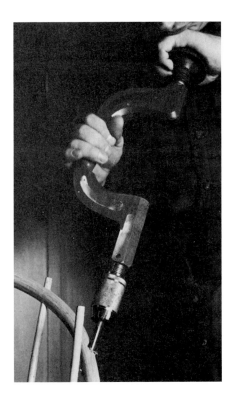
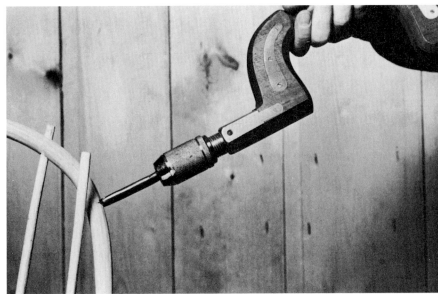

THE FINAL TWO SPINDLE SOCKETS *are the riskiest. Start the bit at a right angle to the bow. Bore slowly and raise the brace to the correct angle as the hole deepens. Whittle a point on each outside spindle to make assemble easier .*

can be heavy.

When the last two sockets have been bored in the bow, whittle a point on the ends of the last two spindles – they should be like sharpened pencils. When the sharpened ends are driven through their sockets, they will not catch on the socket walls and plow a piece of the bow out in front of them. Remove the bow, then trim and sand the burr off the underside of each socket. I do not recommend dry assembling the parts; piloting the two outside spindles into their sockets is so difficult that I do not like to do it twice. Also, there is little that can go wrong in the final assembly because you have already tested five of the seven spindles in their sockets.

ASSEMBLING THE UPPER BACK You are now ready to mount the bow on the back. Begin by smearing glue in all the bow's spindle sockets, and the two sockets for the bow in the arm. Hold the bow above the spindles and set the top ends of the two outside spindles in their sockets. Tap with a hammer next to these two sockets to begin lowering the bow. Throughout the process of driving the bow onto the spindles, be sure to alternate your hammer blows from side to side, working along the length of the bow. If you drive one side too far, the bow might catch on a spindle. Because the bow will not be able to move at this point, it will rack and could break at the hung up socket.

As the bow lowers, two more spindles will line up with their sockets, and you can guide them in. The ends of the bow may contact the arm now also; so insert them in their sockets. Continue to tap from side to side on the bow as you line up and inset the last three spindles in their sockets.

With the bow mounted, turn your attention to aligning it on the chair. The center spindle should appear to bisect the area encompassed by the bow. The bow should not be higher on one side of the center spindle than the other. If it is, tap the high side down or tap under the low side to raise it.

When you are satisfied with the position of the bow, trim the ends of the spindles and the bow with a coping saw. Leave about ¼ in. protruding from the sockets. Split the ends of the spindles with a chisel at a right angle to the grain of the bow, and wedge them. Wipe glue on the wedges before driving them in. When driving the wedges be careful not to drive too aggressively and split the bow. The change of tone should tell you when you are done, just as it did when wedging the tenons in the seat

When all seven spindles are wedged in the bow, invert the chair and wedge the ends of the bow into the arm. It is not possible to get at these from straight on, so you will have to work at a slight angle, holding the chair still on the bench with one hand.

Set the chair on the floor again and trim all the spindles flush with the bow. I shave them with a shallow gouge. Then scrape and lightly sand the end

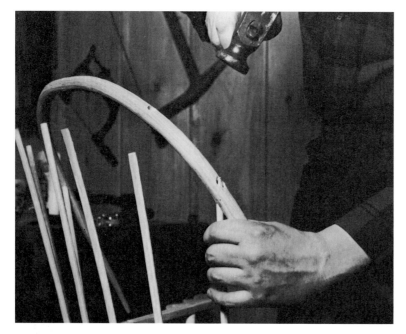

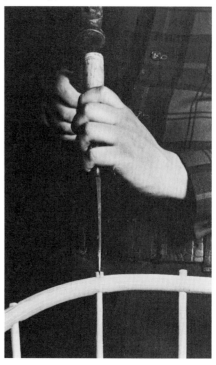

GUIDE THE OUTSIDE SPINDLES INTO *the sockets and then tap near the sockets to begin lowering the bow (left). When all spindles and the ends of the bow are in their sockets, tap the bow into alignment so that it is symmetrical around the center spindle and of equal height on both sides (below, left).*

WHEN THE POSITION OF THE *bow is satisfactory, split the ends of the spindles (above) and wedge them into the bow (opposite, right)*

grain of the spindles and the top surface of the bow.

Do not shave the ends of the bow flush with the underside of the arm. The wedges will have created a slight mushroom on each end, which is thicker than the diameter of the socket. Should these joints ever loosen; the mushroomed ends will not be able to pull through the socket. The pull of someone sitting back in the chair will tighten the joint. Although the joints will not lock, as do the leg joints in the seat, they remain tight as long as there is weight against the bow. If the ends pulled through, all the stress would be transmitted to the long spindles and could cause them to break.

This completes the assembly of the sack back. Clean off any spilled glue while it is still soft. You can do this by either shaving it off with a chisel, or scraping. You might want to try out the results of your chairmaking by carefully sitting in the chair. But after you do, set the chair aside so that the glue

in the joints can harden. This will take a couple of hours and by then; the chair will be ready for its finish.

The old guys referred to assembling a chair as framing it. Framing a sack back in a class has not changed much since 1983. Most of our steps were developed to make the process easier to understand. I will only describe what we have added. To set the stumps use the same technique as for the front legs. Ream the stump holes along their sight lines and insert a dummy leg with a tapered tenon in the first hole. From this tweak as necessary to achieve the new model's slope angle (10 degrees) and the flare angle (14 degrees). Check with two bevel squares set to these angles. Adjust the second stump using the 10 degree flare angle and a pair of winding sticks to make the two parts coplanar.

To give the back the incline necessary for

REST THE ARM ON THE *bench top to wedge the ends of the bow. Shave the spindle ends flush with the bow.*

comfort the arm's rear curve has to extend beyond the seat ⅞". It also has to meet the sloped long spindles at the desired height. To do this, use a 1¾" spacer block. Ours is a strip of pine screwed to a post so its top edge is 26" from the floor. Push the seat's rear edge against the spacer and lay the arm on top of the spacer, pushed against the post. This establishes the ⅞" gap between the arm's inside edge and the seat's outside edge.

Now, locate one stump hole, drill it and ream it. With the arm on that first stump, locate the second stump hole by examining the arm's symmetry relative to the seat. With both holes drilled and reamed adjust the arm to the new desired height (9⅝" at the stump and 9⅛" at the rear, top-to-top.)

With the arm in place find use a square to find the center spindle hole. Walk off the other three pairs with a pair of dividers set to 2⅝".

Locate the short spindles by eye.

Clamp the arm and drill the long and short spindle holes in the arm using a ⁷⁄₁₆" bit. (In the new sack back all holes in the arm are now ⁷⁄₁₆") Use the corresponding angles from the template. Because the arm and seat planes converge, these angles are not exact; they work because the difference is so little and the back so flexible. Use the template sight lines as well. Set a marker at the point in front of the arm where the sight lines

converge and aim at this target.

Drill the bow holes after you have assembled, wedged and cleaned up the arm. Locate the holes by placing a winding stick across the seat, pushed against the front of the stumps. Rest the other winding stick on the arm between the two short spindles. Adjust this stick to eliminate wind. This establishes the bow square to the curve of the arm. Drill the holes at 41 degrees. This sight line is in space, just off the inside edge of the corresponding hand. Protect the front short spindles from the emerging bit by clamping a board across them, just under the arm. Don't forget the C clamp to keep the arm from splitting.

Using a drawknife and spokeshave, whittle the ends of the bow to fit these two holes. Mount the bow and drill the holes the same way as in 1983. In the new chair, locate the holes using these measurements: first pair, 3⅛ in. from center; second pair 3¼"; third pair 3½". Adjust these measurements if needed. The bow height (top of seat to top of bow) is approximately 21".

Whether you are making the 1984 chair or my new design, protect the long spindles while driving them into the seat by sliding a length of ½" PVC pipe over them. The tube supports the spindles by preventing them from flexing and shattering due to an over-forceful hammer blow.

Chapter Eleven
Assembling the Continuous Arm

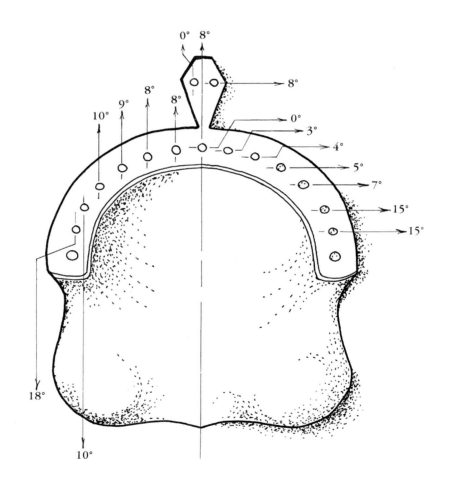

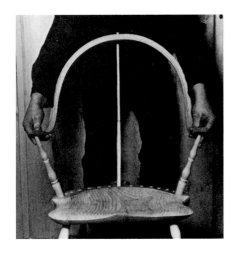

To locate the first stump socket, position the arm symmetrical to the spindle sockets and mark the stump position on the hand. *To bore the stump socket, clamp the arm, and a backboard to the bench top. Remember to start the bit perpendicular to the hand, and then lower it to the proper slope and flare angles as you turn the brace. Ream the socket slowly, checking the fit with the tenon as you go.*

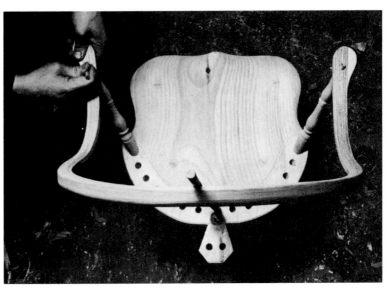

When you sight over the *arm to mark the second stump socket, you should see something like this balanced, symmetrical relationship to the seat.*

POSITION THE CENTER SPINDLE ON *the arm and mark its socket. Walk off the position of the two sockets on either side of the center with a pair of dividers.*

THE SOCKETS ON EITHER SIDE *of the center socket have both slope and flare angles. Start the bit perpendicular to the arm, and then gradually move it to the correct angels.*

After boring the first five spindle sockets in the arm, dry-assemble the chair.

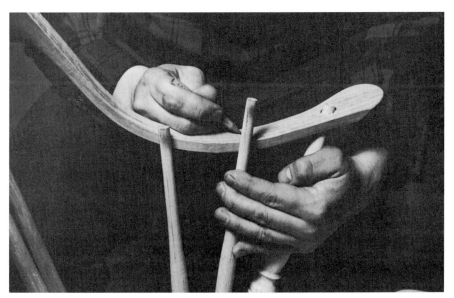

MARK THE POSITIONS OF THE *sockets for the short spindles on the arm. To bore the sockets for the short spindles, start the bit at a right angle to the arm. Notice the C clamp.*

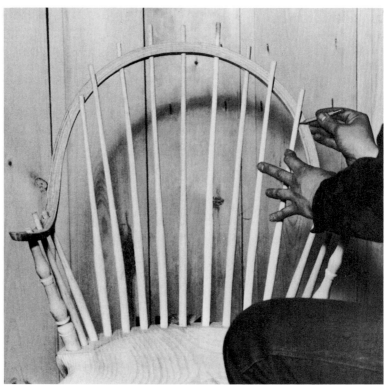

MARK THE BLIND SOCKETS FOR *the outside long spindles on the underside of the arm. Trace the spindles' angles as a guide.*

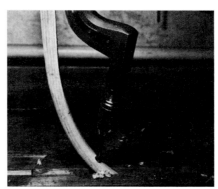

THE OUTSIDE SOCKETS ARE AT *extreme angles to the arm. Raise the bit gradually to the correct angle as you deepen a hole. Check the surface of the arm with your finger, and stop boring when you can feel a dimple form from the pressure of the bit.*

SPREAD GLUE ON THE WALLS *of a socket, then insert the corresponding spindle. The spindle will push glue out of the socket, but the glue that remains on the socket walls will be sufficient to make a strong joint.*

MEASURE AND ADJUST THE HEIGHT *of the arm and make sure it is symmetrical to the back edge of the seat. Then trim and wedge the center spindle to fix it in place.*

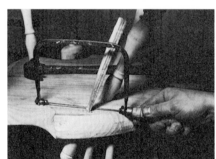

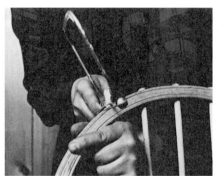

WEDGE AND TRIM THE REMAINING *spindle and stump tenons. Make a split for the wedge with a chisel perpendicular to the grain direction of the arm, and drive the wedge with a hammer. Listen for the dull sound that tells you the wedge is set.*

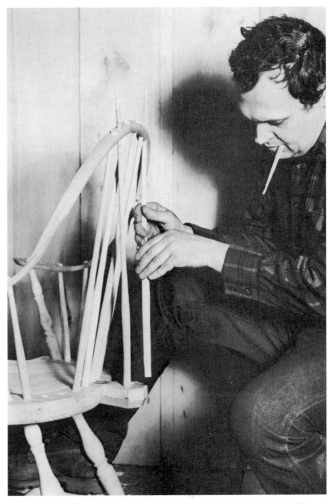

BORE THE SOCKETS FOR THE *bracing spindles by aiming the brace and bit at the spindle sockets in the tail piece. Slide the brace spindle into place after gluing the sockets.*

MARK THE LENGTH OF THE *remaining spindles so they will butt against the bottoms of the blind sockets.*

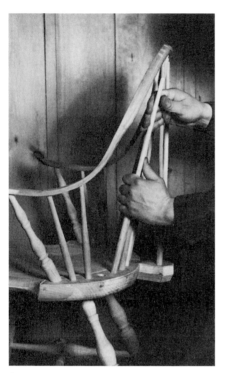 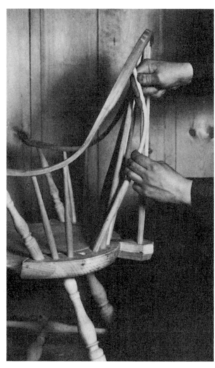 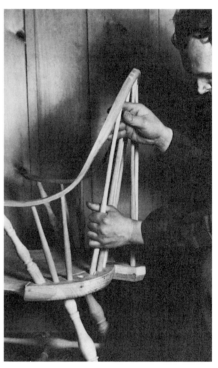

REMOVE THE PLIABLE SPINDLE FROM *the steam box and quickly push the tenon into its seat socket. Space your hands apart on the shaft and bend the spindle until you can push its end into the arm socket. Straighten the spindle while it is still flexible.*

Chapter Twelve

Finishing

All that remains to do is apply a finish to your chair. But before this can be done, the surface of the wood must be prepared. The first thing I do is wipe the saddled area of the seat with a wet sponge. This raises the grain and most of the dents or scratches in the seat. Also, glue will not absorb water, so any glue that was spilled or squeezed out of the joints will show up on the moistened seat. This glue should be scraped off, because it will not absorb a finish. When the seat is dry, I sand the saddled area with #220-grit sandpaper.

While the seat is drying, you can clean up the other parts of the chair.

Scrape off excess glue; clean up any ragged edges on the bottom of the feet with sandpaper. The grain of green wood parts will raise slightly as the parts dry, and this surface roughness can be removed by light sanding. I use #220-grit paper and stroke in the direction of the grain, not across it. I am careful not to round or soften any of the details of the turnings or remove any tool marks from the hand worked parts. The surface will be smoothed even more when the first coat of finish is rubbed down.

The spindles that were added to the continuous arm chair by bending need some attention. Steaming raises the grain considerably, and it can create purple stains on oak, as well as give the entire surface a slight grey cast. All of this is best removed by scraping, followed by a light sanding.

SELECTING A FINISH Traditionally, Windsors were painted. This is the finish I prefer and the only one I will consent to put on a chair for a customer. But painted furniture goes against current taste. We are surrounded by plastic, chrome and other man-made materials, and the wood we use in furniture is a cherished tie to the natural world. I suspect, however, that we have come to revere the wood more than what the craftsman has done with it. When I make a chair, I put a lot of myself and my skill into it. A clear finish draws the viewer's eye to the wood, diverting it from my statement. Stain, which emphasizes the grain is an insult added to injury. A paint finish allows the viewer to see the chair instead of the wood.

The lines of a Windsor chair are its most important visual element. The curved lines of the seat contribute to its three-dimensional, sculptured form. The legs have bold, turned outlines and are set at pronounced angles to support the chair visually as well as physically. The spindles, bent bows, and bent arms are strong lines, carefully placed to achieve symmetry. A paint finish coalesces all these lines, and in addition, separates the various parts of the chair from the background.

The comment is often made that Windsors were only painted to cover the fact that so many different woods were used in the chair. On the contrary, I think the craftsmen who developed the

Windsor forms had a painted surface in mind from the beginning - to a great extent, paint dictated what Windsors would look like. If a clear finish had been intended, the craftsmen would have relied on design techniques other than line for the chair's visual success. Instead of thin, whittled and turned parts, for example, the chair would have had broad surfaces that allow for a showy display of carefully selected woods. The joined chairs traditionally made by cabinetmakers were designed for such displays; the fine lines of a Windsor were designed to be shown off with paint.

MILK PAINT During the eighteenth century, when Windsors were being developed, they were finished with paint made with white lead, turpentine, linseed oil, and earthen pigments. Looking at old Windsors, I have concluded that the chairmakers skimped on the lead, which was the most expensive ingredient. The resulting paint was thin bodied, translucent, and slightly glossy. The painted surfaces were not uniform, but subtly mottled. Part of the mottle was wood peeking through the thin paint. More mottling occurred as the fugitive earthen pigments began to change color, and as the linseed oil yellowed. (Pigments that fade with exposure to light

are called fugitive.) This mottled effect is very subtle – even a photograph cannot capture it. Modern glossy paints produce garish surfaces, and the matte and flat paints are too uniform and dead. I feel that a good Windsor is deserving of a finish that is at least as interesting as the chair.

I have found that milk paint produces surfaces comparable to the old paints. The origin of this ancient finish has been lost in time, but it is available today in a powdered form that requires only the addition of water. (I buy milk paint from The Old-Fashioned Milk Paint Company, Box 222, Groton, Mass. 01450.) Powdered milk paint comes in a lot of colors; I am partial to the Lexington green. The manufacturer recommends mixing this green with black to get the "old Windsor" color. I disagree, and use the Lexington green straight from the container. I also like the barn red, pumpkin, and mustard colors; the black is dramatic but use it with caution for it can make a chair visually overpowering.

For those who would like to make their own milk paint here is a formula from The Mechanics Own Book, published in Portland, Maine, in 1847, (At that time the term mechanic meant a craftsman or tradesman.)

Take fresh curd and bruise the lumps on a grinding stoned, or in an earthen pan or mortar, with a spatula. After this operation, put them in a pot with an equal quantity of lime, well quenched, and become thick enough to be kneaded; stir the mixture well without adding water, and a whitish, semi-fluid mass will be obtained which may be applied with great facility-like paint and which dries very rapidly. It must be employed the day it is prepared, as it will become too thick the following day. Ochre, armenian bole, and all colors which hold with lime, may be mixed with it according to the color desired; but care must be taken, that the addition of color made to the first mixture of curds and lime, contain very little water, for it will diminish the durability of the paint.

When two coats of this paint have been laid on it may be polished with a piece of woolen cloth or other proper substance, and it will become as bright as varnish. This kind of paint, besides its cheapness, possesses the advantage of admitting the coats to be laid on and polished in one day; as it dries speedily and has no smell.

If you cannot bring yourself to paint your chairs, you will find that an oil and wax finish is easier to apply than varnish and shellac. An oil finish can be applied by wiping, rather than with a brush. Also, it does not require rubbing down as do shellac, lacquer, or varnish. Rubbing down one of these hard finishes on a Windsor is time-consuming and difficult because of all the joints and closely spaced parts.

APPLICATION Milk paint bonds best to wood that has never been finished. If the wood is left uncovered for several months, enough grime will settle on it to slow the paint's penetration. Therefore, I advise that you finish your chair as soon after completion as possible.

Mix the dry powder with water in a clean container following the manufacturer's instructions. I mix the paint in a coffee can and stir it with an egg beater attachment in an electric drill. This method of stirring will chew up a throwaway paper bucket and might shatter a glass jar. Wait an hour or so for the froth whipped up by mixing to settle, then the paint should be water thin. Milk paint does not keep well, so make only enough for your immediate use. You can put the paint in a refrigerator overnight, but it will not last much longer than a day or two before it spoils and loses its ability to bond.

Apply the paint with a small brush, about 1½ in. wide. Use a cheap, throwaway brush with natural bristles – avoid nylon bristles, which do not hold the water-based paint as well. Milk paint is differ-ent from other paints, so forget your experiences with oil or latex paints when you use it. It is quickly absorbed by raw wood and you cannot draw out the first coat. You almost have to daub it onto the chair.

The first coat will dry quickly – in the time it takes the water to evaporate. When it is dry, the chair will look terrible, and you will be in a state of panic thinking that it is ruined. Do not worry. Rub down the first coat with scotchbrite, which will polish the paint and smooth any grain raised by the water in the paint. Then, dust the chair well to remove all the dust before applying the second coat.

The first coat seals the wood so the second can be drawn out evenly with the brush. This coat will also dry dead flat, but there is no need to rub it down with scotchbrite. Because the paint is so thin, even two coats will not cover completely. Try three coats if you like, but I find that a third coat makes the surface too uniform and does not produce the effect that I like.

To complete the finish, apply a thin coat of wiping varnish, also called wiping poly. You can brush it on, or wipe it on with a rag. Let the wiping varnish stand about five minutes and dry all surfaces with an absorbent rag. Do not remove all the finish, just what is standing or dripping. Set the chair aside overnight to dry. The wiping varnish will harden enough so that you can sit on the chair the following day.

Over the next several years, the paint will undergo complex changes. Like wine, milk paint improves with age. The wiping varnish will continue to harden, and the degree of polish that it takes will depend on the amount of friction received from hands and clothes. The resulting surface will have a whole range of textures that do not reflect light uniformly. There will be brightly polished areas, those that are less glossy, and even some that remain flat. Upon application, the wiping varnish will cause the paint to change color slightly; gradually, as the varnish ages, it will yellow even more. Some of the pigments used in milk paint are fugitive, and will fade slightly as they are exposed to light. The yellowing oil and fading pigments will not change uniformly, giving the surface a very subtle mottle, best seen when closely examined under bright sunlight. The chair still looks green, of course but the mottled milk paint surface is much more interesting than a single, uniform color.

As the chair is used, the paint will wear through and expose the wood wherever there is the most friction. I am very fond of this appearance; it testifies to the use and enjoyment that the chair has given to people who consider it an old friend.

Chapter Thirteen

Sack-Back Plans

Sack-Back Windsor
Scale: ⅛ in. = 1 in.

Note: *The drawings are of a model chair. Your chair may vary from these measurements, so use them as a rough guide as you follow the instructions in the text.*

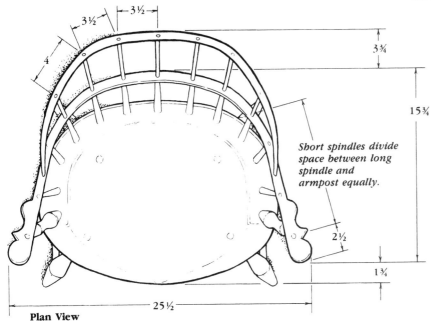

3 ½

3 ½

3 ½

4

3 ¾

15 ¾

Short spindles divide space between long spindle and armpost equally.

Note: *Long-spindle sockets in bow and arm are ⅜ in. in diameter. Short-spindle sockets and armpost sockets in arm are ⁷⁄₁₆ in. in diameter. Bow sockets in arm are ⅜ in. in diameter.*

2 ½

1 ¾

25 ½

Plan View

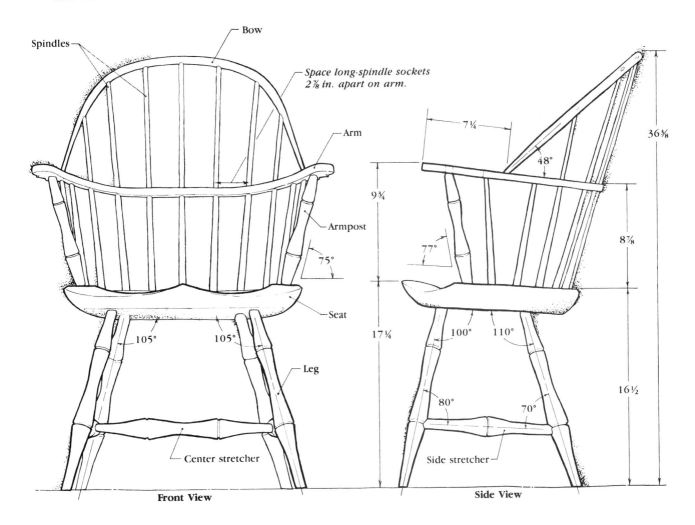

Spindles

Bow

Space long-spindle sockets 2⅞ in. apart on arm.

Arm

Armpost

75°

Seat

105°   105°

Leg

Center stretcher

Front View

7 ¼

48°

36 ⅜

9 ¾

77°

8 ⅞

17 ¼

100°   110°

80°   70°

16 ½

Side stretcher

Side View

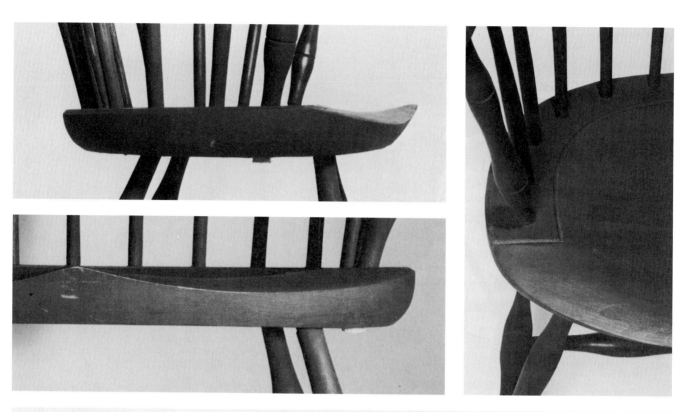

Sack-Back Seat
Scale: ¼ in. = 1 in.

Note: *Light lines indicate depth of excavation.*

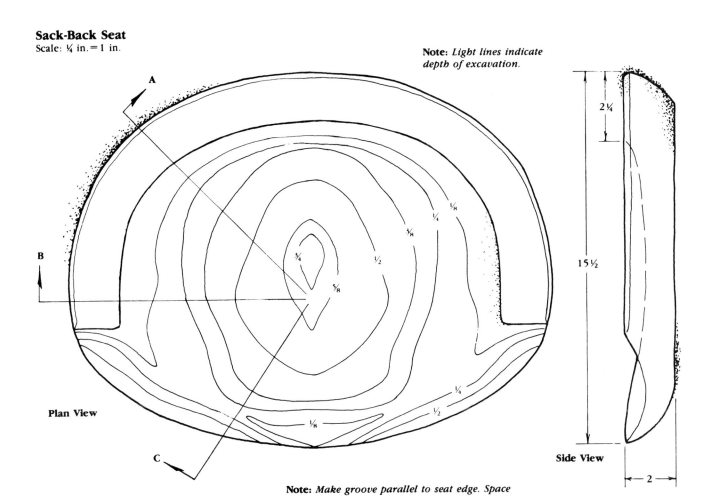

A

B

Plan View

C

2 ¼

15 ½

2

Side View

Note: *Make groove parallel to seat edge. Space sockets about midway between groove and edge.*

Centerline

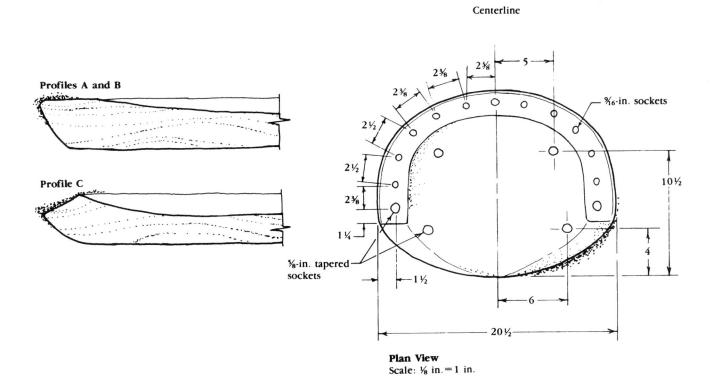

Profiles A and B

Profile C

⅝-in. tapered sockets

5

2 ⅜

2 ⅜

2 ⅜

2 ½

2 ½

2 ⅜

1 ¼

⁹⁄₁₆-in. sockets

10 ½

4

1 ½

6

20 ½

Plan View
Scale: ⅛ in. = 1 in.

Stretcher Patterns
Scale: ⅜ in. = 1 in.

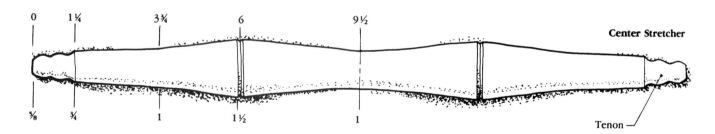

0   1¼   3¾   6   9½   **Center Stretcher**

⅝ ¾   1   1½   1   Tenon ——

Note: *Top dimensions are lengths; bottom dimensions are diameters. Stretchers are symmetrical around centerlines. Be sure to alter stretcher lengths to suit each chair.*

0   1¼   4¾   6¾   ——Tenon   ——Shoulder

Side Stretcher

1½   1   ¾   ⅝

Make rings about ⅛ in. wide and ¹⁄₁₆ in. deep.

Locking Tenon
Scale: ¾ in. = 1 in.

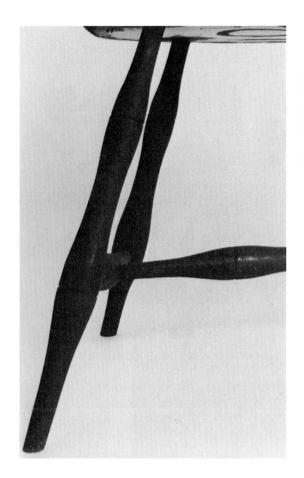

Leg and Armpost Patterns
Scale: ⅜ in. = 1 in.

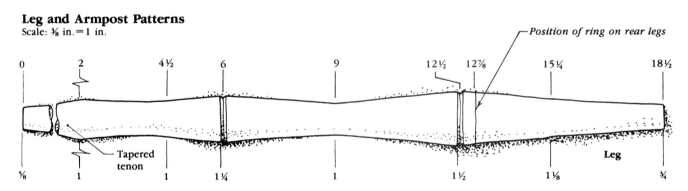

—Position of ring on rear legs

| 0 | 2 | 4½ | 6 | 9 | 12½ | 12⅞ | 15¼ | 18½ |

Tapered tenon

| ⅝ | 1 | 1 | 1¼ | 1 | 1½ | 1⅛ | ¾ |

Leg

Note: *Add at least 1 in. extra to the foot to allow for leveling the chair.*

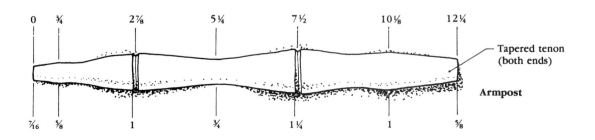

| 0 | ¾ | 2⅞ | 5¼ | 7½ | 10⅛ | 12¼ |

—Tapered tenon (both ends)

| ⁷⁄₁₆ | ⅝ | 1 | ¾ | 1¼ | 1 | ⅝ |

Armpost

Arm, Bow and Spindle Patterns
Scale: ⅜ in. = 1 in.

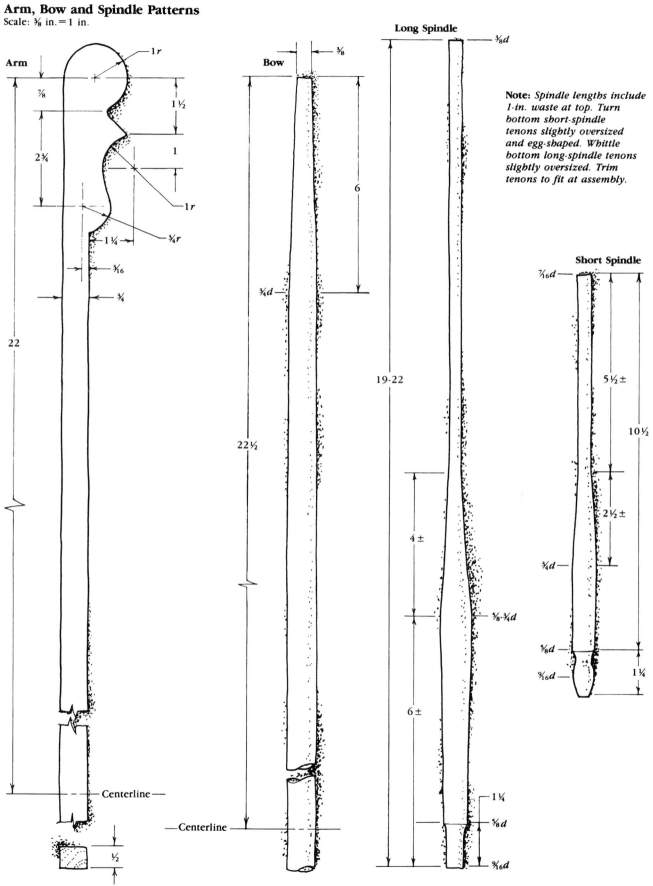

Arm

1r

⅞

1½

2¾

1

1r

¾r

1¼

³⁄₁₆

¾

22

Centerline

½

Bow

⅜

¾d

6

22½

19-22

Centerline

Long Spindle

⅜d

Note: *Spindle lengths include 1-in. waste at top. Turn bottom short-spindle tenons slightly oversized and egg-shaped. Whittle bottom long-spindle tenons slightly oversized. Trim tenons to fit at assembly.*

4±

⅝-¾d

6±

1¼

⅝d

⁹⁄₁₆d

Short Spindle

⁷⁄₁₆d

5½±

10½

2½±

¾d

⅝d

⁹⁄₁₆d

1¼

Chapter Fourteen

Continuous Arm Plans

Continuous-Arm Seat

Scale: ¼ in. = 1 in.

Note: *Make groove parallel to seat edge. Space sockets about midway between groove and edge.*

Note: *Light lines indicate depth of excavation.*

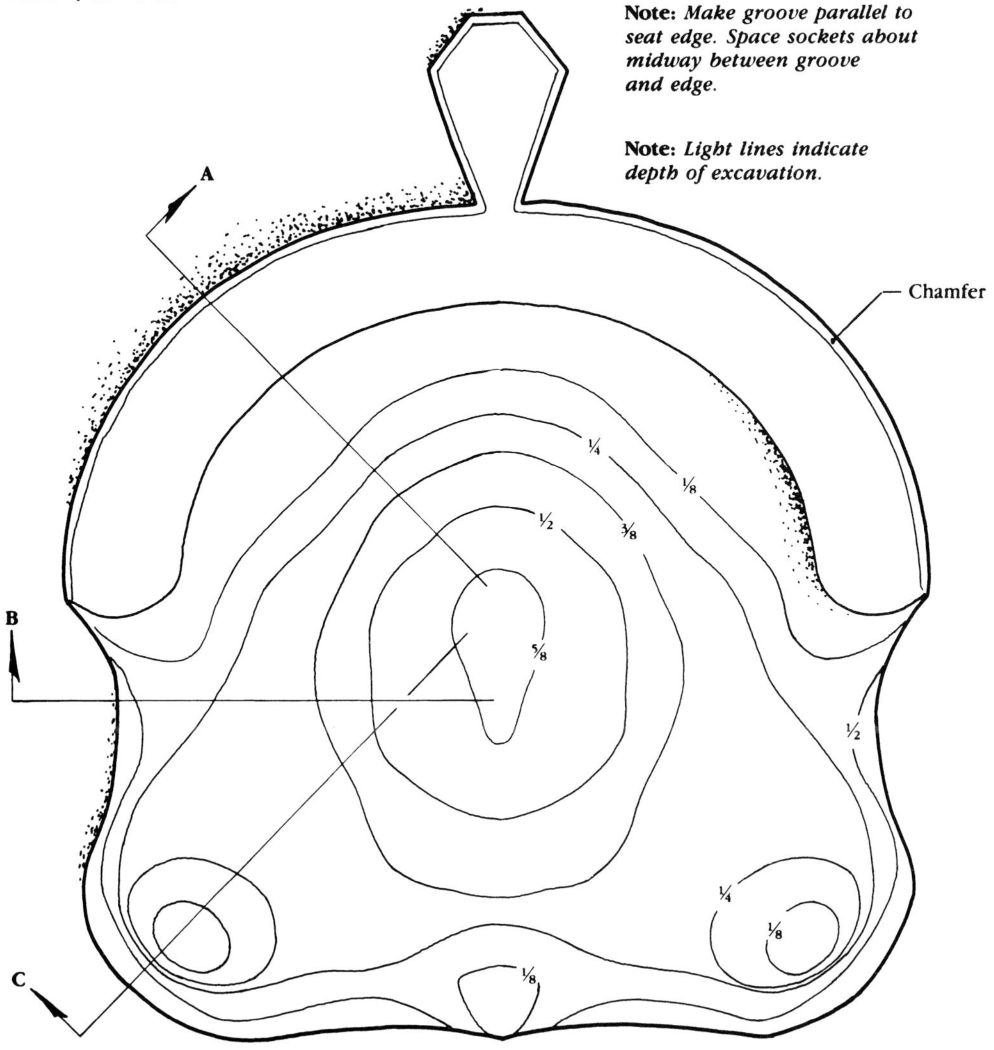
A
B
C
Chamfer
¼
⅛
½
⅜
⅝
½
¼
⅛
⅛

Plan View

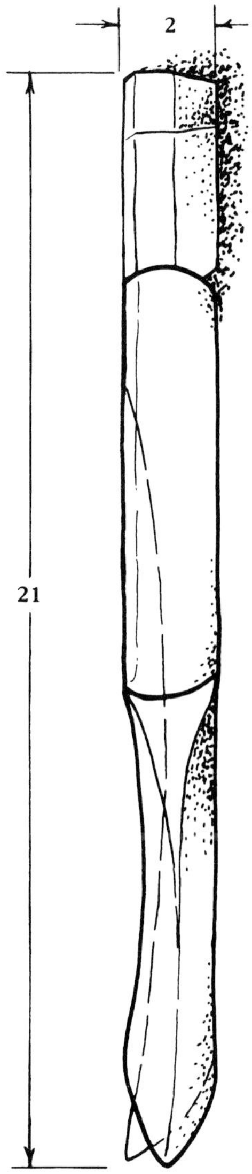
2
21

Side View

Profile A

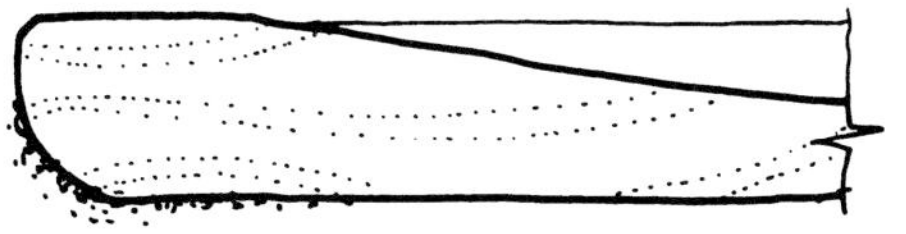

Profile B

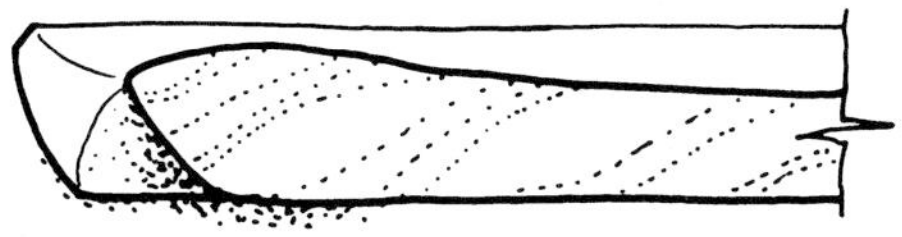

Profile C

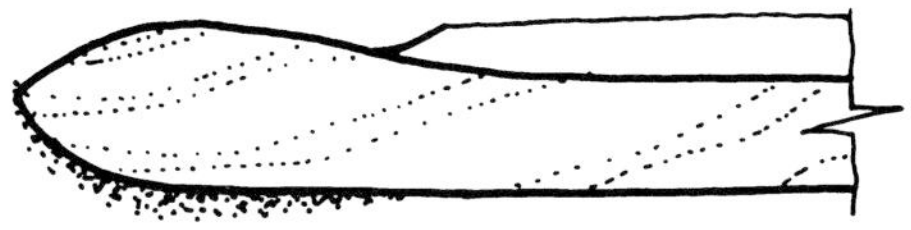

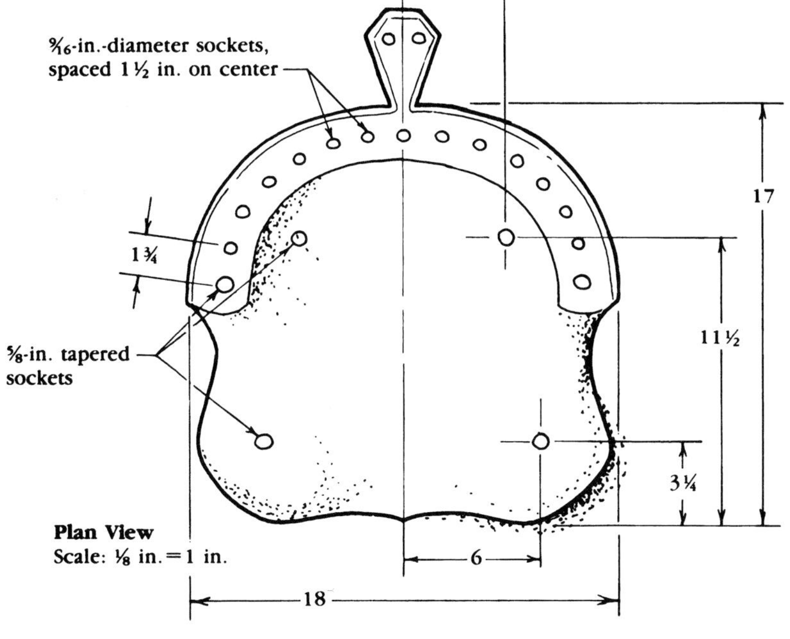
4½
⁹⁄₁₆-in.-diameter sockets, spaced 1½ in. on center
1¾
⅝-in. tapered sockets
17
11½
3¼
6
18

Plan View
Scale: ⅛ in. = 1 in.

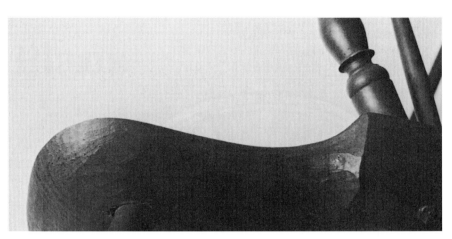
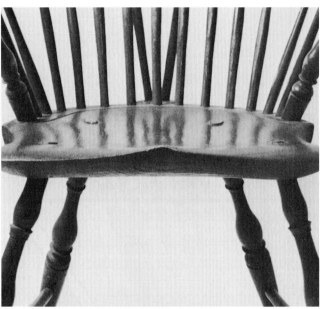

Stretcher Patterns
Scale: ⅜ in. = 1 in.

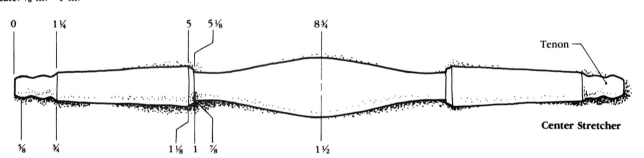

Center Stretcher

Note: *Top dimensions are lengths; bottom dimensions are diameters. Stretchers are symmetrical around centerlines. Be sure to alter stretcher lengths to suit each chair.*

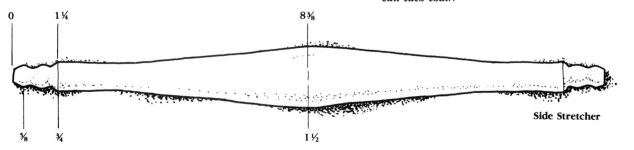

Side Stretcher

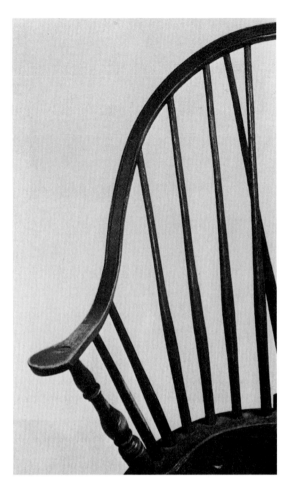

Leg and Armpost Patterns
Scale: ⅜ in. = 1 in.

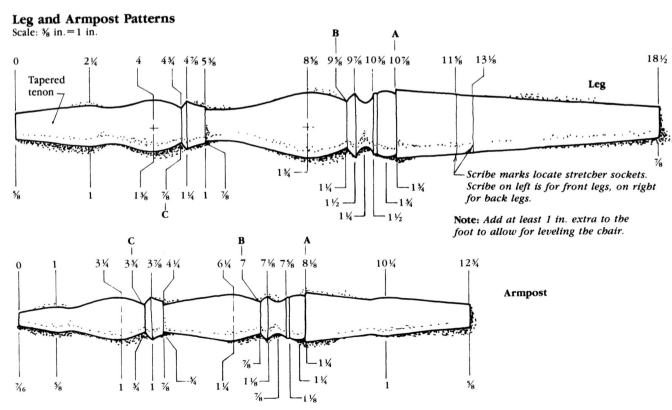

Scribe marks locate stretcher sockets. Scribe on left is for front legs, on right for back legs.

Note: *Add at least 1 in. extra to the foot to allow for leveling the chair.*

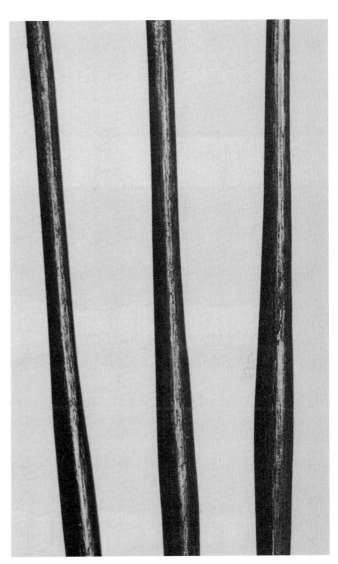

Arm and Spindle Patterns

Scale: ⅜ in. = 1 in.

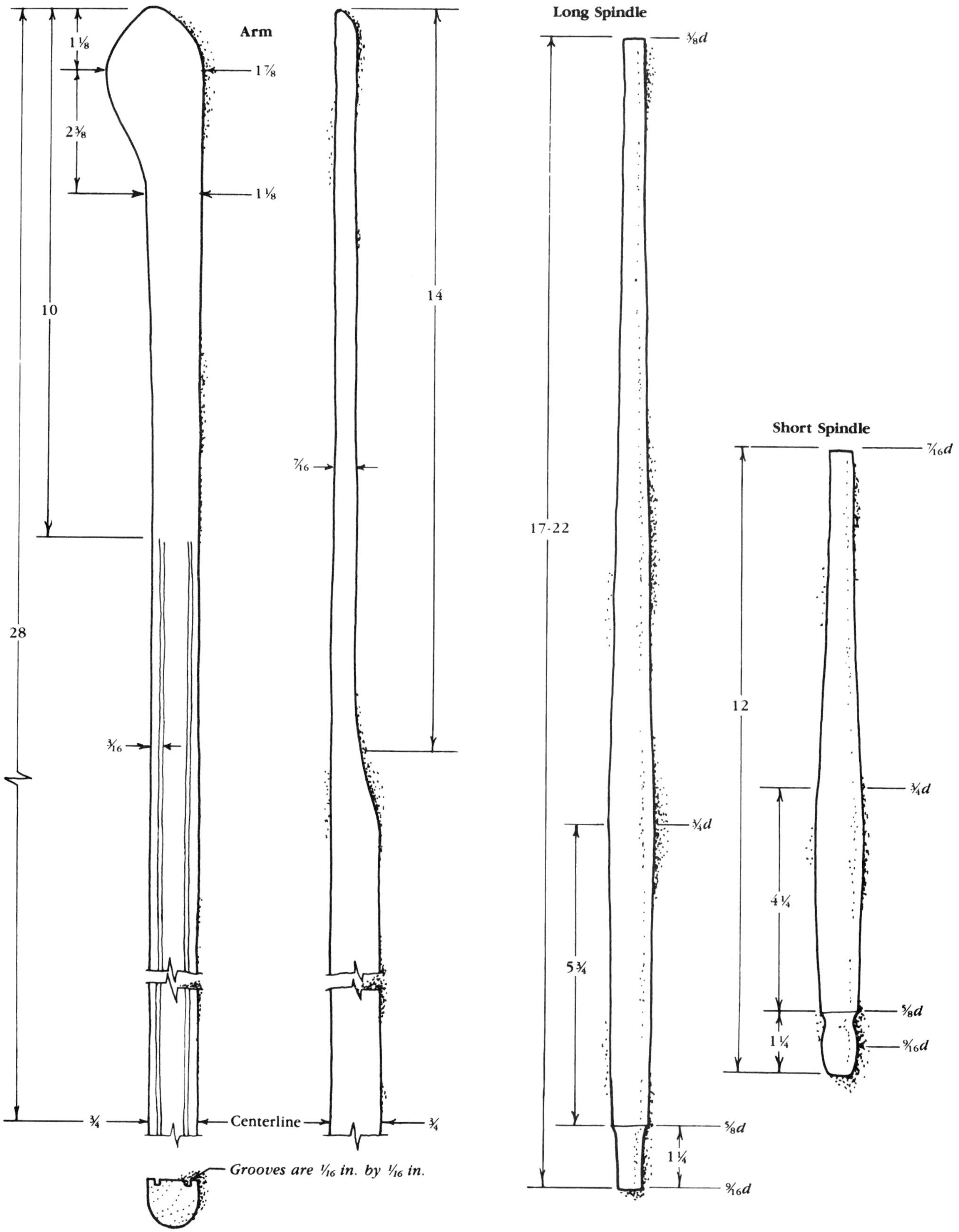

Arm
1⅛
1⅞
2⅜
1⅛
10
28
3/16
¾
Centerline
Grooves are 1/16 in. by 1/16 in.
14
7/16
¾
Long Spindle
⅜d
17-22
¾d
5¾
⅝d
1¼
9/16d
Short Spindle
7/16d
12
¾d
4¼
⅝d
1¼
9/16d

Chapter Fifteen

A Windsor Gallery

THIS ROD BACK SIDE CHAIR *is the first Windsor I ever owned and the one responsible for my interest in these chairs. Not long after I purchased it I discovered that it was signed in pencil by its maker Samuel Stickney. He worked and lived in Beverly, Massachusetts and probably made this chair about 1805. There is nothing superfluous about this chair. It is as basic as a Windsor or any other piece of furniture, can be. It has always been painted black, a color that intensifies its starkness. The lack of elaborate detail makes it difficult to focus on any particular feature. As a result the chair works on an almost emotional level. Someday, I would like to make a set of copies to see what effect a group of these chairs would have.*

THE LEGS OF THIS FAN *back side chair indicate that at was made in southeastern New England shortly after the American Revolution. The seat hints that its maker was not formally trained. It is a little too chunky, and its outline is not as refined as are the shield shaped seats of the continuous arm and the bow back. The crest indicates that the maker was influenced by contemporary Chippendale chairs. The two turned stiles that frame the back are much more substantial than the spindles. These stiles are anchored to the seat with wedged and tapered, through socket joints that allow the back to look delicate without being fragile.*

MAKE A WINDSOR CHAIR   **135**

BECAUSE OF ITS DISTINCTIVE BACK *this side chair is called a bird-cage Windsor. I made this chair. Notice the similarities to the Stickney Windsor, on which it is based. The top horizontal spindle is joined to the two posts of the chair back with a typical through socket joint that is then carved to look like a miter.*

THIS CHAIR WAS MADE DURING *the first years of the nineteenth century, during the transition from early Windsors to Sheraton Windsor designs. It retains the double bobbin and H-stretcher undercarriage and the fully developed shield seat of the earlier chairs. The square back, framed by two turned stiles however, became typical of all Sheraton Windsors, though the stiles on this chair are not flattened, as were those on later chairs The crest rail is mortised into the stiles. Although the chair is now painted green, the original finish was red with yellow striping on the turned rings in the undercarriage and stiles.*

DURING THE EARLY NINETEENTH CENTURY, *Windsors were still being painted so that color would unify all the elements of the chair. At that time however, the chairmaker was working in concert with the decorative painter, who was perhaps even more important to the chair's success than the chairmaker. Windsor chairmakers began to evolve designs that allowed the decorator sufficient space to add painted interpretations of the neoclassical designs and string inlay that were being used in formal furniture of the Hepplewhite and Sheraton styles. As a result, these chairs are often known as Sheraton Windsors. This chair is also called a step down Windsor, because of the shape of its crest rail.*

A CONTEMPORARY OF THE STEP *down, this arrow back Windsor is also a decorated chair. Like the step down, it has a box stretcher system and legs turned to resemble bamboo. This type of undercarriage became popular about 1815 and lasted as long as Windsors continued to be made in craftshops by trained chairmakers. The vogue for decorated surfaces resulted even in flattened spindles to accommodate the decorator. Also, the shapes of the seats became more amorphous, perhaps because the bold curves that had been popular earlier conflicted with a decorated surface.*

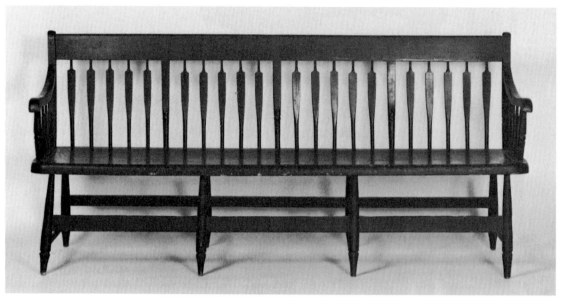

THIS ARROW BACK WINDSOR SETTEE *was probably made in Pennsylvania or Ohio during the 1830s. The settee is painted black although it is a style that should be decorated. Most Windsor settees are basically armchairs stretched to whatever length the customer requests. The only limitation is the length of the seat material that is available. Extra sets of legs are required for strength and are placed to divide the space beneath the seat evenly. Three heavy uprights that mimic the shape of the styles are socketed in the seat and the bottom of the crest rail to strengthen the back. These uprights also break up the back in a manner that suggests individual places for sitters.*

WHEN I AM ASSEMBLING CHAIRS *I find it comfortable sometimes to sit higher than the seat, and other times to sit lower. I made these two stools for such use in my shop; one is 19" high, the other 15" high. The round seats are turned. The low stool was painted with a coat of mustard milk paint, and then sponge grained with a light brown oil paint. The tall stool was painted with a coat of white milk paint, then the rings on the bobbins were picked out in green. The stylized sprigs on the legs are done in red, green, and black oil paint, and the same three colors were used to create a tortoise shell mottle on the seat.*

I MAKE THIS OVAL BACK *chair as my production model side chair. Like the continuous arm, it can be made with or without the tailpiece and brace spindles. I offer this chair in sets with my sack back or continuous arm as the mates. I finished the one shown in the photograph with boiled linseed oil sealed with paste wax to show my customers how such a finish would look. In a couple of years, this finish will age to a good imitation of the old shellac finish often found on antique Windsors that were refinished forty years ago.*

I ACQUIRED THIS SACK BACK *chair long after I had worked out my own sack back design. It was probably made by a formally trained chairmaker working in southeastern New England during the last quarter of the eighteenth century. As a chairmaker, I find the chair intriguing. The maker placed the arm 10 ½". above the seat, leaving only 10" between the arm and the top of the bow. This is the reverse of how I space my sack back arm. The arm on this chair props up the sitter's elbows, rather than allowing them to hang at a natural height. This is not uncomfortable, and the chair still works visually.*

FOR FOUR YEARS I WAS *the chairmaker at Strawbery Banke, a historic restoration project near Portsmouth's city center. Peter Happny, one of the country's finest art blacksmiths, worked there at the same time and he made the bracket for my shop sign. He included a hook at the bottom and suggested I hang a chair from it, so I made a small sack back chair by cutting every dimension of the full size chair by a third. Some small problems with tenon and spindle thickness had to be worked out, but the result was a chair like these, just big enough for a child under five years old. The sack back proved to be so popular that I began to make a small high back as well. I had to regulate how many of these I made a year or I would have done nothing else.*

THIS CHAIR WAS THE INSPIRATION *for my continuous arm Windsor. I do not make exact duplicates of this chair because its distinctive wedge shaped seat would be difficult to reproduce. The seat was riven from a log and as a result, it tapers in thickness from 2" at the back to about 1 in. at the front. The seat appears to be just a wafer of wood which, combines effectively with the overall delicacy of the chair. The chair was made about 1790 probably near the Connecticut – Rhode Island border. That it is still in service proves that it is not fragile. Its existence and the existence of hundreds of thousands of other Windsors that have survived since the eighteenth century are witness to the strength of these chairs.*

A FORMALLY TRAINED NEW YORK *City
chairmaker made this bow back Windsor,
which is contemporary with the continuous arm. The results of his training can be
seen in the seat which is as refined as that
of the continuous arm. Its edges are drawn
so fine that they read as a line rather than
as a surface. This seat strongly influenced
the way I make the seats for my continuous
arm chairs.*

DR. DOROTHY VAUGHAN WAS A *good friend who helped me considerably over
the years with my research. She was a historian and did a lot of her work at the
Portsmouth Athenaeum, sitting at a high clerk's desk. Dorothy said she developed a backache because her desk stool was too high. So, I decided to make a
chair to suit Dorothy and the desk. I made the chair without telling Dorothy,
and since it was near Christmas, I left it at the Athenaeum tied with a red bow
for her to discover.*

*From the seat up, the chair is my production model bow back, without the
braces. The double bobbin legs are not splayed any more than those of a normal side chair, but they form a wider base because they are so much longer.*

THE DOUBLE BEND OF THE *continuous arm is a shape that I have always liked to play with. This tete-a-tete (French for head-to-head) is a result of my amusing myself. The arm is made up of separate pieces that are lap-joined at the location of the center stump. The piece works very well, placing the person sitting on the other side right where you want.*

I finished the chair in mustard milk paint, but picked out the arm and the platform in green. The grain of the seat runs from side to side instead of front to back, as is usual with a shield seat.

KNOWN AS A HIGH BACK *Windsor, this chair is made only as an armchair because without the arm, the spindles would be too weak to support a sitter. Working out this design was easy: from the arm down it is the sack back chair made in this book. The spindles are 27" long and the crest, which is steamed and bent using a clamped form, is 28" long. Despite the apparent fragility of the spindles above the arm, they are strong and supple because they are made of riven wood.*

I USED THE CONTINUOUS ARM *back to make this daybed. I placed the center stretchers so that they run front to back rather than side to side. By so doing, I avoided the problem of arranging the side stretchers in straight lines on either side of the undercarriage. The spindles that connect the crest to the seat are each a single shaft. I padded and upholstered the seat so that it can be used comfortably for long periods of time. A pillow can be suspended from the crest to support the sitter's head in a position suitable for reading. The daybed is finished with black milk paint and its red upholstery outlined with brass-headed tacks.*

THIS FAN BACK ARMCHAIR IS *my own personal chair. I wanted a comfortable place to relax at night and this design allowed me to make a large chair with good proportions. The chair is 44" to the top of the crest and the seat is 17" deep by 24' wide, big enough for a cushion, two dogs and me. The crest is steamed and bent using a form and clamps. The chair has three coats of milk paint: the first green, the second red, and the third black. This produces an interesting effect as the chair wears.*

WHEN MY SON WAS BORN *in 1992, this was his cradle. I copied it from an antique I owned at the time. Today, my wife decorates it with a couple of stuffed bears.*

EVERY CHAIRMAKER MAKES THE FIRST *chair. So did I, and here it is. As embarrassed as I am by the chair, I have to explain that I had never done any woodworking and I had almost no tools. I should also add that the chair is still tight after 41 years. So, I had figured out some things at the very beginning.*

I PURCHASED THIS ANTIQUE BIRD *cage because it has such an interesting seat. It is shield-shape with sharp corners, rather than rounded.*

THIS WINDSOR WAS MADE IN *southeast New Hampshire. I bought it because that is where I live, but also because its original decorated finish is in perfect condition.*

THE REMAINING EXAMPLES ARE CHAIRS *that I have developed as chair classes at The Windsor Institute, where I teach. Each chair presents the student chairmaker with different challenges and allows us to teach new skills. This is a Boston area balloon back, so-called because its in-curved back looks like a hot air balloon. Its undercarriage uses a crinoline stretcher.*

THIS IS OUR NEW YORK *City bow back. It is patterned after the original bow back Windsor shown previously.*

OUR PHILADELPHIA HIGH BACK.

A SETTEE DESIGNED FOR TWO *people*.

A VERY COMFORTABLE ROCKER. IT *is so perfectly balanced that it will continue to rock for 60 seconds after the sitter rises out of it.*

WE CALL THIS THE FAMILY *bench. With the fence in place, it is a rocker for mother and baby. Remove the fence and two adults can rock together. The form is a mid-19th century design, and it bears the appropriate decorated finish.*

OUR RHODE ISLAND LOW BACK *is patterned after an early form unique to Rhode Island. It has an X stretcher and the mid-18th century D seat.*

IN THIS CLASS, EACH STUDENT *makes two chairs; a youth chair for use at the table, and a child's chair.*

OUR LOW BACK SETTEE IS *patterned on an early Philadelphia form.*

OUR WRITING ARM CHAIR IS *a high back with a D seat. It is a very large chair and incorporates an interesting arm that starts out very heavy. After it is bent, it is cut so extra strength remains in the back, while the arms are appropriately thin.*

THIS FORM IS OUR RÉCAMIER. *Although cabinetmakers made récamiers, Windsor chairmakers did not. This is my design. In making it I used details that spanned the Windsor period. The arrow-shaped legs are the earliest, dating to the 1740s. The back reflects Windsor chairs made as late as 1840.*

SHORTLY AFTER 1800
WINDSOR CHAIRMAKERS *began to make what they called "square backed" chairs, as opposed to the earlier forms with bent bows. In this class each student makes both an arm and a side chair.*

I DESIGNED THIS SQUARE BACKED *settee as a companion to the arm and side chairs.*

WINDSOR CONCEPT PROJECT 2004   HUGH CROWE

THIS IS NOT A REAL *chair. It was a joke drawn by Hugh Crowe, one of our students. It would be a nightmare to build, so we labeled it "what chairmakers dream about after eating spicy food."*

Chapter Sixteen

Sharpening Chairmaking Tools

A number of the chairmaking tools used in this book may not be familiar to most woodworkers. I have already discussed how to use these tools, and here will explain how to sharpen them. I will assume that you are familiar with the basic techniques of grinding and honing common woodworking tools such as chisels and planes. If you are not familiar with these techniques, you can find them explained in most introductory woodworking books.

The tools I use for sharpening are quite simple and unsophisticated. They are also readily available and inexpensive. Like nearly every other woodworker, I own a bench grinder. I still use the same machine I bought secondhand some thirteen years ago for six dollars. It still has one of the original wheels on it. I never replaced it because I never use it. I purchased the 5" medium-grit wheel (that I do use) at about the same time as the grinder itself. At the rate I am using it, that wheel will last longer than the electric motor. Long ago, I removed the tool rests from the grinder because I prefer to grind free hand and found that the rests were only in the way.

I maintain the grinding wheel with a diamond dresser. This is nothing more than a piece of round steel stock about the size and length of a cigarette, with an industrial diamond set in the center of one end. Diamond dressers are much faster and more effective than are any other grinding wheel dressing tools that I have used. They are inexpensive and can be purchased from machine-shop supply houses.

The dresser is used to keep the wheel from wearing out of round, which would cause it to wobble. The tool also strips away particles of steel clogging the wheel's surface. A clogged wheel requires more pressure to shape a cutting edge. This pressure increases the friction between tool and wheel, which creates more heat - too much heat and you risk burning the steel and losing the temper.

Hold the dresser at an angle to the axis of the wheel and just touching the wheel's edge, move the diamond across the surface in a steady motion, so that it clears a smooth surface rather than one that is corrugated. (Always wear a face protector when

USE A DIAMOND DRESSER TO *true the edge of a grinding wheel.*

YOU CAN MAKE A BUFFING *wheel from an electric motor and buffing pads impregnated with an abrasive compound (shown in foreground). The wheel is a big help in obtaining a razor-sharp cutting edge quickly.*

using the dresser.)

The only other machine I use in sharpening is a buffer. Buffing replaces the old method of stropping a cutting edge on a piece of leather to create the final, razor-sharp edge. When possible, I also use the buffer to remove the small steel burr that is created on the edge by grinding. This method is less time-consuming than honing on oil stones to remove the burr. When buffing, hold the tool very lightly against the pad, usually for a very short time and be careful not to round over the cutting edge.

I made my own buffer from an old washing

HONE THE ENTIRE LENGTH OF *the radiused cutting edge of a fore plane.*

machine motor which I attached to a wide 2"-thick, pine baseboard and wired to a standard box and switch like those used for light switches in a house. The motor is fitted with a split arbor and two 5" diameter buffing pads. Arbors and pads can be purchased at most hardware stores. I snipped the stitching of the pads about 1 in. back from the circumference with a razor blade to make a 2"-wide, fluffy buffing surface. Impregnate this surface with abrasive compound by holding a block of compound against the pads as they spin.

The remainder of my sharpening equipment consists of several oilstones, an India gouge slip stone, and several files. I am not exactly sure what my oilstones are made of because I either purchased them secondhand or inherited them. One stone for example is amber in color and cuts like a hard Arkansas. It belonged at one time to my great-great-uncle Billy who was a pattern maker after the Civil War. It descended from him to my grandfather, then

to my father, then to me. Anyway, it is what I use to get a final edge. To sharpen all the tools mentioned in this chapter, you will need only two Arkansas oilstones, one hard and one soft, each about 1" by 2" by 6"; a 1" square by 5" or 6" long, soft Arkansas slip stone; and an India gouge slip.

FORE PLANE If you surface a lot of rough-sawn lumber by hand, a fore plane with a convex cutting edge will make your work a lot easier. I grind the cutting edge of my fore plane blade to about an 8 in. radius along its length, and an angle of about 30 degrees. The grinding wheel produces a hollow-ground bezel, which is easier and quicker to sharpen than a flat bezel.

After grinding, hone first on a soft Arkansas stone. Because the cutting edge has been ground to a radius it is difficult to hone it in the familiar figure eight pattern. I work the edge either back and forth, or with a circular motion. While I do this, I slowly move the cutting edge through its arc so

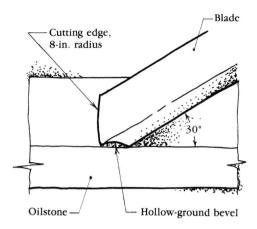

Cutting edge, 8-in. radius

Blade

30°

Oilstone

Hollow-ground bevel

HONE THE CONCAVE CURVE OF *a forkstaff plane blade with a concave India gouge slip.*

HOLD THE DRAWKNIFE IN A *vise and work the stone over the bezel in a circular motion.*

that the entire curve is honed. If the edge has a burr after this honing I remove it by holding the blade lightly against the buffing wheel. Next, hone on a hard Arkansas stone, and gently remove any trace of a burr on the buffer.

As the cutting edge begins to dull you can hone it again on the hard Arkansas stone. This is possible because of the hollow ground bezel; to hone the entire width of a flat bezel you would have to begin with a coarser stone. I can sharpen many times by honing before I have to regrind the bezel. This is why I have been able to live for so long with my old, beaten grinding wheel - I do not use it very often.

I shape the blade of my small compass plane to a 3" radius. It is sharpened in the same way as the fore plane blade. The compass plane blade is made of an old file and is much harder than a bench plane blade. Because I only use it on pine seats, it has to

be honed as seldom as twice a year. I cannot recall having to regrind the bezel more than two or three times in all the years that I have owned and used that plane.

FORKSTAFF PLANE The cutting edge of the forkstaff plane blade is concave, rather than convex. This shape conforms to the curve of the plane's sole. On my plane, this is a 3" radius. I have never had to regrind this blade. I use it only to round sackback bows and one surface of the continuous arm, so it does not need to be kept as sharp as a bench plane. About twice a year, I hone the edge with the India gouge slip and a light buffing.

To hone, hold the blade in a vise so that the bezel is facing you, and work an India gouge slip in a circular motion on the bezel. As you do this, move the stone across the entire length of the curved edge. If you need to grind the blade, it might help to work

USE A ROUND SLIP TO *hone the edge on the inside of the scorp and a flat oilstone to hone the outside edge.*

USE A FILE TO REESTABLISH *the bezel of a spokeshave iron. Hone the blade with a square, soft Arkansas stone. Work the bezel, then turn the burr with the stone flat on the blade.*

the edge of the grinding wheel to a radius with the diamond dresser. Alternatively, you can shape the edge with a half round file, which can remove a lot of metal quickly; a chainsaw file also works in a pinch.

DRAWKNIFE I keep my drawknife up to snuff with a stone that is the equivalent of a soft Arkansas. I hold the blade of the drawknife in my tin knocker's vise, gripping it near one of the handles, and work the stone over the bevel in a circular motion. This is a much less awkward method than moving the knife over the stone. Be careful to hone the entire length and width of the bezel so that the cutting edge does not gradually become rounded. Use the same motion on the underside of the blade to turn the burr over. I hold the stone flat on the underside and do not form a second bezel. A drawknife

maintained in this way should never need grinding. As much as I use mine, I sharpen it in this manner only several times a year.

SCORP A scorp's cutting edge is maintained in the same manner as a draw knife's. Hold the scorp in a vise near one of its handles, and move the stone over the blade. My scorp is bent to a 2" radius, so I use a soft-Arkansas grade stone about 1" square and 6" long to work the bezel on the outside of the curve. The India gouge slip can be used on the inside surface of the blade to turn the burr. Move both stones in a circular motion. It is difficult to grind one of these tools on a bench grinder but if you buy a new scorp, the bezel can be quickly established with a file. After filing, you will have to rely on patient work with a coarse oilstone using the same method as for honing.

USE AN INDIA GOUGE SLIP *to hone the inside surface of a travisher blade.*

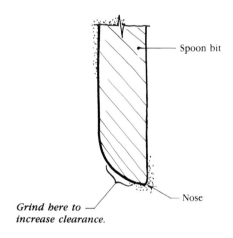

Grind here to increase clearance.

Spoon bit

Nose

A SHARP SPOON BIT SHOULD *cut quickly and produce a crisp, spiral chip.*

SPOKESHAVES My spokeshaves receive a lot of use and their cutting edges need to be maintained regularly. The spokeshave that I use for whittling spindles eventually develops a hollow in its cutting edge, and this has to be removed. The blade is too small to hold on a grinding wheel, and removing the hollow by honing would take too long. I use a file instead. Because the edge is so short, I prefer a triangular file. Grip the blade near one end in a vise and hold the other tang with your free hand to prevent vibration.

Once the file has reestablished the bezel and straightened the cutting edge, hone the blade with a square, soft Arkansas stone. If a heavy burr develops, remove it by buffing, and then return to honing with the stone. Finally strop the cutting edge lightly on the buffing wheel.

TRAVISHER This tool is similar to the spoke shave and is sharpened in the same manner. The square Arkansas stone will not work on the inside curve of the blade. Therefore, I use the India gouge slip on this surface. My travisher is never used on wood other than pine, and even then its only function is to produce a finished surface. Consequently, its cutting edge does not require the same regular care as a spoke shave.

SPOON BITS When sharpening new spoon bits the first step is to make the curve of the nose symmetrical. Once that is done the bit can be honed; otherwise, little work is required to keep the edge sharp. I establish the curve of the nose with an India gouge slip. Set the bit right up on its nose, nearly perpendicular to the surface of the stone. Then, work the nose to a radius by pivoting it from side to side on the slip. When the nose is shaped, buff it inside.

Test the edge of the bit by mounting it in a brace and pushing the nose into a piece of hardwood. Be sure that the edge is at a right angle to the direction of the grain. The nose should pierce the wood easily, and as you turn the brace the typical spiral chip should result. If it merely produces pow-

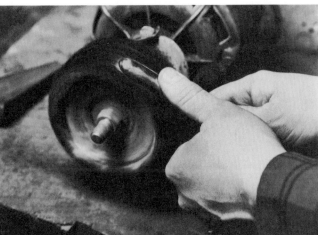

WORK THE NOSE OF A *spoon bit to a perfect radius on an India gouge slip. Buff the shaped spoon bit inside and out to finish the cutting edge.*

der, the bit is scraping and is either insufficiently sharp, or lacks sufficient clearance. If it lacks clearance, grind away a bit of the metal behind the cutting edge, as shown in the drawing.

A properly sharpened spoon bit will cut in a very aggressive manner. After every half dozen or so sockets, I restore the edge by buffing the inside and outside of the nose for several seconds. You can push the nose into the buffing wheel fairly hard - I use more pressure for a spoon bit than for any other tools. Every month or so, I hone the nose for a very short time on the India slip. Never grind the cutting edge of a spoon bit. The edges of the bit's body above the nose never require attention.

TAPERED REAMER The reamer is a companion to the spoon bits. It makes a scraping cut, and when it is sharp, a reamer will produce shavings rather than just dust. To sharpen a reamer, hold it in a vise by its tang and run a file along the two upturned edges, then hone with a medium grit stone. Be careful to file the edges flat. When the arrises become rounded the tool will not cut cleanly and will need touching up with the file and stone.

CABINET SCRAPER I use a cabinet scraper for finish work - smoothing and cleaning up parts that have already been shaped. A small burr of steel running the length of the scraper's edge does the cutting. A sharp scraper will raise a nice curl of wood, rather than dust. To prepare the scraper for this burr hold it in a vise. First, file the edge flat. I use a file held in a saw sharpening jointer to do this. This tool ensures that the edge of the scraper is square to its faces. File the faces to remove any of the remaining old burr; keep the file flat on the faces.

Next, hone the edge and faces with a soft Arkansas oilstone – be sure not to round the edge. Honing removes the rough marks of the file and makes for a stronger, more uniform burr. I turn the burr with a wheel burnisher, a tool specially designed for this purpose. I hold the scraper in my vise and place the burnisher so that its wheel contacts the edge. I then bear down with as much pressure as my arms will supply, and pull the burnisher over the edge in a single smooth pass. One pass creates a perfect burr. I find this method is fast and foolproof. When the scraper produces dust not

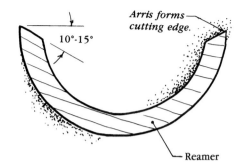

Arris forms
cutting edge.

10°-15°

Reamer

SHARPEN A REAMER BY FILING *its edges flat, then honing with a medium-grit stone.*

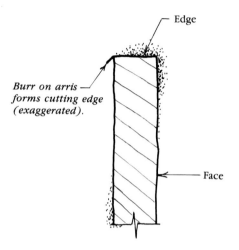

Edge

Burr on arris
forms cutting edge
(exaggerated).

Face

REMOVE ANY BURR ON THE *edge with a file. Hone the edge and faces with an oilstone. Be sure not to round the edge. A wheel burnisher makes fast work of creating a scraper burr. Push the burnisher hard against the scraper's edge.*

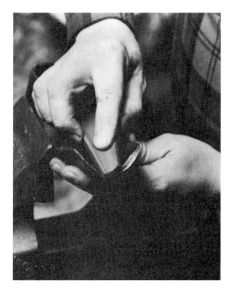

SHARPEN A GUTTER ADZ BY *honing the cutting edge with an India gouge slip and buffing inside and out.*

shavings, it is time to file, hone, and turn another burr.

GUTTER ADZE The gutter adze also has a curved cutting edge. Because I use it only once a week to chop out two pine chair seats, I can maintain the edge by just honing with the India gorge slip, and then buffing lightly. Grip the adze in a vise to hold it steady while honing. Work the slip over the entire length and width of the bezel in a circular motion. (This will remove most nicks; a chainsaw file will take care of heavy nicks.) Remove the burr on the buffer. If you make your own adze, you can create the bezel with a half-round file. I have never had to do anything but hone my adze, and I expect to be able to say the same when I am an old man.

SPLITTING HATCHET I use my Kent hatchet only for riving, so it requires no care. You can remove nicks in the cutting edge with a file, but they will not prevent it from wedging a billet of wood apart. If you want to use your hatchet for cutting as well as for splitting, sharpen the cutting edge as you would that of a regular ax.

FROE I use a froe as a lever for splitting and do not drive it into the wood. So, it should also last forever without sharpening. If you drive a froe to start a split you may want to sharpen its cutting edge with a file. But remember that a froe should split rather than cut. A sharp cutting edge could cut the wood fibers rather than wedge them apart.

BOW SAW I do not think that sharpening bow saw blades is worth the effort. Long before a blade needs filing, it breaks from metal fatigue. Store-bought replacement blades are expensive, so I make my own from ¼ in., six- point bandsaw blades.

Appendix A

The Little Black Chair

This is the first magazine article I ever published. It appeared in the May, 1972 issue of Spinning Wheel, a now-defunct magazine for the antique crowd. In it, I tell about the little, black chair I bought at a yard sale. In the New Introduction I refer to this chair as the singularity of the Windsor chairmaking Big Bang. All 20th and 21st century Windsor chairmaking radiates out from it.

A signature discovered recently on the bottom of a Windsor chair has attributed the piece to a heretofore unknown Beverly, Massachusetts, cabinetmaker. This remarkable rod-back side chair had been in a Worcester, Massachusetts, collection for a year before the name, scratched faintly in pencil on the bottom of the seat, was discovered.

The name, Stickney, can be best seen with the aid of a bright light. The owner, knew the writing was there but never bothered to decipher it. Not until he read in a book on early American cabinetmakers that very often old craftsmen would simply scrawl their names in some unlikely place, did he become suspicious of pencil scratching on the chair. Prior to this the owner had thought, as do many collectors that if a piece did not bear either a brand or the maker's label, it was one of the multitude of unsigned examples.

The owner's next step was to find the name listed in a book of cabinetmakers (*The Cabinetmakers of America*, by Ethel Hall Bjerkoe). There were two Stickneys, one working in Beverly around 1820 and another in Newburyport, Massachusetts, around 1850. The fact that the chair is a Sheraton Windsor ruled out the Newburyport craftsman. He was working too late.

A call to the Beverly Historical Society shed more light on the chair's creator. Historian Ruth Hill indeed remembered a Samuel Stickney, cabinetmaker. He had disappeared from history until some years before when Miss Hill had compiled a list of Beverly Cabinetmakers. Stickney came to light one day when a researcher helping Miss Hill found his name and occupation listed on a deed. She telephoned and said, "I have another cabinetmaker for you." Thus Stickney was saved from the waste-

basket of history. But until his name was found on the chair bottom he had been relegated to semi-obscurity. His only recognition, and that thanks to Miss Hill, was a three-line entry in the back pages of the book where the collector had found his name.

The next stop was to bring the chair to Beverly and allow the Historical Society to compare the signature with copies of Stickney's name signed on handwritten receipts. The president of the Society and Miss Hill both concluded the signatures were the same.

The receipts had been found by Miss Hill while culling a stack of bills bundled together by a Beverly resident in the early decades of the 19th century. Sure enough Stickney had done odd jobs for the fellow and among the slips were the receipts, handwritten and signed, Samuel Stickney.

These bills shed more light on the livelihood of a cabinetmaker in the early 1800s. Stickney was paid "to 8 days work at $1.50 per day - $12.00," the bill dated November 18, 1826. On January 15, 1827, he was paid 50 cents "to fixing a Well Bucket." Several years later on August 10, 1835, he was paid "to Sundry Jobs at thee (sic) house - $1.50; 1 Set of Casters - $.75; . . .for twine & Nales (sic) -$ 0.34," for a total of $2.59. It seems cabinetmakers filled their spare time with tasks more mundane than making furniture.

The house Stickney occupied for the first twenty years of his marriage is at 168 Cabot Street within a block or two of the Beverly Historical Society. It is there presumably that he had his shop and would have made the chair owned by the collector. The house is covered with brown shingles and its condition is undoubtedly worse than it was while he lived there. On the street level there is still a storefront, now occupied by a small mattress concern. Possibly it is where Stickney kept shop. Two apartments, one of them vacant, are over the store. The building is so altered that all there is left to hint that it has a history extending back to the 18th century is a small pediment over a side doorway.

There is evidence that Stickney was well known in the community and a man of no mean ability. He was born in Boxford, Massachusetts, November 6, 1771, and was married in Beverly, December 14, 1794, to Edith Wallis. He died August 23, 1859. From records at the Historical Society we learn that his body was found in the woods around Beverly where he had been walking. He was pronounced a victim of a heart disease. He would have been 88 that November.

During his life Stickney was an Ensign of the First Light Infantry Company of Beverly. On the Fourth of July, 1807, he accepted an "elegant standard," which was presented to the Company by the ladies of Beverly. The Stickney Family Genealogy remarks that Ensign Stickney "made a brief and pertinent reply." He must have been a typical Yankee, terse, and concise. Stickney was also a member of the Massachusetts Missionary Society, an original member of the Salem Mechanic Association, and a Life Member of the Beverly Mechanic Association.

Stickney and his wife, who died four years before her husband, in 1855, had six children, four boys and two girls. The first son, Samuel, lived less than a year. A daughter also died before her first birthday. His sixth child, a son, also named Samuel, did survive, although there is no record.

The rod-back Windsor, all that Stickney is known to have left as an example of his craft is indeed a remarkable and beautiful piece. It was found by the collector sitting atop a pile of items at a rural yard sale. The seller, unaware of the chair's value, parted with it for a mere $10. Thus, the piece is reassurance to despairing collectors that "real finds" and even discoveries of historical significance are still available.

It is not known where Stickney learned his trade but Salem, just across the bridge from Beverly, is noted for the high quality of its furniture and the artistry of its craftsmen. Possibly, some of this Salem talent rubbed off on this Beverly cabinetmaker.

The chair, although its design is of the early 1800s, is reminiscent of the last quarter of the preceding century. Most rod-backs compromised the grace and pleasing lines of the previous Windsor types to the style of the Sheraton period. Stickney did not.

The chair, of which the front legs have at some time been replaced, is not at all squared or boxy as most of its kind. The legs have a distinct rake as opposed to the almost non-existent splay of the other rod-backs. The members of the legs and H stretcher (instead of box stretcher) are bobbin-shaped rather than having bamboo turnings. These recall legs and stretchers of late bow, arch, and loop-back Windsors. The six-spindled back is framed by two well splayed bobbin-turned uprights and joined by a slender crest. The angle of the uprights recalls the spread of the fine fan-back Windsor giving it the same sense of delicate grace as this earlier type of chair. The seat is boldly shield-shaped, a sharp departure from the typical seat of 19th century Windsors. It is only slightly saddled, however. The leg sockets are bored all the way through the seat and are wedged as usual. Where each end protrudes there are marks, visible only in good light. Some earlier owner had evidently used a power sander to try to make the wedged ends smooth with the surface of the seat. The damage, however, is slight and this superbly turned and constructed chair remains a mute testimony to the art and technique of a long forgotten Beverly craftsman,

Editor's note: Mrs. Nancy Goyne Evans, Registrar, The Henry Francis DuPont Winterthur Museum, informed us of furniture bills signed by Stickney dated 1797, 1801 and 1804 in the archives of the Essex Institute, Salem, Mass. She dates this Windsor chair "ca. 1800-1810 (or 1815)." Mrs. Evans has been researching material on American Windsor chair manufacturers for some years. Her scholarly study of these chairs will be published several years from now.

Appendix B

Bending At Home

The following treatise on wood bending first appeared in serialized form in The Windsor Chronicles, a quarterly magazine I used to publish and mail to our alumni. My purpose in writing this piece was to make available to our students the knowledge they needed to bend successfully at home. This is important information, as I cannot help from a distance. There is no way I can diagnose a chairmaker's problems with bending unless I am present and know the wood's history.

In the digital age, electronic communication is much easier and less expensive than printing and mailing a publication. The Chronicles has been superseded by a monthly essay that I email, and a blog at our website. The paper publication ran from Spring 1995 to Summer 2006.

About once a month I receive an email or telephone call very similar to the one below.

"Help! I made the parts for five chairs and steamed them for 45 minutes. I know that's longer than necessary, but I wanted to be safe. "The first two pieces broke. So, I steamed the remaining ones for another 45 minutes — an hour and a half! All of those pieces broke as well. Only one of the 34 pieces we bent in class at The Institute broke. What am I doing wrong? I am really discouraged."

When I get one of these messages I feel as helpless as the person who sent it. There is nothing I can do to help from a distance. It is similar to calling the doctor and saying "I have a headache. What is wrong?" Unless you go to the doctor's office, he is not able to diagnose your problem either. Unless I am right there with the person having trouble bending; unless I know the history of the wood, I cannot possibly tell what the problem is.

Since I cannot go to the people having these problems, whenever possible, I urge them to bring their parts here and bend them. That way, I can observe their bending technique and be more helpful.

Because so few people can take advantage of that offer, I have decided to write down what we know about steam bending here at The Institute. This information is backed up by 37 years of expe-

rience bending many thousands of chair parts, made from hundreds of logs, of about a dozen different species of wood. I am confident you will not be able to find a lot of this information in this level of detail, anywhere else.

Most Windsor chairs require bent wood parts. It is safe to say that if you want to make these chairs, you have to master this skill. However, steam bending is an art, not a science. No matter how much experience you have, some bendings are going to break. Like a military planner, the chairmaker's goal is to keep the casualties as low as possible. That means you need to have every contingency leaning in your favor, and you cannot take short cuts. If you do, you may accomplish some successful bends, but your failure rate will be unacceptably high.

Begin with wood selection and use the woods most suitable for bending. About 10 years ago, it was popular for woodworkers to make everything out of walnut. Right now, the "in" wood is cherry. I regularly get calls (as I did then) from people who are suffering very high failure rates. When I ask what they are bending, I am told they are trying to make an all-cherry chair (just as it used to be an all-walnut chair.) This is folly, as these woods do not bend well.

Windsor chairmakers traditionally used locally available oak, ash, or hickory for bendings. These are all ring porous woods with long, tough fibers. Today, as in the past, these remain the best woods for this job.

You need to obtain your wood directly from the log. Wood that has been sawn into boards or planks usually does not have straight enough grain to result in a high success rate. Do not buy wood at Home Depot and try to bend it. Do not try to bend wood that has been kiln dried, as wood that has been heated does not bend well. I have had bad luck bending wood that has been heated when it was left leaning against a wall too near a stove.

You have to be finicky and downright fussy when selecting your logs. When trying to describe to people what to look for I say, "Think telephone poles." That is just what you want, trees that look like telephone poles, perfectly straight. The wood inside such a tree will generally look like the tree did on the outside. For that reason, the trunk must be straight, with no curve or twist. If there is, the wood will be bowed or twisted.

There must be no obvious blemishes on the log's surface. A blemish in the log will cause the layers of annual growth to deflect around it, and the stock you obtain will not be straight. Reject out of hand logs with freshly trimmed limbs. It does not matter whether these limbs were live or dead.

Refuse any logs with bumps or burls. Next to the shape of the log, the bark is the best indicator to what is inside. Oaks, ashes, and hickories have coarse bark with striations in it. These lines should all be straight and parallel.

A knot or defect inside the log is said to be "encased." Encased defects will usually disturb the pattern of the striations in the bark and often create "cats' faces." These telltale swirls are a sure give away that the log contains a defect, and should be rejected.

Be on the lookout for folds in the bark. These appear as long (often dark) lines, like a scar on human skin. These folds cover an injury the tree has sustained. Look out also for dark stains in the bark. This can indicate an injury that is still open to water, which can cause rot in the log.

No matter how choosey you are, there is no guarantee that even the best looking logs will not have flaws. You cannot be sure what the wood looks like until you split it open. If you are buying the log at a mill, you obviously incur all the risk. The saw mill owner is not going to let you return a log that you split open.

Avoid logs that are too big or too small. We do not like them to be less than 14" in diameter, nor greater than about 24". Small logs have a greater percentage of juvenile wood - the wood that was once the sapling. This wood usually has too many small encased knots to be good for bending. Logs that are too big cannot be easily handled. Splitting them requires more wedges and backbreaking work. In a big log, the splits made by the wedges frequently miss each other rather than running together and a lot of wood will be wasted.

Here at The Institute, we use forest grown trees. We are a big enough business to be able to buy our logs wholesale from a concentration yard that sells veneer logs to buyers from China and Germany. The logs are delivered here by a big logging truck and a cherry picker. If you want just one log, try a local sawmill or a logger. They also have forest grown trees.

I have successfully used oaks that grew on someone's lawn. However, landscapers and tree ser-

vices usually have urban grown trees and I would recommend avoiding these. We tried to use an urban tree in a class I taught in Atlanta many years ago. The log was beautiful, but we had almost 100% failures. I do not know whether the problem was environmental, but I never wanted to take that chance again.

Finally, determine when the tree was felled. If it has been down too long, it may have begun to decay. Decayed or decaying wood will not bend. If you are buying from a saw mill, the operator may not know this information, but if you are buying from the logger who cut it, he should.

Otherwise, your best bet is to examine the sapwood. This is the band of annual rings about an inch thick and closest to the bark. On oaks, the sapwood is usually a lighter color. The sapwood contains nutrients that attract fungi. These will usually appear as bluish or blackish spots about the size of a pencil point.

In red oak, you can cut away the speckled sapwood and still use the reddish heartwood. I suspect the tannic acid in red oak protects it. However, after enough time even heartwood will be affected by decay.

Trees that are cut in the summer or late spring are more likely to decay quickly. At that time of the year the tree is in its growth cycle and the sap is up. The weather is also much warmer. A tree dropped in July when temperatures are in the 90s can begin to decay in a week. A tree dropped in October when the tree is dormant and the weather cool, will remain fresh much longer. In fact, we like to put in a large supply of logs in the late fall, as they remain frozen from December through March. In the warm weather we buy small numbers of logs, and more frequently.

The problem is that other than in the sapwood, you cannot always see the early stages of decay, a breakdown of the wood that makes it brittle and incapable of bending. Although over the phone or via email, I cannot diagnose why wood will not bend, I suspect that decay is most often the culprit. Your best protection is to know a tree's history — when it was dropped and where it has been in the meanwhile.

No matter how fresh your log, it will not remain that way. This means you need to get to work on it right away. There is no difference between wood taken from a log that has been at the mill for six months and one that has been lying in your back yard for the same amount of time.

This is the analogy I use when describing wood selection during a class. Think of yourself as a farmer putting down a cow for meat. You will not take the cow out into the field, drop it, walk away, and return three months later to cut off a steak. The meat needs to be processed right away. Once it is cut up you have two choices – freeze it or dry it into jerky.

Treat a tree the same. Split it up right away. Then, you have two options, freeze it or dry it. Here at The Institute, we have a large 6 foot chest freezer which we fill with riven wood for our classes and for sale.

Unfortunately, back in the 1970s working wood that has been split from the log was been dubbed "green woodworking." As a result many people think the wood needs to be kept wet. This is wrong, and results in a lot of ruined wood. Some people try keeping the billets submerged in water. This is unnecessary. Others wrap it in plastic. Still others wax the ends. These steps only promote decay.

If you cannot freeze your wood, allow the billets to air dry. Although successful steam bending requires the wood to be wet, the steam box will take care of that. Treat the billets like you would any other wood you buy. Keep it dry and off the ground. I remember one fellow who called because his bends were breaking. It turned out he had stored his billets on the ground under his back porch. Of course, the wood began to rot just as would a board stored on the ground.

The best place to store billets is in a garage or other unheated building. Unless you live in a desert, it will not air dry much below 10% - 14%. Wood stored this way will be good for years. I have successfully bent air dried wood I split into billets a decade earlier.

Here at the Institute we split our logs with a log splitter. Every couple of months we have what we call a "spilling party." The guys and I, along with a farmer who lives down the road, split enough wood for our upcoming classes and for sales. The farmer, Kevin, drives his tractor down here with a four-foot splitter mounted on rear. Splitting the logs this way saves us a great deal of back breaking labor.

If you are a chairmaker working on a smaller scale you will most likely split your logs by hand. Using a maul and splitting wedges, split the log into halves. This is called riving. Use a hatchet to snip any wood that is tearing from the two halves and holding them together. Otherwise, these tears may lengthen and waste good wood. Next, split the halves into quarters and then, the quarters into eighths. These eighths - called billets - have a cross section that looks like a slice of pie.

With a maul and wedge split away the pointed piece of the pie. This is the tree's juvenile wood, and it is seldom useful. Next, use a drawknife to peel the bark off each billet. Remember, the tree's living growth layer is right under the bark. It is wet and rich with nutrients. If left this way, boring insects will quickly make your riven billets their home.

After our splitting parties we take these billets and carefully following the grain, cut them into arm and bow blanks on our Hitachi band resaw. We use this big saw because we are cutting enough stock for as many as six classes at a time. You are not likely to place these demands on your equipment and so, can use your shop band saw. To make the stock more manageable, you might want to split your billets one more time, into sixteenths.

Once the oak has been sawn into bending stock it is ready to be worked. In our experience, stock that has been set aside for even a couple of days and has lost a bit of water will bend better than wood that is dead fresh. As I explained last issue, the use of the term "green woodworking" leads many people to think that wetter is better. However, as long as wood is not heated by kiln drying, being placed near a stove, or stored in a hot attic, moisture content is largely irrelevant. The steam box will provide the necessary moisture.

The type of chair you are making determines the stock's shape and dimensions. When sawing, the goal is to keep the blade in one layer of growth as much as possible, as doing this perfectly results in stock with no grain direction. Following one layer of growth may result in stock that is not perfectly straight and that has a slight bow. This is not a problem, as the part is going to be bent anyway.

Like most other human endeavors sawing bending stock is not always possible to do perfectly. As a result, when shaping the wood into chair backs there will sometimes be places in the stock where you will be cutting with the grain and other times, against it.

When a tool begins to dive or choke, it is necessary to cut in the opposite direction. The greatest risk occurs when using the draw knife. This tool's open blade can dive as it follows the stock's grain and ruin the part. A light test cut is always best.

Do not be concerned by the light colored sapwood. In our experience it bends well. However, it does best when in compression. Therefore, when it is present, we plan our work so that it will be on the inside of the bend. In other words, so it will be placed against the bending form.

Pin knots are a real hazard, as they create weak spots. It is best to plan your work so they are removed while shaping the part. If this is not possible, we again prefer to place them on the inside of the bend so they are in compression.

When sapwood, pin knots, or some other risk

is present, our habit is to mark the area with large, dark Xs made with a Sharpie permanent marker. When the part comes out of the steam box, this reminds us that when making the Xs we had determined a preferred placement on the form.

Since Windsor chair parts are bent from the middle, it is necessary to locate and mark the center. You have about 45 seconds to bend a part. While, this is more than enough time, you do not want to be delayed by problems that could have been avoided.

We also mark the centers of our bendings with a Sharpie, as it leaves a dark, easy-to-find mark. Do not skimp on this important step by making a faint or incomplete mark. Make the center mark all the way around a round part and on all four sides of one that is rectangular. When you take the hot, wet part out of the steam box, you do not want to waste precious time looking for your mark.

Do not use a mechanical pencil or a ball point. Steaming gives the wood a slight gray cast, and the faint mark made by a mechanical pencil can be hard to find. Steaming will bleed ink out of the wood and the mark will disappear.

Remember steaming wood is an art, not a science. Some parts will break, even when you are doing everything right. The goal is to keep these failures at an acceptable level. This means you want to have as much in your favor as possible. The process we use at The Institute does just that. An average of two parts out of 34 will break in a sack back class. In some classes, there are no breaks at all. In others, there are more than two.

In our experience, bending goes better some days than on others. Over the years I had observed this and began to look for the cause. The following may seem like folklore, but it is quite true and accurate. The best bending days are those that are bone dry and crystal clear. These are the days that make you feel like you have boundless energy. Wood taken from the steam box on these days feels dry and not very hot.

The least favorable bending days are wet, gloomy, and dreary. These are the days when there is not enough coffee in the world to wake you up. Wood out of the steam box feels wet, and is so hot we end up juggling it from hand to hand as we carry it to the bending form.

This observation runs counter to what one would assume. Since wood needs to be hot and wet to bend, it seems a wet day would be our favor. However, this is not the case.

We found an indicator that would tell us when bending conditions were good. We found it in a very unlikely place — a piece of wood called a weather stick. These are specially cut twigs from Maine that are sold by some of the country living type catalogs for about $8. Please, Google "weather stick" rather than calling me for a phone number.

When the weather is dry and providing a good bending day, the stick points upward. When the weather turns dreary and overcast, the stick turns down. Obviously, the wood in the twig is responding to the relative humidity of the surrounding air, and the particular way it was cut makes it go up and down.

The weather stick further underscores how much successful steam bending is art and skill. I would never recommend becoming a slave to the weather stick. However, if you are not in a hurry and have the flexibility to wait for a better day, I would. At home, you have an advantage in that you can wait for a good bending day. We have to bend on the first day of each class so the parts are dry and ready to use later in the week. Regardless of the weather, we fire up the boxes and go to work.

To successfully bend wood it has to be both hot and wet. The temperature should be at least 185 degrees F. with 25% moisture content. With both these properties the wood is said to be plasticized, which means capable of being bent.

The steam box we use is the one we developed and perfected here at The Institute. We call it The Ultimate Steam Box because it is so efficient and because it solves the problems associated with other ways of making these devices.

To make the box we use Schedule 80 PVC pipe. (Schedule 40 will not take the heat and will crinkle up like a pretzel.) Wood steam boxes require a lot of steaming time just to become saturated and tight. Unless insulated, metal boxes radiate off a lot of the heat that should be plasticizing the wood. If you touch an exposed part of a metal tube you can get a good burn. PVC is both impervious and a good insulator. I demonstrate this to a class by holding my hand on the PVC tube. Only ¼ inch away from my skin is live steam.

We boil water on a 160,000 BTU burner originally designed for cooking lobsters and crawdads. This burner creates a rolling boil and lots of steam. Electric hot plates and the camp stoves that I used early in my career, make the water simmer and do not provide the volume of steam created by these new burners.

We boil our water in 5 gallon steel utility cans. Needless to say, we buy these new, and never put gasoline in them. Five gallon capacity is more water than most chairmakers will need. However, in a sack back class we bend 34 arms and bows in about 2½ hours, and having to continually fill the boilers is a nuisance. For most chairmakers a two gallon can is sufficient.

The steam box and boiler are connected by tight fittings. This ensures that all the steam that is generated in the boiler is conveyed to the steam box. Because the PVC is impervious and a good insulator, the steam goes right to work doing its intended job of plasticizing the chair parts.

If the steam box did not have some relief, the test caps on either end would be blown off as pressure developed in the tube. We make a ½ in. relief hole in the bottom of each end of the tube. The steam enters the tube in the middle and travels in both directions, escaping out the vent holes. This ensures an even distribution in the box. When our boxes are running at full steam a plume of water vapor blows down from the ends of the tube to the ground. We can look out the classroom window and tell how things are going in the bending area.

Because heat rises, the parts should not sit on the bottom of the box. There they are bathed in cooler, condensed water. Instead, they rest on a rack made of stainless steel bolts that pierce the tube. Regular steel bolts would leave dark purple stains on the parts.

As little as 15 minutes is all that is required to plasticize red oak chair parts. This time can vary somewhat according to the circumstances. The wood we use is freshly cut before each class. That means our bendings already have 25% moisture content and that all we need to do is heat them. If your wood has been stored for a while and allowed to air dry, it may be around 14%. You should steam a bit longer, perhaps 20-25 minutes.

Chairmakers who live in the Rocky Mountain States or at other high elevations, have another problem. Water boils at a lower temperature the higher you are. I ran into this problem in 1980 and 1981 when I taught chairmaking classes at BYU in Provo, Utah. We managed to bend successfully by steaming our parts even longer than usual. We left them in the box 40- 45 minutes. Because the wood was noticeably cooler than at lower elevations, we worked even more quickly.

Adding fabric softener to the water in the boiler has been suggested in some woodworking magazines as a way to soften the wood's fibers and make it bend more easily. I have tried that trick and have not found that it makes any difference.

Before removing a piece of wood from the steam box, be sure that everything else is prepared and ready. You only have about 45 seconds to complete the bends before the wood becomes too cool, and you do not want to waste any of that time fumbling. Always check the form to make sure it is securely clamped to the bench. Be sure that the bending strap is easily accessible. Check that you have the required number of wedges and pins, as well as a hammer. I always go through this mental checklist. For beginners, I recommend refreshing the bending process in their minds by first pantomiming it.

Remove the wood from the box with a pair of tongs. We use the ones sold in a supermarket for picking ears of corn out of boiling water. Before you open the steam box remember what you learned in your high school physics class. Released steam will rise. To avoid a burn, always open the box and approach it with the tongs from below.

Remove the part from the box, and moving quickly place it in the bending strap and secure it to the bending form. While you want to move quickly when setting up the bend, remember that as you bend, speed is your enemy. You must give the wood time to compress. If you move too quickly, you shift the outside edge of the bend from compression into tension. While wood compresses very well, it has a very limited ability to stretch. Tension will cause failures. Avoid it by bending slowly and deliberately.

"Do you wear gloves?" is a common question asked by students. I advise against them. As you gain experience bending you will discover that you can sometimes feel problems in time to correct them. We will sometimes feel a piece beginning to weaken, and turning the part around bend it successfully in the other direction. Roll up too, can be felt by a pair of experienced hands. You will never develop this "feel" for the wood if you wear gloves.

While steamed wood is quite hot, you can juggle it back and forth while carrying it to the form, and can switch hands while bending. The wood needs to be this hot, and if it is not you will experience more failures. I always tell students, "If you're not swearing, it's not hot enough." You cannot tell if the wood has been sufficiently heated when wearing gloves. Furthermore, bending requires dexterity. Gloves make your hands too clumsy.

While we have few bending failures at The Institute, they do occur. Failures are a fact of life that a chairmaker has to accept, as bending wood is an art, not a science. Four types of failure can occur when bending. They are: delamination, tension shear, compression failure, and roll up.

Delamination is by far the most common failure. In this case, a layer of wood peels off the outside edge of the bending. A tension shear occurs when the wood fibers rupture, tearing like cloth across their width. In a compression failure, the wood on the inside of the bend fails to compress evenly, and kinks up like ribbon candy. Roll up occurs only in pieces with a rectangular section, such as the sack back arm rail. In this case, the part does not remain in a plane as it is bent. Instead, the rear edge rolls upward.

A failure is not necessarily catastrophic and can frequently be fixed. The difference between a bending going into the scrap pile or into a chair is usually a matter of degree. If it is not too large, a delamination can be tacked back into place with glue. It is best to wait a day or two before making the repair. This will allow the wood to dry a bit.

A small tension shear can be consolidated with cyanoacrylate glue, which with a sufficient number of applications will actually fill the void. We saturate small compression failures with cyanoacrylate and when it is dry, smooth the crinkled, ribbon candy effect with a plane or spoke shave. We remove roll up by clamping the bending flat between two boards and setting it aside to dry.

The first three failures can frequently be prevented by bending in a slow, steady motion. As I said above, speed is the enemy. Roll up results from one of two causes. If the part's edge against the bending block was not made at a right angle to the upper and lower surfaces, the part's section is a parallelogram rather than a rectangle. In this case, the rear edge will lift as the front edge is pulled tight.

Second, when bending, it is common for students pulling the part towards themselves to actually twist it forward. We suggest students be conscious of this and counter it by purposefully twisting the part away from themselves. If in spite of these efforts a roll up begins, we can minimize it by allowing the bend to ramp up the side of the block. When it is cool we drive it back flat against the back board.

Once a part has been bent it has to dry before it can be used in a chair. For single plane bends such as sack back and bow back side chair, we wait until the part is cool. We then tie the bending with a string and remove it from the form. The c-arm is bent in two planes and has to dry on its form. Crests are bent in a press and have to stay clamped in this device until dry.

At The Institute we dry bendings in the furnace room, which we use as a kiln. During the heating season the furnace keeps the temperature around 100 degrees. Because humidity is very low in the winter, the warm room will dry bendings in several days. In the summer we maintain the same temperature with a heat lamp. We lower the summer humidity with a dehumidifier.

At home, you can allow a part to dry on its own, if you have the time to wait. In the winter you can speed it up by placing a bending on a heating duct, or above a radiator. In the summer, a part will dry in about a week if left in the sun. When I taught on the road, we would dry summer bendings by placing them in the backs of pickup trucks with black bed liners.

If you want to dry your parts more quickly build a small kiln out of foam core board. In a pinch you can also use the kitchen oven. Set it to its lowest possible temperature and crack the door to allow the moisture to escape.

Anyone who has ever read an article on steam bending knows that it is necessary to over bend to allow for spring back. While everyone knows this, it is flat wrong. It seems to be one of those things, that having made its way into print just keeps getting repeated. When wood is sufficiently dry it compresses further. We can tell with a glance whether or not a bending is dry. As it comes off the form, the string is taut. Once the part is dry, the string droops. Obviously, the part did not spring back, but moved in exactly the opposite direction. When it dries, a c-arm will compress so that the wedges that hold it on its form will loosen and fall away. A fully-dried crest will fall out of its press.

In fact, this extra compression presents problems for a chairmaker who bends a long time before being ready to put the part in the chair. The compression set makes the amount of curve too extreme for the chair. We have had good luck correcting over compression by filling the kitchen sink with hot water and soaking one side of the bend. Once it has become wet, we can force the bend back open. We then repeat the process on the other side. Once you have restored the part to the desired shape, use it in a chair immediately. Otherwise, it will compress again as it dries.

As I pointed out earlier in the series, most of the problems people have bending chair backs is caused by decay. However, other things can go wrong and result in repeated breaks. This is an example of a problem with the equipment. During a class a couple of summers ago one of the other instructors called me out to the bending area. On the ground were four or five broken arm and bows. Over a little less than half its length, each part was a strange purple-brown color, and each had broken within this discolored area. However, the other end of each part had bent well.

First, we examined the broken parts then, the steam box. I discovered that instead of being level, one end of the box was significantly lower than the other. The landscapers had recently replenished the crushed stone in the bending area, and one end of the saw buck that supports the steam box had sunk into the fresh stone. The Institute's steam boxes have vent holes on both ends. These are drilled through the lower surface, just before the end caps. Since these vents are the only escape, the steam flows evenly through the tube in both directions. This two-way flow plasticizes the entire chair back uniformly.

Because the box was at an angle with one end lower than the other, the steam entering the tube in the middle rose and exited only out the higher end. None was flowing down through the lower end. However, the jet of steam entering the middle of the tube and rising did heat the air in the lower part of the tube without wetting it. This hot dry air not only failed to plasticize the wood, it began to toast it. That explained the discoloration we had observed. The parts on the ground had all broken in the end that was lowest in the tube.

As I described earlier, in order to bend wood it has to be both hot and wet. This wood was only hot and wet on one end, and hot and dry on the other. In fact, it was so dry and so hot, it had begun to char. We leveled the steam box and every part after that bent as it should.

We quickly made replacements for the students whose parts had broken, and these too, bent without trouble. I saved one of the discolored parts and hung it on the shop wall. I tell this story to each class and use it to illustrate my tale.

During a writing arm class one year we also experienced a series of breaks. I went out to the bending area to watch and help. As I assisted a student bending his arm I commented that the wood seemed too cool. Sure enough, it broke. Polling the staff and students, I learned that all the breaks were coming from one box. Those from the other box were bending properly. This ruled out bad wood. As I studied the box, I observed that very little steam was coming out the vent holes. Ordinarily, plumes of water vapor blow down to the ground from each end of the tube. Assuming the boiler was running dry; I took it by its handle to shake it. I expected it to be nearly empty and thus, light in weight.

All I remember is a moment of surprise at how heavy the boiler was, because as I began to agitate the boiler a geyser of hot water and steam erupted from the filler spout. Next, I was running across the lawn with the skin of my face stinging. After lots of cold water and aloe I was sufficiently recovered to look for the cause of the accident. We use utility cans as our boilers. About six months earlier the old boiler on the problem steam box had rusted through its bottom. Unable to immediately find a replacement boiler of the type we prefer, we had bought another brand. This brand of utility can had a fine mesh screen at the base of the spout, which was intended to act as a filter.

Over time, the steel screen began to rust and the tiny holes became more and more constricted. Eventually, this constriction cut down the flow of steam up the spout, creating back pressure in the boiler.

In the filler spout we have a wooden plug with a funnel though its center. This allows us to maintain the water level in the boiler without shutting down. As the water begins to boil, the wooden plug becomes wet. It swells and tightens. When I agitated the can the plug let go. The water and steam trapped in the boiler by the constricted mesh filter erupted out the filler spout.

Fortunately, my head was not directly over the hole. Most of the hot spray passed by my face; only some of it landing on my right cheek and neck. For several days I looked like I had an odd-shaped sunburn. However, I healed quickly.

Like most accidents, this one could have been avoided if I had exercised plain old, common sense safety. The lesson — always shut down a steam box before working on it.

Appendix C

Sandpaper Sharpening

Windsor chairmaking and sandpaper sharpening are forever joined at the hip. Sandpaper sharpening is part of the universe created by the singularity that created the Windsor Big Bang – the little, black chair in Appendix a. While teaching chairmaking on the road I was forced to come up with a fast, easy way to sharpen with commonly available materials. I worked out this system. It is so convenient, I still use it.

This is a subversive article. Woodworking gurus and companies that make expensive sharpening equipment don't want you to read this, because when you discover that sharpening is both easy and inexpensive, they are all out of a job.

When I began teaching Windsor chairmaking in 1980, I was an itinerant. I traveled from city to city and provided a tool list for the students in advance. When the class began, I was amazed at the tools that showed up. Few were ready to use. Many were brand new and had never been sharpened. Others had been on the barn wall where great-granddaddy had hung them, decades ago.

These tools were not in working order because the students who had brought them did not know how to sharpen. That meant that I either spent the first morning of a class sharpening tools, or the class would be a disaster.

My problems were compounded by the absence of suitable sharpening equipment. None of my hosts ever had a dedicated sharpening station, and any paraphernalia they could provide consisted of a few water or oil stones. I had to develop a solution, or stop teaching.

These were my criteria. I had to do more than just hone an edge. I had to be able to reshape an entire blade in very short order. My classrooms were full of unusable tools and I could not spend a lot of time on each one. A lot of chairmaking tools have curved blades, but we also use both chisel and knife edge tools. So, my eventual solution would have to be versatile. Finally, I would need supplies that were easy to find and provide. Hosts were not going to buy expensive equipment just for me.

Three things I could find in any host's work space were sandpaper, a flat surface and small pieces of wood. This was my answer. It was not so much a "eureka" moment as it may appear. I had already been using sandpaper on plate glass for a decade to lap plane soles. I was really taking a process I already used and expanding on it.

Sandpaper sharpening solved my problem. It had an added benefit. It is so easy and simple that once shown, my students got it and were able to sharpen their own tools. Other advantages are that you will never again burn an edge, and you will be able to use this system to sharpen just about anything, from your best plane to a lawn mower blade.

The primary piece of equipment, and the one that will probably cost the most (but not much) is a suitable hard, flat surface. In the beginning I used plate glass, as glass is easy to find. However, it breaks. While no one was ever hurt, I worried. Today, I use ½" thick aluminum plates that I bought from a metal dealer. You could also use a piece of granite counter top. Whatever you select, it should be long enough to hold numerous strips of sandpaper of various grits.

The actual sharpening is done with sandpaper. I prefer aluminum oxide, as it seems to hold up best. You can adhere the paper to the lapping plate with spray adhesive, or purchase self-adhering rolls. I do both. Purchase the rolls from a sandpaper catalog and the adhesive at a hardware store.

You will need a variety of grits. We use #80, #120, #180, #220, #330, #650, #1,000 and #1,500 grits. The last three grits are wet and dry paper available from automotive supply dealers. Do not confuse these sandpaper grits with water stone grits. They are not the same measurement.

You will also need a stiff brush for keeping your paper clean of loose grit. I use a wallpaper brush. Single edge razors and a holder help remove worn out paper. Paint thinner dissolves any leftover adhesive. These are all available at a paint store. Finally, you will need a variety of ¾" hardwood blocks of a size that will fit comfortably in your hand. Pieces of dowel of various diameters about 4" long complete the equipment.

Setting up your sandpaper system depends on

your needs. I keep a strip of #80, #120, and #330 grit on one side of the plate and the wet and dry papers on the other. You will be better able to plan your own set up by reading on.

A lot of the problems woodworkers have with sharpening stem from not knowing, or not being able to envision what they are trying to accomplish. A sharp edge is simply two flat, polished surfaces intersecting at an angle that will cut wood cleanly. While that is a simple definition, it is very demanding, in that anything less is not sharp. The definition permits no short cuts, no half measures.

How to proceed depends on whether you are starting with a new, factory ground edge; an old beat up, nicked and rusted edge; or a well maintained edge that merely needs to be honed. It will also depend on whether the tool has a chisel edge or a knife edge. As you can see, this requires some judgment. Sharpening is not a rote process of so many strokes of this surface, followed by so many strokes on another. You need to combine whatever variety of processes your tool needs to achieve our definition.

Factories usually create an edge by coarsely grinding the two surfaces. This is the condition of many cutting edges on newly purchased tools. The grinding leaves behind a series of parallel scratches. If you were to magnify these scratches, each one is a tiny furrow in the metal. Where each furrow intersects the cutting edge it creates a dip. Under magnification, this row of dips looks like the teeth on a saw. Imagine trying to push a saw blade across a piece of wood. It would take a lot of force and the result would be a row of scratches. That is what happens if you try to use a factory edge.

A beat up edge, as you frequently find on second hand tools, usually has nicks and rust. A nick is similar to a furrow as described above, but nicks are not evenly spaced and are frequently bigger. Rust will pit the steel, and these pits too when they intersect the cutting edge act like the furrows. They leave scratches and require more force to work the tool.

Furrows, nicks, and pits need to be removed. This is the reason for the #80-grit. It will cut metal fast.

Chisels — Let's start on a chisel edge as it is the one most woodworkers recognize. Remember our definition. An edge is TWO flat, polished surfaces. The wide surface is the back and the narrow sloping surface is the bezel. No, this is not a typo. It is actually the precise word. The dictionary defines a bezel as the sloping surface of a cutting edge. In other words, all bezels are bevels, but not all bevels are bezels.

Begin by flattening the back surface. Place it flat on the strip of #80-grit. It is imperative that the blade remains flat on the paper, and that you never lift or rock it. This will round the surface. The action on sandpaper is side to side, rather that front to back, as you would hone on a stone. I shift my weight on my legs and move my body with the blade. This helps to avoid rocking the tool, or applying uneven pressure. After a dozen or more strokes, examine the results. It is best to do this under natural light, and I will usually step to a nearby window. Use a magnifying glass or a jeweler's loop if your eyes like mine are aging, and no longer see small details very well. You will see scratches left by the #80-grit. These have begun to remove the surface grinding, and reduce any nicks and pits. You may also detect low spots in the surface. It is not uncommon to discover that a blade is not actually flat.

Continue this action on the #80-grit until these blemishes are completely replaced by an even matt of sandpaper scratches. The exception is a nick or pit directly in the cutting edge. These may not completely disappear until you work the bezel.

Our definition does not mention how wide those two flat surfaces are. So it is not always necessary to flatten the entire back of the blade. A couple of inches are usually sufficient. You will probably feel the tool grow hot. It may even get too hot to keep your fingers on it. I usually blow on the tool to cool it. The good news is that you could not possibly hold the tool long enough to burn the edge. That old bugaboo does not occur with sandpaper sharpening.

Use the brush to clean away any loose grit that remains on the lapping table. This is an important procedure to perform at every step, as this grit will damage later stages of the process. Move to the next grit, in my case #120. Repeat the side to side lapping, the same as before. If you look at the results after about a dozen strokes, you will see the finer scratches beginning to replace those created by the 80 grit. This is a light bulb moment for someone learning to sharpen. The polishing part of our definition is really a process of replacing coarse scratches with finer ones. You have completed the work on the #120-grit when this matt of finer scratches has completed replaced the previous, coarser matt. If you look at this surface in a good light you will see what appears to be a shadow moving within it. That shadow is you, beginning to reflect on a surface that is becoming increasing more polished. Now, move on to the #180-grit and repeat the process of replacing the #120-grit scratches with an even finer matt.

At this point, I will usually focus some attention on the bezel. This is a narrower surface and flattening and polishing it does not normally require the coarser grits. However, if the blade has nicks or pits that were not removed in flattening the back, you may need to work the bezel with a coarser paper. The bezel is one of our two flat surfaces and you need to be careful to not round it. No need for a honing jig. The trick is to place the bezel on the paper on its heel. Now, lift the back until you feel the cutting edge make contact. It is a positive feeling that you cannot easily miss. This is the angle. Apply even downward pressure as you go back and forth, and you should have no trouble maintaining the angle.

The remainder of the process of sharpening a chisel edge is moving through the finer grits. You will notice that your reflection takes on more definition with each finer grit. By the time you reach the wet and dry paper, you should be able to recognize that handsome face looking back at you. In fact, #1,000-grit will create a polish so fine you cannot detect any scratches in the metal, and by looking closely you can pick out individual hairs in your eye brows. Examine the cutting edge by looking directly at it and rolling it slowly up and down. You should see no metal glinting back at you. This is because you can see a dull edge, but a sharp one disappears. If the tool is as described, it should be razor sharp. Test it by paring end grain. You should be able to slice off a shaving that will hold together, and the resulting surface should be glassy smooth.

Gouges – Chisels and jointer plane blades all have the classic straight cutting edge. A gouge is essentially a chisel, except the blade is rolled like a rain gutter. To complicate our jargon even more, a chisel's bezel is called a cannel, and a gouge can either be out cannel, or in cannel. A mere word does not change our definition of sharp. If you cut a section of a gouge's cutting edge, it is still two flat, polished surfaces.

Most gouges you will use are out cannel. In this case, the problem is to flatten the blade's back surface, which is a concave curve. I do this by applying strips of various grits of sandpaper to appropriately sized dowels. The larger the gouge, the larger the dowel's diameter, up to about 1 in.

If the gouge's condition requires, I will start with #80-grit and move on up through finer papers. The trick is to lay the dowel flat on the gouge's concave surface. This means you have contact all along the dowel. Unless you are trying to create a knife edge on a carving gouge, you do not want to round over the concave back surface. Work the dowel down one side of the curve and up the other. Repeat this until you have a uniform matt all the way out to the cutting edge. Repeat this through the grits.

When you reach #120-grit start to work the cannel through the same grits as your dowels. (Depending on the size of the gouge, some judgment is required here.) The cannel is worked on the lapping plate. Once again, find the correct angle by placing the heel on the paper and raising the handle until the cutting edge makes contact. Now, roll the bezel on the paper. Roll up to one corner of the cannel and back to the other. Try to make this a smooth, fluid movement. Check the width of your cannel to make sure it is uniform.

An in cannel gouge is easier to sharpen. Flatten the back by rolling it from one edge to the other while moving it side to side along the paper. To work the cannel, use various grits of sandpaper applied to dowels.

Crested Plane Blades – The cutting edges of jack and smooth plane blades are crested. In other words, the profile is an arc that looks like a finger nail. This is very easy to do on sandpaper. In this case, I shape the edge before flattening the back. Place the blade on its bezel and find the correct angle by lifting the end until the cutting edge makes contact. You are going to use a side to side motion, but it will also be arced. Begin on one corner applying pressure there with the fingers of one hand. As you slide along the edge, gradually shift the pressure to your other hand, so that by the time you reach the other corner the weight is all on those fingers. By moving the blade along an arc and shifting the weight, you will abrade more metal from the corners. Keep up this motion and the blade becomes crested. How much you crest the cutting edge depends on the plane's purpose.

Once the cutting edge is crested, flatten the back of the plane blade as you would a chisel. As you proceed through increasingly finer grits, return to the bezel and work it in conjunction with the back.

Knife Edge – Many tools have a knife edge. A knife edge is most desirable when a tool cuts down into wood and back out again. Most knife edge tools are used for fairly rough work such as shaping. An ax, adz and scorp (inshave) are examples of knife edge tools. A drawknife is also a knife edge, but is a slightly different matter. I do not use the lapping plate for knife edge tools. Instead, I use wood blocks or dowels with paper adhered to them.

The two sides of a knife edge are symmetrical. Although they are slightly rounded, their shape only defines the angle of the cutting edge. Our definition of sharp still applies, for at the very cutting edge the surfaces are still flattened and polished.

Ax – The ax is the simplest knife edge tool. So, let's start here. I adhere several grits of paper to ¾" thick hardwood blocks about 3" by 4" I have a small hand with stubby fingers. If you have a big hand, use a block that fits you comfortably.

Because I am running a block over the blade with the cutting edge uncomfortably close to my fingers, I like to have the tool well-secured. If a knife edge tool will not rest stable on a bench top, I will typically hold it in a vise.

If I am working a new tool that has been coarsely ground, or one that is beat, I begin with 80 grit. The process is one of stroking the block along the cutting edge, starting at the edge itself, and then over lapping the strokes down the curved surface. Work both sides the same and keep at the process until all blemishes have been removed. Once again, the result will be an even matt of scratches. Move through the finer grits, repeating the process of polishing. With each grit be sure to work right up the cutting edge on both sides of the blade and then back down.

Scorp and Adz – Both these tools are concave. While a block works well on the convex surface, you have to use dowels on the inside curve. The only difference between them and an ax is that the stroking is done along inside and outside curves.

Drawknife – This is a modified knife edge. Unlike the other examples, a drawknife's cutting edge is not symmetrical. Like a chisel edge, one side is flat, while the other is rounded. This point is not appreciated by most modern drawknife manufacturers, who typically grind the tool to a chisel edge. This shape edge prevents the tool from being able to slice into the wood and out again, in the way that knife edge tools are supposed to work. Instead a chisel edge on a drawknife causes the tool to dive into the work, frustrating the poor user.

Begin by flattening a drawknife as you would when lapping a chisel or plane blade. However, the tool's handles prevent this from being possible on a lapping plate, and you need to use a wood block. The back is as much as 1⅜" wide and usually 8" to 10" long. I typically begin with #80-grit, as there is so much metal to remove. With the back flat and with a uniform matt, work the curved upper surface as you did on the ax. Overlap your strokes all the way out the cutting edge. Repeat across the blade until you have the same uniform matt as on the flat bottom. Now, move through a progression of finer papers until you have the degree of sharpness you desire.

These are the steps for sharpening a new tool fresh from the factory, or a second hand tool that is worn. Some new tools (such as Pfiel carving gouges) are sharpened by the manufacturer. They, and any tool you have sharpened will eventually dull and will have to be sharpened again. This is

a slightly different category. Think of it as maintenance, as opposed to the preparation described above.

A tool usually dulls due to friction and wear resulting from use. The keen cutting edge created by the arris of two flat intersecting surfaces, rounds over. Instead of engaging the wood and shaving it, the rounded cutting edge begins to skate. Engaging it into the wood is only possible by using more force. You can see if an edge is dull. Take the blade to a source of natural light and examine it closely. Again, magnification will help weak eyes. Roll the edge in the light and you will see the rounded edge reflecting the light back to you. Remember, you cannot see a sharp edge, so this is visual proof that it is time to hone.

The good news about honing is that it usually pretty fast. Unless the blade has been nicked, you can usually begin on a medium grit such as #180 or #220 (for a large tool and even finer for a small one.) Hone a chisel edge by lapping the back until the rounded edge on that side is completely removed and the uniform matt extends all the way out to the edge. Remember, there are no short cuts and half measures. Here's a trick that may help as you learn to sharpen. Color the rounded edge with a red Sharpie and lap until that red disappears. Now, hone the bezel until the rounding on that side of the edge also is removed and the red ink is all gone. You can polish through as many finer papers as you need to achieve the desired result.

For a knife edge the process is similar. Only here, use a medium grit paper on a block or dowel to remove the line of polish that reveals a rounded edge. Now, work in the same way through the finer grits.

Routine honing restores a sharp edge for a while. However, repeated honings will eventually remove enough metal from the cutting edge that you begin to change the blade's angle. The angle can increase to a point where it no longer cuts well. If the blade is mounted in a tool such as a plane, it can even loose the clearance behind the cutting edge. In most sharpening methods, this requires going to the grinding wheel. With sandpaper sharpening, you return to the 80 grit and reestablish the original angle through the aggressive abrasion of a coarse paper. Now, hone the newly shaped edge with finer papers.

Below are some general thoughts and advice on sharpening, as well as answers to some FAQs. Every shop should have a dedicated sharpening system. You should work with sharp tools. It is easier and safer. You are less likely to stop and hone a tool that is beginning to skate if you have to dig out your sharpening equipment and set it up.

Sandpaper sharpening is a complete system. I not only maintain all my personal tools with it, we maintain the many score of tools we provide for our students' use. When sharpening as many tools as we do, one wants a system that is fast. However, there is no reason why the method cannot be blended with other equipment you may already own or prefer. For example, diamond hones will work in place of wet and dry paper applied to a wood block.

How flat is flat? I receive emails and read comments from people who are unsatisfied with a lapping plate. When tested with a dial indicator or other precision equipment it is out of flat by some otherwise imperceptible amount. There is an important point to remember: don't go crazy here. Over the years obsessive compulsive authors and letter to the editor critics have convinced too many of us that we cannot work wood unless we are accurate to three decimal places. Remember, when lapping we are sharpening woodworking tools not making equipment for NASA's Mars Rover.

How sharp is sharp? The answer to a lot of woodworker questions is "It depends." In this case, it really does. Not all tools have to be equally sharp. A tool one woodworker relies on for finish work, such as a plane, another may use for rough stock removal. Generally, speaking chisel edge tools will need to be sharper than knife edge tools. The former are more commonly used for finish work, while the latter are for shaping and heavy stock removal. I only take my draw knife up to #330-grit, but my best Bedrock 404 smooth plane is honed to a bright mirror polish on #1,500-grit wet and dry paper.

What angle should I use for my cutting edges and how accurate do I have to be? This answer com-bines the last two: it depends, and don't get crazy. The more acute the angle the more easily it will cut. However, the more acute the angle, the more fragile the edge. So, the heavier the work you do, the less acute (or more robust) the edge. For example a jack plane blade's edge will have less angle than a smooth plane. Mortise and firmer chisels have more robust edges than paring chisels. Don't get wrapped up in how accurate your angles are relative to what you read or hear. If someone writes the proper angle for a tool should be 35 degrees, do you think it will matter if you really get 37 degrees? No. In other words use your judgment.

I think (insert any other sharpening system here) results in a sharper edge. Imagine there is a sharpening scale of 1 to 100. If your tools were only at 50 on this scale, would you complain if a system resulted in 93, as opposed to another that created 95? I once visited a shop run by a real sharpening fanatic. He was so proud of his edge that he gave me jeweler's loop to watch the action as he shaved hair. It was not like shaving your beard; he shaved along the follicle like you would whittle a stick. I asked how long such a sharp edge would last in a plane. He replied "About a half dozen strokes. Then the super edge wears to merely sharp."

How often do you sharpen? Sharpening is a function of use, not time. Simply put, sharpen when you need to. A dull tool requires more force and does not create a cleanly cut surface. You can also see the rounded edge under good light.

What about micro bezels? I don't use them and my tools cut fine. Sandpaper sharpening is real easy, and I don't like to complicate what can be done easily.

Appendix D

Milk Paint

While I included a chapter on using milk paint in the original edition of Make a Windsor Chair I have used the product for several additional decades and have refined my technique. Also, a book chapter is limited as to space. The material I gathered below is more in depth and is worth reading before you finish your chair, or if you wish to use milk paint on other furniture. You'll like the stuff. However, it is not the authentic 18th century finish for Windsors. The old guys used lead paints. Milk paint is the best simulation of the original that I have found.

Woodworkers have been painting their furniture for thousands of years. Over that time, they have used many different types of paints. In fact, what you will find at the paint store is pretty limited in historic terms. Modern paints are also pretty limited in the appearance they produce. To put it simply – they are pretty boring. Old paints looked a lot nicer.

If you plan on painting a piece of furniture you probably don't want to be mixing a bunch of hard to find ingredients in order to get a better appearance. Also, some of the ingredients used in paints in the past are poisonous and are today illegal. However, you do have a safe and easy-to-use option – milk paint. Woodworkers have used milk paint since antiquity. It remains a desirable finish today for the same reason it was favored by the ancients, and every generation of woodworkers in between.

Milk paint is quick, easy, and forgiving. It results in a rich, lustrous, and complex finish that improves with time. Yet, it can be applied in an afternoon. Milk paint does not chip like regular paints and it does not produce the boring, perfectly uniform color of modern products. Instead, it has subtle differences of shading that make it much more like the lead and oil paints used in centuries past. As a piece of furniture finished in milk paint is used, the paint polishes where it is contact with hands or body and takes on different levels of sheen. This is very subtle, but results in a finish that is complex and lively. Because of the way this wear plays with light, a milk paint finish actually gets better as it ages.

Milk paint is nothing more than a mixture of lime, casein, clays, and any one of a variety of earth pigments. In the past, woodworkers mixed their own milk paints using a simple formula that had been handed down from one generation to another. Today, it is far easier to buy it from Old-Fashioned Milk Paint Co., 436 Main St., Groton, MA 01450-0222 (978) 448-6336.

The paint arrives in powder form and is mixed with water. It has a distinctive earthy smell, but it is not disagreeable. There are no fumes and it can be washed down the kitchen sink. The manufacturer warns that prolonged exposure to lime can burn wet skin and can injure eyes. In 30 years of use I have never experienced any of these problems and to my mind the finish as perfectly safe.

Milk paint is not difficult to use. However, it is very different from modern latex and oil paints. Unless you understand these quirks you may not get the best results. Most of these differences stem from the fact that milk paint is water based. Oil and latex paints are much thicker than milk paint and sit as a skin on the surface of wood. There is limited penetration into the wood. When struck or scratched these paints will chip.

Being water based, milk paint and has far less body. It is much thinner and lays on in much thinner coats. Also, much of the water based milk paint soaks into the wood. Because it penetrates the wood antique collectors have always dreaded stripping this stuff. The good news is that milk paint does not chip. In normal use it will only wear.

MIXING

To make milk paint, just add water. The manufacturer recommends one part water to one part paint. My method for mixing it is simple. I use a clean wide-mouth plastic jar. The wide mouth makes it easier to dip the brush. I prefer plastic over glass because I don't have to worry about it breaking. In is a minor concern, but accidents can happen. Peanut butter jars are perfect. In a pinch, I will use a 1 quart coffee can with a plastic lid for mixing milk paint. Because milk paint is mixed with water, avoid a cardboard paint pot. It may soak through and may fall apart before you are done.

You can mix the paint with a stirrer driven by an electric drill. However, I just shake it up like a bartender making a martini for James Bond – shaken, not stirred. It doesn't take long to mix the paint. About a minute of shaking is more than enough. The shaking or stirring will result in a paint that is frothy and full of air like whipped cream. You will not be happy trying to use this foam. I let freshly mixed milk paint sit for about an hour. This allows the foam to break back down into a liquid.

Because milk paint is water based, the solids will not suspend like they do in oil and latex. They settle out fairly quickly. I always keep a stirring stick in the jar. I stir before I start painting and I stir regularly during the process.

Depending on the surface you want, you can strain your milk paint. Unstrained milk paint results in a slightly more grainy finish. It is more matte, like an exceedingly fine sand paint. I usually do not strain, but when I do, I pass the mixed paint through an old pair of pantyhose. You can also buy a strainer at a paint supply store.

Once you have opened a packet of powdered milk paint it will slowly absorb moisture from the air. As it does, it gradually loses its ability to bond. In other words, milk paint has a shelf life. For that reason, I prefer 1 pint bags. If I have some powder left over, I don't feel too badly throwing it away. The unused product will last a lot longer if you seal the bag carefully and store it in a dry environment. I'm a pretty frugal guy, but holding on to an open bag of paint strikes me as penny wise, pound foolish. I feel much safer opening a fresh bag.

Mixed milk paint too, has a very short shelf life. Simply put — it spoils. It is a good idea to use it only on the day it is mixed. If you are not able to complete the finish in one day, you can stretch the mixed paint's working life by keeping it in the refrigerator. After two days, throw it away.

Surface Preparation

If my project has any small holes or blemishes I fill them with Plastic Wood. This material will take the paint. The water used to mix the milk paint will soften latex fillers. This may cause the milk paint to wrinkle. Remember, milk paint has almost no body. You cannot use it to fill small holes the way oil or latex will. You have to take care of any voids before you begin.

I generally take of the next steps in preparing my project while I am waiting for the froth to settle out of the paint. Milk paint is water based and the water will raise the grain of the wood. If you apply milk paint directly to a freshly sanded surface, you will have to sand again between coats. I would rather not have to do this extra sanding. So, I raise the grain before I apply the first coat. I spray the wood I am painting with water. I use a spray bottle, the type available at any hardware store. The trick here is to moisten the surface thoroughly but not like you were washing a car. If the water puddles or runs, you are being too liberal with the water.

There is another advantage to wetting the surface first. Any glue spills or glue smears that would prevent the milk paint from bonding will become quickly visible. They can be easily removed by scraping. I use a scraper, a chisel, or even a pocket knife. Once the wood is informally wet and all the glue removed, allow the wood to dry. On a warm day or in a heated shop this happens very quickly. Do not put your project out in the sun. You may cause parts to warp or split.

Finish sand the wood and dust it with a clean, soft cloth. You can also use a tack rag. Milk paint dries very quickly and unless wiped up immediately is difficult to remove. To protect my work bench I put down a layer of newspapers or builder's paper. I'm not beyond cutting open a large cardboard box. I also paint wearing an apron to protect my clothes. I don't bother with gloves. The paint washes off my hands easily.

Brushes

I apply milk paint with a natural bristle brush. I buy the cheap ones with unfinished wood handles and blonde bristles. They sell for about $1 apiece at paint, hardware, and craft supply stores. Their prices reflect the quality with which they are made, and during the first coat numerous bristles will pull loose and stick in the paint. I flick them out with my fingernail. If I miss any, they brush away when the paint is dry without leaving a blemish. By the time you are ready to apply the second coat almost all the loose bristles have dropped out.

For a chair, I prefer a 2 in. brush. Wider ones are better for woodwork with a lot of broad surfaces. The manufacturer also recommends using a foam brush, although I have never found these easy to work with. I do not use a nylon bristle brush, as the plastic bristles do not pick up a lot of paint.

First Coat

The manufacturer recommends wetting the surface before applying paint, as this makes the application easier. I do not do this. In my experience it easier to apply the first coat this way, but the water used to moisten the wood thins the paint so that a third coat is usually required for complete coverage. So, I end up doing more work in the long run.

Milk paint draws into the wood as quickly as it makes contact. This means that you cannot successfully draw it as you can an oil or latex. The action is more like daubing. Do not let milk paint puddle on the wood. Draw it and work it to a thin film. You do need to work it so it spreads and is absorbed uniformly. In this way too, milk paint is different. It has to be worked vigorously with the brush. Remember to stir the paint regularly.

If you do leave milk paint too thick or it puddles or runs, you will still not usually have a blemish. When the paint dries the thick areas will become crusty. Generally, the excess paint will brush away as a powder. At worst, you may have break up the crust with your fingernail.

The tendency of milk paint to soak into the wood makes it difficult to cut in — the process of drawing a fine line of paint with a brush. It is not impossible to pick out areas or parts in a different color, but you do have to be careful. If possible, paint separate parts before they are assembled.

Milk paint dries through evaporation, and so on a large piece the paint has dried where you began, long before you are finished. Allow the first coat to dry completely. Drying time is a function of the shop's environment and will take longer on a muggy summer day than in a heated shop in the winter.

The first coat will look like something the cat dragged in. It is splotchy and uneven. This is no time for a faint heart. If you are trying to achieve a very smooth surface, rub down the first coat with Scotchbrite. You can use #000 steel wool, but it leaves a lot of dust.

Rinse out your brush with running water and store it in a jar of water. If you do not keep the brush wet, it the paint will dry and you will not be able to use it for the second coat.

Second Coat

Before beginning to apply you second coat, remove the excess water from your brush. I do this by wiping it over the paper layer on the bench.

The first coat of paint sealed the wood. Applying the second is much easier in that you can draw the milk paint in a manner similar to oil and latex paints. Because the paint is no longer being absorbed almost as fast as it is applied, the second coat usually takes a lot less time than the first. You still need to work the paint to spread it evenly and thinly. You want to avoid puddles and runs.

Like the first coat, the second coat of milk paint too, will give the first time user fits of panic. The paint has dried dead flat. It is flatter than anything you have ever seen; as flat as chalk. You can still see brush overlaps and areas that you touched up. Again, have courage. If you want a very smooth surface, rub the second coat too, with fine Scotch Brite. Or, rub hard and vigorously with a soft cloth.

Over Coat

The paint needs an over coat whose purpose is twofold. It pulls the whole finish together and gives it a darker, but deeper, rich color and luster. Also, it protects it from spills that can cause spots on raw milk paint.

I use wiping varnish, also called wiping poly. Apply the mixture with another of those cheap natural bristle brushes. Be liberal, ensuring that you wet all the painted surfaces. Do this over the entire piece. Overlaps and thin areas in the paint will stand out for several minutes, but slowly begin to blend together into a uniform color. Allow the liquid to stand for about ten minutes. Then, wipe off as much as you can with a soft absorbent rag. Let the varnish dry for a day before using the piece. If you want more sheen, apply a second coat of varnish the same way as the first. Add a coat of wax if you like. I do not.

Like the human face, the young finish is beautiful, but has no character. This develops with time. Use the piece as you would normally and enjoy the increasingly subtle and complex finish.

For some projects, milk paint is more restrictive than oil and latex paint in that it only bonds well to fresh, raw wood or to itself. I have never had good luck using milk paint over another finish. If a chair has been left unfinished for a long time so that the exposed wood has case hardened, or areas of the chair are sealed from dirt and oil from human hands, I will not use milk paint. The manufacturer sells a product called Extra-Bond that will cause milk paint to adhere to just about any other surface; glass, metal, and plastics. However, I have never used it and cannot confirm the claims.

On the other hand, there are a number of neat tricks available to you with this product. New colors can be created by mixing the contents of different packages to suit. A favorite finish among chairmakers is to paint a chair several different coats of different colors — the most common sequence being Lexington green, barn red, and pitch black. Over time, the wear caused by repeated use will cut through the various colors, creating a close approximation of the old paint so prized by antique collectors. Pitch black over barn red produces a subtle tortoise shell.

Thinned to 1½ parts water to 1 part powder, milk paint works well as a colored wash. Thin it even more and more and it makes a nice colored wiping stain. On reproduction pieces made of cherry, I frequently apply a coat of red mixed this way. I brush the mixture onto only one area at a time. I let it sit a minute and wipe away the excess with an absorbent cloth.

Below is a blog posting I wrote inform-ing Windsor chairmakers about Colonial Williamsburg's recreation of the original Windsor green. The conclusion surprised me, as I had always though it to be Lexington green.

There was a very interesting article in eighth anniversary issue of Antiques & Fine Art maga-zine. It was written by Christopher Swan, a fur-niture conservator at Colonial Williamsburg. Mr. Swan is aware (as are many students of old furni-ture) that period paints were far more brilliant than most of us realize. Many have the misconception of the past as a world of honey colored wood and pale colors. Many museums are now making an effort to show us that brightly colored world as it really existed. Frequently, the effect and can be quite jar-ring. Other times, it can be illuminating.

Prior to the mid -1970s when restoring a house, museum people usually scraped a painted surface down to the first layer. Looking that the first layer, they painted the room in the color they observed. As a result, a lot of colonial and federal period house interiors were painted muted colors – creams, beiges, grays.

During the mid-1970s chemists and research-ers working for some museums began to study old paint. The Society for the Preservation of New England Antiquities (now known by the much eas-ier name Historic New England) in Boston was at the forefront of this research. They discovered that what you see when you look at old paint, is not usu-ally what they original owner saw. Old paints are fugitive, meaning they change color. Two things (among others) happen to paint over time. One, the pigments change color in response to sunlight. They often fade, but can also darken. Two, the oil will yellow, changing the paint's appearance.

Unaware of this, early restorers really skewed the public's perception of period colors. Our ances-tors came to be viewed as having been quite drab, when the real story was the exact opposite. They loved color. They loved lots of it and they loved it bright. The particularly loved it on wood. The rhap-sodic fascination with the "natural beauty of wood" is a 20th century obsession, not 18th.

Mr. Swan is part of a new generation of researchers, building on the foundations laid in the 1970s. As with all research, techniques improve and knowledge grows. He recently painted two repro-duction bow back side chairs with paint mixed to match an original green paint recovered from a pair of labeled Windsors made by Andrew and Robert McKim working in Richmond, VA ca. 1795 – 1805. Today's Windsor chairmakers are going to be sur-prised at the results.

Let me first tell a story. I had known since 1971 that Windsor chairs were originally painted, and that by far and away the most common color was green. In fact, the street name for Windsors was "green chairs." That was reinforced by a 1787 advertisement by Ebenezer Stone in The Institute's collection. Stone advertised he made, "Warranted Green Windsor Chairs" in Boston.

When I first started making and selling chairs, I did the same as the first house restorers. I examined early Windsors that retained their original green paint, or that showed traces of it. It was always a dark green. So, this was the color I used.

I switched to Lexington green milk paint dur-ing the late 1970s. That color was similar to what I had observed, so I felt comfortable with it.

Another event made me very comfortable with Lexington green. Sometime during the mid-1980s I received a phone call from a woman named Ann Jackson. I immediately put my foot in my mouth. Ann told me she owned the Rockler store. Having spoken at several Rockler stores, I knew there were a fair number of them. I asked which store she owned. She answered, "All of them." Ann was gra-cious and overlooked my faux pas.

She explained she was taking a course, and she was writing a paper on Windsor chairs. She hoped I would take the time to talk to her about Windsors and Windsor chairmaking. I did.

A while later, I received a call from a curator at SPNEA (now Historic NE.) He explained that the society was preparing to reproduce a couple of their Windsor chairs, and these reproductions would be sold through the society's catalog. The plan was to offer the chairs in a natural finish, as well as some various colors of stain. The curator's call was to ask me what would have been the typical original finish.

I told him Windsors were almost always painted green. I further added that being a museum with an educational function, it would only be proper for SPNEA to also offer the chairs painted. At the very least, they should inform people buying their chairs that Windsors were originally painted green.

The curator called back a while later. He had presented my argument to the people making the decisions, and it had worked. SPNEA agreed that the chairs should be offered in green, even know-ing that most people would surely buy them stained (that natural beauty of the wood fixation.) Did I per-chance know the exact shade of green?

I explained that I had always used Lexington green milk paint, but could not confirm it was the exact color. I knew enough about the growing field of paint research to realize that possibly it was not. The curator made note that SPNEA did have a paint analysis laboratory, and he thought perhaps they could do the research. However, he would need some paint samples taken from old Windsors. I offered to let the analyst take samples from chairs in my collection.

Yet another phone call from the curator. He had spoken again with the people who make the decisions. He thanked me for my offer to provide samples, but the society felt it more proper to obtain the samples from the chairs being copied. Thought stripped, there were small areas where samples of the original green paint could be obtained.

The major problem was the lab. Its work would need to be funded, and there was not enough money in the curatorial budget. It appeared the idea of offering the reproduction chairs in green paint was going to be a dead letter.

I recalled my conversation with Ann Jackson and had the idea that maybe Rockler would like to help. Ann was agreeable and financed the paint research. A month or so later, I received a color sample from the curator. Guess what? Lexington green. From then on I was very comfortable with that color for my chairs. Furthermore, I recommended it to anyone wanting to reproduce the original Windsor green.

It is now 25 years later. As I noted above, technique and knowledge march on. We've come a long way since the development of paint analysis in the mid-1970s, and a long way from the state of the art in the mid-1980s. Christopher Swan has gone a big step beyond the earlier research. He not only analyzed paint samples taken from the McKim chairs, he also mixed a period formula to make a Windsor green. I think his method and results described in his article are trustworthy.

Swan's pigment was verdigris, as called for in the formula he used. He points out that verdigris is a mixture of various copper acetates and produces a blue-green color. Swan points out that in contact with an acidic medium like linseed oil, verdigris will turn brown, and eventually black. This same darkening will occur if it comes in contact with light and oxygen. To slow these processes that darken verdigris, chairmakers either mixed varnish in their paint, or applied varnish overcoats.

The varnish could only slow the dual process caused by the acid in the oil, and light and oxygen. Eventually, verdigris darkens. This is why Windsor green usually is thought of as a dark green. That is how we received it, but not what it originally looked like.

Today's Windsor chairmakers, who want to recreate the look of old chairs in their work, will now have to make an adjustment if they want to keep up with Mr. Swan's research. Forget Lexington green. Swan's results are best recreated with Tavern green milk paint. Two top coats of wiping varnish will recreate the glossy appearance of an original finish. Remember, original paint was protected from darkening by the varnish mixed into, or applied over the paint. It too, was shiny.

Chairmakers who have studied here at The Institute probably remember the writing arm Windsor in the show room. I did that chair in Tavern green. To better help you if you have never see that chair, imagine this comparison. Lexington green is the color of mature foliage in mid to late summer. Tavern green is closer to the color of young leaves in the spring and early summer.

By the way, if you are visiting Colonial Williamsburg, and wish to see the chairs Christopher Swan painted, they are on display in the Wig Shop.

Refining Windsor Design

In the new edition of Make a Windsor Chair I explain that I no longer make the designs I did in 1984. Below is an explanation of how I fine-tuned my designs, eventually arriving at a steady state, designs that I think are as refined as possible. It is an article first published in the April, 1998 issue of Woodwork magazine. This area of inquiry - refining Windsor design - is still wide open to exploration and I hope the next generation of Windsor chairmakers will take it to a higher level of understanding. The universe of Windsor chairmaking created by that singularity in Spring, 1972 (the little black chair) continues to expand.

I have recently begun using a fascinating technique to help fine tune my Windsor chair designs. It has taken some time for me to understand it and to learn how to put it to use. In fact, I am sure I have a long way to go. That's why I'm writing this article; I hope as more people use it, more and more of the system's potential will be revealed.

To understand this method, it is necessary to understand how Windsors are engineered. Other furniture forms, such as chests, shelves, tables, or beds, bear loads that are directed straight down. The most effective shape for bearing these loads is a square or rectangle. Most furniture can be thought of as boxes with parts joined at right angles.

A chair made like a box would work well if a person sitting on it rested still like a sack of potatoes. However, that is not how we sit. We cross our legs, we reach for things, we squirm, and we lean back. These movements create rotational forces that stress the joints. If a chair were built like a box it would have to be quite massive in order to resist these strains; otherwise, it would quickly break. Building a light weight chair requires that a chairmaker rely on a geometric shape better able to resist such forces. One shape that does this well is the regular trapezoid, a form with two converging sides. In a Windsor chair we have essentially an assembly of regular trapezoids: the side stretchers; the seat and arm rail; the stumps and short spindles; the pairs of legs. Because a regular trapezoid is a truncated isosceles triangle, each pair of legs has a point of convergence.

When I started making Windsor chairs I quickly encountered a nagging design problem. My first production chair was the sack back, and when making it I was very careful to build the arm rail parallel to the surface of the seat. But the first time I stepped back to admire my finished chair, I was stunned to see that the arm rail and seat appeared to diverge. The arm was higher in the back than at the arm stumps. How could I have been so careless?

Yet when I re-measured the arm rail, I confirmed it was indeed parallel with the seat. The divergence I saw was an illusion. After the same problem occurred in subsequent chairs, I decided to counter this unwanted effect by building the chair so that the plane of the arm rail actually converged with the plane of the seat. I placed the arm rail ½ in. lower in the back at the center spindle than in the front at the stumps. This solved the problem. The arm rail now appeared to be parallel with the seat, even though it was not. I made the two planes appear parallel by making them converge.

From time to time, I would examine my production models (the chairs I copied from and kept around my kitchen table) and conclude that some of their elements seemed out of place and needed to be moved in one direction or another. For example, on my early sack-backs I observed that the stumps flared too much and needed to become more vertical. At another time, I noticed that the front legs splayed too much and needed to be brought together. Gradually, I changed the placement of these parts, as well as others, until they looked right. Sometimes I would overcorrect and have to move elements back in the direction of their original placement.

This long, gradual process eventually resulted in a major change in the shape of my sack back seat. As it appears in my book Make a Windsor Chair the seat is more oval than the one I use today. The change was necessary because the earlier seat shape would not permit the stumps and short spindles to line up in a way that to my developing eye looked best. Today my current seat template still contains traces of numerous old sight lines that have been erased and replaced with newer ones, evidence of this ongoing process of changing angles.

Visually, Windsors are a very dynamic composition of flowing lines that attract the viewer's gaze and guide it through the piece, the same way that an artist uses line to guide one's eye through a painting. I believe that this is why Windsors have a universal and timeless appeal; the viewer experiences this "passage" through the chair as a pleasant experience. A maker who does not understand and allow for this is bound to encounter design problems.

The process of adjusting individual parts by trial-and-error required a lot of time. I had no method for what I was doing and I could not communicate the process to anyone. I could only say that one part or another just did not look right.

When I started teaching, I was forced to do a great deal of thinking about my chairmaking; I had to be able to describe why I did something a certain way and why I found that to be the best way. But I was still not able to explain good design. I just assumed that it was subjective and beyond definition and description.

All that changed in 1992 when I was teaching a sack-back class at a woodworking store in Michigan. I was showing the class how to mount the arm rail and describing to them how

I made the seat and arm rail planes converge to counter that illusion of divergence. I explained that I did not know why this happened; only that it did, and that I overcame the effect by means of an intentional distortion.

One of the students, a designer for Ford with an art background, stated matter-of-factly that it was because the chair worked in perspective. It is no exaggeration to say that I was stunned by his observation. I stopped the class while I tried to absorb what he had said. I knew in an instant that his comment had completely changed the way I understood Windsor design.

He was right. In this chair, the planes of the arm and seat converged at a distance behind the chair. As he and I, together with the class, examined the chair, it became apparent that all its major lines pointed in the same direction. He observed that when the arm rail was parallel to the seat this foreshortening did not occur. As a result, the arm rail stuck out like a sore thumb and consequently, appeared to actually diverge from the seat. The same effect would occur in a painting if the artist failed to direct a feature such as a doorway toward the vanishing point. It too would appear distorted and stand out.

At the time, I was too busy to take this discovery much further, but as I continued to teach classes I would describe this observation. Sometimes people would speculate about where the vanishing point was located. I always assumed that it was a

large area, perhaps the size of a basketball, somewhere behind the chair.

A couple of years later another student added one more significant element. He wondered where the center lines of the legs would converge if continued above the seat and how they were related to the chair's perspective.

Last summer I decided to find out. I placed my production sack back on a work bench. I ripped thin strips of wood from a long board and clamped these strips to the chair, using them to extend the chair's major lines until they converged.

I was surprised by the results. The back's lines converged not in a cluster the size of a basketball, but rather, the size of a tennis ball. That cluster was located only 6 ft. 6 in. behind the seat's rear edge. Although the stretchers created a separate plane, their center lines converged at the same distance. When I extended the front legs upward their center lines converged on a line that connected the top of the bow to the vanishing point.

I did not know what to make of all this. It seemed too complex to be simply a coincidence, so I began showing my pictures to everyone I thought might have some insight. Several people said my wooden strips looked very similar to a system developed by architect Jonathan Hale and explained in his recent book, *The Old Way of Seeing – How Architecture Lost its Magic and How to Get It Back*.

Hale sought to understand why pre-1830 buildings are so much more harmonious than those built since – especially those built during the 20th Century. To do this he developed a system to demonstrate how buildings work visually. Overlaying photos of building facades he drew what he called "regulating lines" to show how certain design elements are used to create a united composition. Hale suggested that architects could use regulating lines to find the problems in their designs and to make the necessary adjustments. More importantly, the reasons buildings do or do not work could be concretely demonstrated. Good design was more than subjective.

I realized that this system could be used both to design chairs and to diagnose problems in an existing design. I also realized what I had been doing all those years when moving various chair parts. I was subconsciously lining them up with a vanishing point of which I was not even aware. As Jonathan Hale would say, I was "seeing intuitively." Using wooden strips and a vanishing point, I could at last show others what I was seeing in my mind's eye all those years.

I began testing other chairs to see what the system revealed. The second chair I examined was my continuous arm. A number of years earlier (bowing to customer requests) I had increased the seat width at the stumps from 17" to 17¾". I was never again happy with the chair. That ¾" – such a minor change – created a disharmony that nagged at me. Using the same trail-and-error techniques that refined my sack back, I regularly tinkered with the chair's back, trying to correct what felt wrong.

Applied to my continuous arm my wooden strips showed that the back worked very well in perspective - the major lines all converged at a common point. However, the rear legs were too close together relative to the front. The center lines established by the side stretchers converged at a point much closer to the chair than did the lines in the back. The problem I was seeing was not in the back at all. Instead, it was in the under-carriage.

To make the stretchers converge at the same distance would require that they be connected to the medial stretcher at an angle of only 5 degrees - very close to parallel. To effect this change I would have to relocate the rear leg joints in the seat to make them further apart. Their four points on the floor would create almost a square instead of the more pronounced trapezoid I regularly used. My knowledge of chairmaking warned me that this nearly square arrangement would not be as strong as a chair whose rear legs are located more directly under the sitter. This placement seemed extreme to me and made me doubt the value of this new technique I was using.

A short time later, while reading Nancy Goyne Evans' American Windsor Chairs, I noticed at photograph of a New York side chair (which like the continuous arm has a shield-shaped seat) turned upside down. The legs on that chair were arranged just as my wooden strips had indicated they should be. Two hundred years of use, and they had passed the test of time. Knowing that the chairmaker had sacrificed some strength for the sake of appearance convinced me that he too had worked either consciously or unconsciously with perspective.

I changed my rear leg locations and their sight lines to match my calculations and those of the antique chair. That new placement corrected the problem. Without the continual tinkering by trial and error I had managed to bring the chair's design to where I wanted it.

I now knew exactly what this system could accomplish.

Like Hale's regulating lines, the wooden strips are a way to highlight design problems by showing which elements to line up on a vanishing point. When making or designing a Windsor, a chairmaker can either arrange those converging sides so they point in generally the same direction (toward a common point somewhere behind the chair) or can ignore them and allow them to point to a variety of random locations. To aim them all at a common point results in unity and harmony. To randomly scatter the points of convergence of the various parts produces visual dissonance.

My experience with this system is still limited to the sack back and to the continuous arm, and to the bow back side chair that I make to match them. I do not yet completely understand how it works with crested chairs such as the high back and the fan back. However, my limited experience has shown it to be a valuable tool for today's chairmakers. Many people making Windsors live in areas where they cannot see a lot of the originals. Pictures in books are not enough. As a result, they are designing randomly on their own. Because they lack a connection to the best of the 18th-century Windsors, their designs lack the order of the originals.

Without this grounding, chairmakers are more likely to be influenced by the trends of fashion.

Here are some examples of how this system can be used. A common problem for modern Windsor chairmakers is scaling a chair's back. The backs tend to be too high relative to the chair's under-carriage. Less often, the back is too low. Using this system, the best scale for a sack-back bow or continuous-arm back can be accurately determined by first finding the vanishing point. Next, continue the center lines of the front legs upward until they converge. This depends on using the normal (and strongest) 14 or 15 degrees of front leg splay.

Connect this point of intersection to the vanishing point. The top of the back should touch this line. Side chairs should have the same back height as their matching arm chairs.

The continuous-arm is the apex of Windsor design and sooner or later every chairmaker wants to make one. This chair's design is very complicated and delicate. Without a way to order it, a continuous-arm easily becomes awkward and clumsy. One common mistake is to make the arms (the area under the sitter's elbows) curve upward like the bottom of the letter "J." This upswept arm directs the eye up into space away from the chair. Another error is to make the straight section of the arms too short, making the chair look uninviting. Still another pitfall is to make the plane established by the arms parallel to (or even diverge from) the seat. The first case results in the same undesirable illusion as with a sack back. In both cases, the back looks as if it is trying to push the sitter out of the chair.

The straight section of the arm on this style of chair is one of the back's major lines. Thus, it cannot be curved. It also needs to be long enough to establish a line, and that line should be directed towards the vanishing point. When a continuous-arm is ordered in this way, many of the problems chairmakers have with this style of Windsor are resolved.

All this is a preliminary report. However, like any new tool, the more people work with it, the more uses will be discovered. For example, while shooting the photos for this article, the photographer decided to take a series of views of my continuous-arm from the front, side, and rear. While he was setting up the rear view he placed his camera at the vanishing point. I got my face down close to the camera. Like everyone else, I have always seen chairs in three dimensions. However, at the vanishing point the chair becomes two-dimensional. I tried the same point of view on other chairs that do not set up perfectly. The parts that are out of alignment with the vanishing point remain in three dimensions while the rest of the chair magically becomes two. Although this technique is not as precise as the wooden strips, it is far faster and easier. It has the added advantage of being more appropriate to use in a museum or in an antique shop.

I have a couple of final thoughts. I do not claim this system is the be-all and end-all of Windsor design. It is just a tool. However, as Hale's study shows, good design is not simply subjective. It can be analyzed and the reasons why it works revealed. Also, while it is not necessary to slavishly copy antique chairs in order to create a good design, some things - such as scale - are constants. Still, I urge chairmakers to be as familiar as possible with old chairs. In design, as in history, those who do not learn from past mistakes are doomed to repeat them.

Finally, if you try this system, use it as a tool for identifying problems. Do not let it become a quest for some model of perfection. Strict adherence to any system results in designs that are sterile. Truly great design occurs when tension is introduced by purposely breaking these design "rules" at selected places, but only someone who truly understands the system can accomplish this. To my eye, an absolutely perfect chair is also lacking an essential ingredient: the slight imperfections of hand work that give it character. Bench-made chairs are fashioned with the manufacture of risk and some will always come out better than others. Some chairs built using perspective will line up perfectly while others will be slightly off. It is the understanding that major lines should be directed towards (rather than always directly at) a vanishing point that is important. As in horseshoes, you earn points for getting close. If you try this system I would be very interested in hearing about your experiences.

The Shave Horse Invective

The commentary below is self-explanatory. I wrote it in annoyed frustration and posted it on my blog.

Sigh. Another one of the woodworking magazines has printed a picture of a chairmaker sitting at his shave horse. In doing so, the magazine joined the long list of sources that continue to undermine the craft of chairmaking. How do we ever advance as a craft with such odds so stacked against us? A single misleading picture mailed to several hundred thousand readers has more negative impact than can be undone by 10 years of teaching classes.

When I run across a fellow practitioner of our craft I quietly assess the guy's work and rank his abilities in my mind. The shave horse is one of the standards I rely on. For me it is a shibboleth. A shibboleth is something that separates two groups, and something one of those groups uses to identify its members, sort of like a secret handshake. The shave horse divides chairmakers. The two groups are the guys that are serious and those who are quaint. Guess which group I belong to.

I do not use a shave horse. When asked why, I answer, "Why would I impose a pay cut on myself?" That is the result of using this tool. It is so limiting that it slows down the chairmaker and costs him income. I prefer a vise. Using a vise I am standing, not sitting, and I am far more productive and efficient. I work far faster, using less energy.

Consider the two postures. Sitting at a shave horse you have the work secured immediately in front of you. The muscles available to operate the draw knife are predominantly in your shoulders. You are limited as to how you can use the tool. You can do very little slicing, which means you are also misusing your knife. Remember, the tip from the Staff Tip Sheet you received in sack back class? "A drawknife is a slicing tool, not a two handled hatchet."

Using a vise, you are standing. You bring into play the muscle groups in your legs, butt, back, and shoulders. Leaning into the work and progressively shifting back on your ankles, your slice can be several feet long. That's a major advantage when making a four to six foot long bow. Students have commented that when working I remind them of a ballet dancer or an aerobics instructor. (Either way, that's a pretty good comparison for a guy that's 65 years old.) Yes. When using a vise the body's motion is fluid, graceful, and almost effortless. Above all, it's fast.

Suspended in air in front of me I can access about 300 degrees of the part's circumference. I do minimal stopping to turn the piece. Students remember the myriad of grips I show them for using the knife most efficiently. Those grips are possible because with a part projecting in space I have access to most of it. I move my body and my grip, rather than the part.

That raises the question, "With all its drawbacks, why would anyone use a shave horse?" A lot of chair makers are into being quaint. I think it is a throw back to the Hippies who got into woodworking in the 1970s. Sitting on a shave horse you look like you stepped out of a picturesque and bucolic past; or at least the commune. Editors don't know better. They're general woodworkers, with at most a passing knowledge of the various specialized crafts. Besides, a guy sitting at a shave horse does make a good picture; one that evokes a picturesque and bucolic past; or at least a 1970s commune. In other words, it's a vicious circle. Chairmakers want to look quaint, the editors like quaint pictures. So many pictures of chairmakers sitting at a shave horse have been published our imaginations have been overwhelmed. In woodworkers' minds the shave horse and chairmaking go together like a horse and carriage. (Wait a minute. That's love and marriage.)

Both the chairmakers working on shave horses and magazine editors are ignorant of the Windsor chair's origins. Windsors are an urban chair, developed in major furniture making centers like Philadelphia, New York, Providence, and Boston by highly trained craftsmen. In their minds, editors and the guys on sitting on shaving horses have confused Windsors with (at best associated them with) the Appalachian ladder back. Nothing could be more wrong.

This is another point of confusion. Working languidly away on their shave horses, these chairmakers (and the editors that publish photographs of them) are unaware of how fast urban chairmakers worked and how productive they were. The old guys produced chairs in prodigious quantities and would never have tolerated a production-killer like a shave horse. Old chairmakers regularly advertised that they could outfit a ship with a cargo of Windsor chairs at a moment's notice. They regularly advertised the large numbers of chairs they kept on hand (frequently in the thousands.)

So, if you are an editor, please, please, please, stop publishing photos of guys working on shave horses. If you are chairmaker that uses a shave horse; get off your butt and get to work.

Appendix G

Four Woodworking Objectives

I wrote the piece below for a woodworking magazine, because it applies to all furniture, not just chairs. However, the discussion is lifted from my opening remarks to a sack back class. In that discussion I explain the four objectives a woodworker seeks to accomplish when making a piece of furniture. The discussion arrives at the conclusion that when it comes to building a Windsor, objective number four governs. Rather than being a slave to dimensions on a drawing we make adjustments as we work. We share this in common with boat builders and coopers; many of our dimensions are determined by the chair.

When you build a piece of furniture, you have four primary objectives. You may not be consciously aware of them, but they are part of your decision-making process. The four goals are function, comfort, durability, and appearance. Although these are somewhat obvious, and all very fundamental to woodworking, they deserve to be explored from time to time.

FUNCTION The first objective is axiomatic. The piece of furniture you are making has to do its intended job. Function implies a generally accepted definition of purpose. For example, a chair is a piece of furniture designed to be sat on and on which a person can sit. Therefore, if you are making a chair, it has to hold your backside off the ground. If it's a table you have to be able to sit at it, and you have to be able to lie in a bed. A lot of ink has been spilled in the art furniture debate—for example, is a chair that you can't sit in truly a chair? For most of us who accept function as an extension of purpose and definition, the point is absurd. Calling something you cannot sit on a chair does not make it a chair.

COMFORT This objective is a corollary to the first. A piece of furniture not only has to do its intended job, it has to be comfortable and commodious. If you are making a chair, it must be comfortable to sit in. A rock will keep your backside off the ground, but a rock is not a chair because it is not comfortable or convenient. You must be able to sleep all night long in a bed, and a table must be the proper height and dimensions for its job. A coffee table's height makes it ideal for serving tea and coffee to guests, but makes it uncomfortable to use if you try to dine on it.

DURABILITY A piece of furniture has to be made well enough that it will hold up under its intended use. The life expectancies of different pieces vary and are linked to their particular functions. Adirondack chairs and picnic tables that are left outdoors are not expected to last as long as a chest of drawers or a lampstand—pieces that you expect to leave to your great-grandchildren.

Durability is often confused with quality, but in reality quality requires successful accomplishment of all design objectives, including the next one, aesthetics. A strong but ugly or uncomfortable chair is not good quality.

APPEARANCE In the days of the craft shop, this objective is the one that separated the journeyman from the master. By virtue of his training, the journeyman knew how to accomplish the first three objectives. He knew how to make a piece of furniture that did its job, that was comfortable to use and sturdy enough to last.

However, only the master understood the form well enough to produce the masterpiece. I define a masterpiece as a decorative object that not only incorporates the first three objectives of function, comfort, and durability, but whose success (eye appeal) is also able to transcend time and culture. Imagine entering a museum and coming upon a Ming vase. You are struck by the vase and drawn to examine it. You first observe it in its entirety, standing back several paces to take in the overall statement. Next, you move in closer to examine the vase in greater detail, to appreciate the finer points and to observe evidence of the craftsman's technique. The vase was made centuries before you were born and by someone living in a completely different culture. Yet it speaks to you, a viewer removed from the maker by all that time and space. It accomplishes my definition of a masterpiece.

We all want people to notice our woodworking and to appreciate the effort we invested in making it attractive. And we know intuitively that the things we make will survive us and be used by future generations. We want them to appreciate our work as well.

It is a common mistake to confuse the masterpiece with the fashionable. Both the fashionable piece and the masterpiece are appreciated in the maker's own time and culture. The appeal of the fashionable piece, however, is transitory. Trendy furniture soon looks dated.

The masterpiece's transcendence is frequently not detectable to someone living in the time and place where it was made. This quality only emerges as the winds of time winnow out the merely fashionable. To observe this, look at some early issues of woodworking magazines and notice the stack lamination and Post Modern furniture that was being made 25 years ago by some of the country's best known and most highly regarded woodworkers. Although the height of fashion then, today much of it looks dated. However, a Queen Anne highboy is as fashionable now as it has been for a couple of centuries.

The four objectives are in constant tension and even competition one with another. However, you cannot make good furniture by emphasizing one or more objectives at the expense of another. I point this out when showing my students how to make a Windsor chair seat. I explain that the broad solid surface which supports the sitter's backside satisfies function. However, the seat has to be nearly two inches thick so it can be deeply saddled to make it comfortable. The thickness also allows for deep, strong joints. However, the mass of a thick seat is in conflict with the chair's graceful lines. Therefore, the maker has to carve the edges and upper surface of the seat in such a way as to create the illusion of the seat being thinner than it really is, while leaving it strategically thick at the locations of the joints.

Another good example is the Klismos chair, popular in the young United States and Western Europe starting about 1815. The Klismos is a chair developed in classical Greece and often illustrated on Grecian urns. Although very fashionable and beautiful, the Klismos chair was not a good piece of furniture. Stretchers were not used because they did not look good when combined with graceful saber legs. However, the legs were too thin to create strong joints. The result is that few Klismos chairs lasted very long without breaking. After a decade or two of bad experience, furniture makers began to add stretchers to their Klismos chairs to strengthen a beautiful, but weak design.

Sack-Back Handout

We give the following handouts to sack back students to help them remember the processes we explained and demonstrated for them. These guys have to absorb a lot of information, and these sheets refresh their memories as they work. Later on, when the student is making chairs at home, these handouts help to recall what he learned in class. I have included the handouts here for the same purpose - to help you.

The first three pages explain the process for making the spindles for my redesigned sack back. The first page is a measured drawing of the finished spindle. The second page is a step-by-step procedure. The third is a photo sheet that shows the spindle making procedure in pictures. The spindle at each stage is compared to a completed spindle ready to be dried.

In a class we make the spindles slightly oversized and all 23 in. long. After they have dried and shrunk, second and third pairs of spindles are selected and cut to 22 in. (second pair) and 20 in. (third pair). Next, the top several inches are shaved to pass through a ⅜ in. hole in the Go Gauge so it will fit the bow when it is being mounted. Then, each of the seven spindles is individually fitted to its corresponding hole in the arm, ensuring a snug joint.

The Reaming the Leg Holes photo sheet illustrates the steps we use today when legging up.

Set Ups for Reaming and Drilling the Sack Back Arm is another handy photo sheet. The most convenient ways for securing a curved arm when drilling holes in it, and when reaming the stump holes are not intuitive. We worked out these techniques with much trial and error. You will save yourself a lot of grief if you refer to the sheet when setting up to perform any of these steps.

The stick with three dots projecting forward from the arm in Photo #2 marks the points where the long spindle sight lines cluster and where the short spindle sight lines intersect the center line (taken from the seat). The black line in Photo #3 illustrates the stump hole's sight line, also taken from the seat.

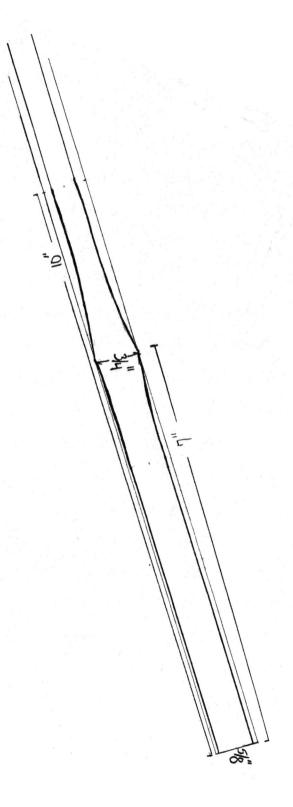

Roughing Sack Back Spindle Blanks

SPINDLES START WITH A BLANK *and are roughed to the shape shown on the right.*

CUT THE SPINDLE BLANK TO *23 in. and using a draw knife, rough the blank to ⅞ in. square.*

ROUND ABOUT ⅔ OF THE *blank's length so the ⅞ in. Go Gauge hole will pass about ½ the length. Note, this rounding establishes the bottom of the spindle, not the top.*

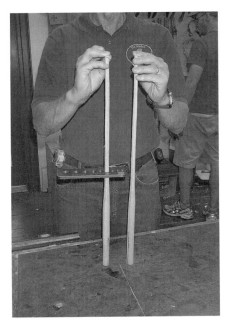

FORM THE NARROW, UPPER END *of the spindle by squaring about ⅔ of the length of the spindle to ½ in. Round the upper end until it passes about half way through the ½ in. hole in the Go Gauge.*

Reaming the Leg Holes

USE A BEVEL SQUARE SET *to 14 degrees against the dummy leg to establish the splay angle. Use another at 10 degrees for the rake angle. The first front leg is the bench mark from which all the other leg placements are determined.*

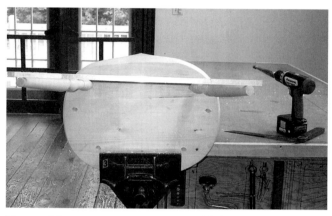

USE THE **14** DEGREE BEVEL *square to establish the other leg's front splay. Use the winding sticks to make the two front legs co-planer.*

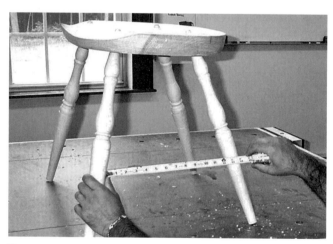

REAM BOTH REAR LEG HOLES. *Remember, there are no rear leg angles. Determine rear rake by measuring between the legs where the stretchers will go and accomplish a length in the target range of 12 ¼ in. Anything from 12 to 13 works, but you must have the same stretcher length on each side.*

PLACE THE FRONT LEGS ON *the edge of the bench and a winding stick on both sides. Use a bevel square to compare the two sides. Adjust as necessary, remembering that rear splay is the least important and you have a lot of latitude.*

Set Ups for Reaming and Drilling the Sack Back Arm

USE THIS SET UP TO *drill the stump hole in the hand. The dark line is the sight line and the angle is 19 degrees.*

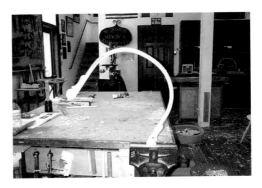

TO REAM THE STUMP HOLE, *hold the arm by its hand in this position. You are looking at the bottom surface. The sight line is vertical to the bench top.*

USE THESE SET UPS TO *drill the spindle holes in the arm rail.*

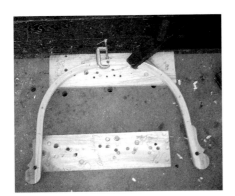

#1 CENTER HOLE

#2 THE OTHER SIX LONG *spindle holes*

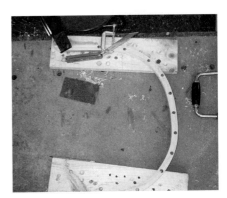

#3 SHORT SPINDLE HOLES

Mistakes

The following is explained in the first paragraph. I consider this the most important woodworking article I ever wrote.

After having seen me help a student recover from a mistake, someone in the class will usually take me aside say, "You know, you need to write an article on fixing mistakes." I always explain that I prefer to teach how to avoid making mistakes.

While my staff and I have a lot of experience fixing things that have gone wrong, I have really compelling reasons for focusing our attention, and that of our students', on avoiding mistakes in the first place. When they happen, mistakes have four very undesirable consequences for me.

First, mistakes cost expensive materials. We cannot tell the student "Too bad you ruined that piece of wood. The class is over for you." We have to replace it. Second, I have on my hands a student who is angry with himself. Everyone is aware of his funk and it is a drag on the class morale. Third, fixing the mistake will take time. The student will fall behind and it will be more difficult to keep the class on schedule. Fourth, I have to fix the problem, increasing my workload. If the mistake is really bad, I will have to cut a staff member loose to help me. As a result, other people who may need help do not have it as readily available.

These are the same four reasons that you too, want to avoid mistakes when working on your own. At home, it is you who has to replace expensive materials. It cuts into your woodworking budget, or if you are a pro, your bottom-line. You are now angry with yourself. Your satisfaction with woodworking is diminished and your ego takes a pounding. It will take you time to fix the mistake or remake what you have ruined. You lose precious shop time, or for a pro, your hourly rate just took a hit. Finally, like me, you're the one who has to fix it, and fixing mistakes is no fun.

As you can see, mistakes are expensive in several ways, other than just wasting materials. They adversely affect your efficiency by cutting into productivity. While this is a tangible problem for a pro, it is equally annoying for the hobbyist. The hours you are able to set aside for shop time are limited and precious. You want to leave the shop at the end of the day with something to show for your efforts.

Mistakes are linked to safety. You are more likely to get hurt if you are rattled or angry.

Few of us will tackle a project that we know is beyond our capabilities. So, we do not usually make mistakes because we are overwhelmed. Most mistakes occur in repetitive operations, and much of the work in any piece of furniture is repetitive. Seldom do you cut one mortise or one tenon. We generally mess up when we become distracted or confused. This most often happens when we are doing something more than once. We get into working mode, and as our mind wanders or we get mixed up, we make a mistake.

In my shop our mistake avoidance methods divide into three categories. I recently interviewed three professionals for whom mistakes are not an option because the consequences are so disastrous. They were a surgeon, and airline pilot, and a nuclear power plant technician. The mistakes avoidance techniques they use are all remarkably similar to ours.

You will also note that a lot of folk wisdom is woven through our mistake avoidance. You will be reminded of such sayings as "A stitch in time saves nine." Or, "An ounce of prevention is worth a pound of cure."

Layout

This is your first shot at avoiding mistakes. While good layout is no guarantee that you won't make mistakes later, incomplete or poor layout will make errors more likely.

Most woodworkers are reluctant to make a lot of marks on wood. Perhaps it is because they know they will have to clean them off later. Thus, their layout marks are small and light. Layout that is hard to see is only slightly better than none at all. While I tell my students I appreciate their frugality, pencil lead is cheap. I urge them to be wildly extravagant with this commodity.

When doing layout, make big, dark marks and notations that can be seen across the room. This way, they are obvious and clear when you pick up a piece of stock. I prefer a #2 pencil because the lead is soft and dark. I have no use for mechanical pencils. They make very thin lines that are too hard to see. Laying out rough stock, I use a red marking crayon because it can be seen and read at a distance. Chalk too, is good. All these marks remove very easily with a sharp plane, a scraper, or sandpaper.

Mark all surfaces, not just the ones you are going to work. Knowing where you don't want to cut is as important as knowing where you do. For example, if you are laying out table legs, bundle them together as they will be placed in the piece and draw a square on the top. The square will orient the outside and inside corners for you. However, also identify the other surfaces by writing "front" or "inside" on them. Indicate top and bottom. When working, all those legs are going to look alike and a complete layout will make it easier to orient them.

Of course you must check your work. After you are done with the layout, arrange the parts again as close as possible to how they will be oriented in the completed work, and be sure you have not made a layout mistake. For example, in a set of table legs, make sure all the mortises will align by placing the laid out joints against other.

When parts look alike, or when you have multiple marks, color coding is a good idea. In laying out shoulders and tenons, we teach our students to mark shoulders in red and the ends of the tenons in green. The red mark is visible at a glance and says, "Danger! Warning! Do not cut here!" The green mark reassuringly says, "It is safe to cut here." When a student ignores this technique and uses a pencil, or two marks of the same color, he usually cuts off at least one tenon by cutting at the shoulder.

You can also use color to code different parts that look similar. In making a door or a carcass with several panels, the top and bottom rails can look a lot like the center rails, but they only have a groove in one edge, not both. Colored painters tape effectively identifies the various parts. When you are done, it easily peels off without leaving any mastic that will affect the finish. If you need further identification, you can write notes and reminders to yourself on the tape with a Sharpie.

Painters tape is equally good for telling you where not to cut. Put a piece over a surface where you might mistakenly cut an extra mortise, or trim a piece of stock. In a Windsor chair the medial stretcher can be confused with the side stretchers. We put a strip of tape around the center to identify it during layout and to prevent anyone from drilling a hole at that location during assembly.

Sometimes layout is best done during the first test assembly. For example, if you are making a table with tapered legs, dry assemble to test the joinery. With the legs all in their proper locations it is pretty clear which surfaces need to be tapered. This is a good time to mark them – clearly and obviously, of course.

ORGANIZATION

With the parts all laid out, it is almost time to go to work. It is almost time, but not quite. You first want to organize your work. Working in an organized, orderly manner will avoid a lot of mistakes.

Don't try to work a jumbled pile of parts. Arrange all the same parts in an orderly manner. Cluster all the parts with space between clusters of other (especially similar) parts. Orient the parts all the same way. For example with a set of table legs, have all the top ends going the same way. This way, when you pick up a part you know where you are going to work and you can quickly confirm it by checking your layout. Not only do you avoid confusion by being orderly, you save a lot of time trying to figure out which end or surface is which.

Have as few parts on hand as possible. Put away parts that will not be involved in this operation. Extra pieces on your workbench, or at your station create visible clutter at a time when you want things crystal clear.

Do not co-mingle parts. Work from a To-do pile to a Done pile. After you have performed an operation, do not return the part to where you got it. Start a separate pile. As you work, the To-do pile should shrink and the Done pile should grow. This way, you do not have to keep picking up parts to find the ones you have not already worked. Also, you don't think you have finished the operation and disassemble your set up, only to later discover that you skipped a part. Avoiding these scenarios also saves you precious working time. The picture we draw for students when describing the problems of poor organization is a fish flopping on the deck.

PROCESS

Layout and organization are done and it is time to cut wood. After all the work you have invested in layout and organization you don't want to confuse yourself now. You are a lot less likely to make mistakes if you practice good woodworking habits.

When you perform a repetitive operation do all of it at once. Don't jump back and forth between different steps. For example, cut all your mortises and then, cut all your tenons. We have a limited capacity for retaining information. The more you are juggling in your mind, the more likely you are to make a mistake. If you stick to an operation and complete it, you can erase all the information it needed from your mind and focus only on the next step.

As you perform a repetitive process always work the same way. Just as you don't want to jump back and forth between operations, you don't want to use different techniques. For example, if when dovetailing you start out cutting tails first, keep doing it that way.

This advice does not apply to just the job at hand. To avoid mistakes whenever you are working, develop consistent working habits. By doing a process the same way every time, you can take advantage of muscle memory. Eventually, your body remembers how it felt when you were performing this operation before. This not only speeds you up, but when something doesn't feel right, it probably isn't. Learn to listen to your body.

Also learn to listen to the little voice in your head. Besides always working the same way, a good technique for avoiding mistakes is to always use the same tools. For example, in making chairs there are times when we have to use two bevel squares set to different angles. You can see the potential problem. Confuse the bevels and you have a mistake to fix, or a new part to make.

All my working life I have owned two bevel squares that are easily distinguishable. One is much larger and its handle is made of a much darker wood. I always use the bigger square for certain angles and the smaller for certain others. I never vary, and I never will. When I am distracted and pick up the wrong bevel the little voice starts screaming. When I pause to figure out what set him off, I find I have picked up the wrong bevel.

If you use more than one marking tool (such as bevel squares or marking gauges) only once or occasionally, you will not be able to develop a habit. In this case, find a temporary way to distinguish them. Again, painters tape with a written notation indicating the setting or the job will avoid confusion. Remember to peel off the tape when you put the tool away so it doesn't confuse you next time.

Here's another good tip. When you are done with an adjustable marking or layout tool, collapse it. You can't use it mistakenly if it is closed up. Every one of my students has watched me collapse a bevel square when I am done with it. Holding it up for them to see, I proclaim, "The only safe bevel square."

When I am helping students, I will use his tools so he can see how they should work. If the student has made a mistake that I need to fix and things are a bit tense, I follow the rule of always using the same tools. I only fix things with my own tools. They are comfortable in my hands and I know them intimately.

Here is another example of how I avoid mistakes in process. I am obsessive about only using my tape measure. I will walk across the shop to find my tape measure while numerous students offer me theirs. All my life I have used a Stanley 10 ft. Powerlock and I know and recognize its blade.

We teach students to stay as much as possible in the same relationship to their project. In our case, this means staying in front of the chair as much as possible. We call it the Chairmakers Position. Try to do the same in your work. You are more likely to become confused if you keep changing your body's orientation to the piece.

Also, as you work try envisioning the completed piece in front of you. Being able to see what is not there helps make sense of what you are doing. Before you cut, hold the part as it will fit into the piece, or place it as it will go into the partially assembled work. I do this with miters. I hold the piece and then I draw angled lines the way the miter will go. They are rough, so they cannot be confused with the exact line I will make with the miter square. Checking the line I drew with the part held up in position, I do not trace the angle the wrong direction. I learned this one the hard way, but it has since saved me a lot of grief.

When you get to my age you talk to yourself a lot. While this not desirable in social situations, it is a good woodworking technique for avoiding mistakes. Your mind is less likely to wander if you are describing to yourself what you are about to do. When they are working, my airline pilot, my surgeon, and nuclear plant technician all have another person present who describes for them what they are to do, often by reading a procedure. Most woodworkers work alone. To help keep you focused, talk to yourself. Turn off the radio so all you hear is your own voice.

If you foresee the possibility of confusion looming, work out a mnemonic to keep you on track. If it works once, remember it and make it a habit. Every student who has ever studied with me recognizes "Top of leg, to top of leg." and "Front is back, back is front." I suspect you can easily figure out what mistakes we are avoiding with these bits of doggerel.

Similarly, before you actually cut wood, pose to yourself the question, "What is the result of what I am about to do and, is the answer believable?"

By imagining the result you will sometimes find you are about to do something backwards or in the wrong direction.

If you are about to undertake a complicated process write out a procedure in advance. Use the procedure. Read each step rather than trying to remember what comes next. Check off each step as you work. We have already done this for our chair-making classes. We give them printed procedures for the most complicated steps.

NEXT TIME

If a project was worth making once, chances are good you will end up doing it again. Take notes on what you did so you do not have to figure it out all over again. It is a bummer to avoid a mistake the first time only to make it the second. Especially take notes about the mistakes you did make. If you wrote a procedure, make corrections or additions while the process is fresh in your mind. Taking pictures is another good way to keep a record of how you did things. Just as we give our students written procedures, we supply them with photo sheets for steps when a picture is the easier way to refresh their memories.

WHEN MISTAKES DO HAPPEN

No matter how seasoned a woodworker you are, you will make mistakes. When they happen, follow the advice we give our students, "You can't get out of a hole by digging." By this we mean, call one of us for help rather than trying to fix it by yourself. However, at home it means take a break. You are at the greatest risk for making another mistake or getting hurt when you are upset. Put down your tools and get a cup of coffee, or take a walk. Come back to the job with a clear head and you will be more able to dispassionately access the situation.

Learn from your mistakes. Your first reaction when you discover a mistake is to snap the piece in two and throw it in the burn barrel. Don't. You may want to get your mistake out of your sight, but out of sight is out of mind. You are more likely to learn from a mistake if you look at it frequently. This can literally mean, hang it on the wall. In our shop we avoid a lot of mistakes because of our "Wall of Shame." We save mistakes students have made in the past, and as we are teaching a process, we show the current class the applicable mistakes. Why? Because humans learn better by seeing than by hearing, and knowing that a mistake can and has happened helps avoid it.

Treat a near miss as a mistake. Just because you got away with something this time does not mean you will be so lucky the next. Use a near miss as a reason to take a break, and to contemplate what nearly happened. Decide how you can avoid that problem in the future.

Finally, do not let the fear of mistakes paralyze you. Mistakes will happen, and you will have to fix them. However, by paying attention to layout, organization, and good working habits, you will avoid a lot of them.

Read This Important Safety Notice

To prevent accidents, keep safety in mind while you work. Use the safety guards installed on power equipment; they are for your protection.

When working on power equipment, keep fingers away from saw blades, wear safety goggles to prevent injuries from flying wood chips and sawdust, wear hearing protection and consider installing a dust vacuum to reduce the amount of airborne sawdust in your woodshop.

Don't wear loose clothing, such as neckties or shirts with loose sleeves, or jewelry, such as rings, necklaces or bracelets, when working on power equipment. Tie back long hair to prevent it from getting caught in your equipment.

People who are sensitive to certain chemicals should check the chemical content of any product before using it.

Due to the variability of local conditions, construction materials, skill levels, etc., neither the author nor Popular Woodworking Books assumes any responsibility for any accidents, injuries, damages or other losses incurred resulting from the material presented in this book.

The authors and editors who compiled this book have tried to make the contents as accurate and correct as possible. Plans, illustrations, photographs and text have been carefully checked. All instructions, plans and projects should be carefully read, studied and understood before beginning construction.

Prices listed for supplies and equipment were current at the time of publication and are subject to change.

About The Author

Say the words "Windsor chairs" and most wood-workers think of Mike Dunbar – with good reason. In the early 1970s Mike set off the Windsor Revival, the rediscovery of the long dead craft of Windsor chairmaking. For more than 40 years he has worked tirelessly to advance that craft and to promote handmade Windsor chairs. Since 1994 he has taught at his school, The Windsor Institute. Mike is the author of seven woodworking books. He also wrote the eight-volume Castleton Series, an adventure series for young teens and adults that are young at heart. He has written more magazine articles than he can count. Mike lives in Hampton, NH with his family.

Dedication

I dedicate this book to my beloved wife Susanna. Besides taking good care of me, Susanna is the vision and driving force behind our school, The Windsor Institute. Although content to remain anonymous, I and all others making Windsor chairs today, are in her debt. I also recognize my son Michael, my pride and joy, who grew up at The Institute. I am in awe as I watch his career blossom. The music made by him and his band mates is a source of continuing pleasure in our home. I also acknowledge our dog, Menlo, whose furry face I love to nuzzle.

Metric Conversion Chart

TO CONVERT	TO	MULTIPLY BY
Inches	Centimeters	2.54
Centimeters	Inches	0.4
Feet	Centimeters	30.5
Centimeters	Feet	0.03
Yards	Meters	0.9
Meters	Yards	1.1

Distributed in Canada by Fraser Direct
100 Armstrong Avenue
Georgetown, Ontario L7G 5S4
Canada

Distributed in the U.K. and Europe by
F&W Media International, LTD
Brunel House, Ford Close
Newton Abbot
TQ12 4PU, UK
Tel: (+44) 1626 323200
Fax: (+44) 1626 323319
E-mail: enquiries@fwmedia.com

Distributed in Australia by Capricorn Link
P.O. Box 704, Windsor, NSW 2756 Australia
Tel: (02) 4560 1600; Fax: (02) 4577 5288
Email: books@capricornlink.com.au

Visit our website at popularwoodworking.com or our consumer website at shopwoodworking.com for more woodworking information projects.

Other fine Popular Woodworking Books are available from your local bookstore or direct from the publisher.

ISBN-13: 978-1-4403-3481-8

17   16   15   14   13   5   4   3   2   1

Acquisitions editor: David Thiel
Cover Designer: Daniel T. Pessell
Designer: Angela Wilcox
Production coordinator: Debbie Thomas